It ENDED *in the* LIGHT

Grief is not a destination...
It is a journey.

DIANE C. SHORE

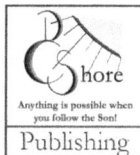

hore
Anything is possible when
you follow the Son!
Publishing

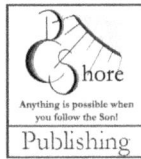

DCShore Publishing
dcshorepublishing.com

DEDICATION

For you, Jesus, because without You, my Lord, I have nothing. And with You, I have everything I need. You are my eternal Hope! *The Lord is my Shepherd, I shall not want.* Psalm 23 (NKJV)

For you, Philip Andrew Shore, because without you, my son, I might not realize how much I need Jesus. And with you, I will always have a reminder of what Heaven holds for those who will believe. *Blessed are the poor in spirit. For theirs is the kingdom of heaven.* Matthew 5:3 (NKJV)

For you, Charlotte Beyer, because without you, Grandma, I wouldn't have had a lifetime of watching a faith walk through grief. And with you, I have seen that, *weeping may stay for the night, but rejoicing comes in the morning.* Psalm 30:5 (NIV)

I love you more, Phil.

CONTENTS

In the morning watch, neath the lifted cloud,

You shall see but the Lord alone,

When He leads you on from the place of the sea

To a land that you have not known;

And your fears shall pass as your foes have passed,

You shall be no more afraid;

You shall sing His praise in a better place,

A place that His hand has made

Red Sea Place
By: Annie Johnson Flint

.

A WORD FROM THE AUTHOR

I write this note to you on November 14, 2014, Phil's 13th anniversary in Heaven. My granddaughter, Laila, and I were just talking about Phil's Homegoing. Our six grandchildren know about their Uncle Phil. They are looking forward to meeting him one day. It is good to get comfortable talking about Heaven, and about those who are there. I want our grandchildren to grow up with the knowledge that life goes on when we leave here because we have Jesus as our Savior. I want them, and everyone, to know that death is not to be feared, but to be acknowledged. And that Heaven can and should be looked forward to when that time comes. Yes, sometimes departures come too soon—and sometimes they linger too long. But discussing Heaven, as believers, should be the norm, since it is our future eternal Home. As you begin to read this book full of stories about my own journey through grief, I hope it will begin to open up discussions with your family and friends—maybe about things you hesitate to talk about.

This book is based on the reality of Jesus Christ, and all that He has provided for those who will believe in Him. These writings are shared to point you to the Truth of the Gospel. If you don't know Jesus as your Savior, there's no time to waste—not in today's world with all the crazy things going on. If you turn to page 347, there's a prayer there that can help you invite Jesus into your life. Truly, it is the only way to find healing, and the only way this book will make any sense, so you should probably go there first.

I pray these stories will contain useful tools to help you find Jesus' healing power in your own circumstances. Jesus told us He would be returning to take us Home one day. Not all of us will die a physical death. But all of us who believe in Jesus will live together in Heaven one day. Be sure to be counted among those the Father calls His own children.

Living in Jesus' saving grace,

Diane

INTRODUCTION

"No one lights a lamp and hides it in a clay jar or puts it under a bed.
Instead, they put it on a stand, so that those who
come in can see the light."
Luke 8:16 (NIV)

Just yesterday we finished "It Started in the Dark." I say "finished,"
because it is nearly so. One more look at a final proof that will arrive in
two days, take care of any last minute changes needed, and then we will
be ready to order copies for the Gala/book signing party planned in just
three weeks. Nothing like having a deadline to meet for motivation to
get it finished! It really is a good idea because the process to take a
book from manuscript to book form is not an easy task. It has taken just
about three months to do it—a lot of sweat and, yes, even some tears
along the way.

When bringing a project like this into finished form, there is a spiritual
battle going on. It has given me a whole new appreciation for any
Christian author, any Christian speaker, and especially our pastors each
Sunday morning. I just told my friend, Ann, today, "If we really
appreciate the Truth preached on Sunday morning, we better be
praying for our pastors. They will certainly be attacked for what they
have said!"

My sister, Karen, finished reading a proof for "It Started in the Dark,"
and called with her comments on it. Thankfully, they were mostly good,

and VERY encouraging; but before she hung up the phone, she emphatically warned us that attacks will be coming after speaking such Truth. Jim (my husband) and I almost chuckled at that point. The attacks had been coming so fast and furious over the last weeks and even months, that we were WELL AWARE of the high stakes of this process by now. Not only from the outside; but also emotionally. There were times I hated the book, loved the book, wanted to trash the book, etc... But I did appreciate her warning us, and even understanding the "cost" of this project, not to mention, the HIGH COST of the subject matter itself...living without our son each day!

There are two moments that I would like to share with you, about these writing projects, before we dive into the book you now hold in your hands. Because you have this book, you have probably read "It Started in the Dark" already, but maybe not. That is okay. My sister said the first one can truly stand on its own. So much so, in fact, that she doesn't know what I can possibly add to it in this "sequel." I laughed and said, "I don't know what I will be writing either. But I didn't know what I would be writing in the first one. So we shall see." Obviously, once again, if you are holding this book, God has given me something to write about. I certainly hope it will be worth reading. And perhaps it will stand on its own, too. Another friend, Lynn, had the boldness to say just yesterday, "I think this will be a trilogy." Oh my. Just, oh my.

The two moments I want to share with you are these. One day I was standing at my kitchen sink. The spiritual warfare was raging, I was tired, and not feeling my normal self...suffice it to say, I had a bit of depression—all part of the warfare—I don't normally struggle much with depression. The thought that came to me in that moment was, "Let's get out of here...let's go do something fun...let's run away from the struggle and bury it under some kind of exciting time." I almost shook my head to clear out the fog and confusion in those thoughts. That's exactly what I was NOT talking about in my first book. It wasn't even what I normally did. It was not the spiritual discipline that I had learned in dealing with grief. I took those thoughts, and it might be said, I put them in the garbage disposal and ground them to a pulp. I then left the kitchen, found my Bible, and sat down to go to the real source of Help, God's Word. That is the cure for what ails us, and not the Band-Aid we seem to want to so quickly run to.

Story number two: I was talking with my friend, Denise, on the phone about a month ago. She lives in a beautiful area in the mountains, and loves to use her home as a place of retreat. During our phone conversation, she invited me to come up and spend some time with her, to go out on their houseboat on the lake, and just get some R and R. The tears just filled my eyes, and spilled over, running down my cheeks at just the mention of that R and R time. It caught me by surprise. I am not easily moved to tears. The very next day, I was telling another friend about Denise's offer, and once again, the tears started in—a clear warning that I was over my eyeballs in spiritual warfare. I chose a day, packed my bag, and headed to the hills.

When I got to Denise and Mark's place, I settled in. Denise took off for a meeting, and her husband Mark sat outside reading a book. I decided to lie on the bed and read. It seemed like a huge, peaceful treat. It had been a while since I had done that. I turned to Psalm 91 in my Bible, which I was working on memorizing. As I worked through the verse, I drifted off to sleep. Once again, unlike me to nap in the daylight hours. When I woke up, God gently spoke very encouragingly to me. He showed me that what I had just done was what Jesus had done when the crowds pressed in on Him. He would go alone to the mountain to pray. God reminded me in those few moments upon awakening that I had gone to the mountain, sought time with my Father, opened up His Word, and prayed. I had not turned to shopping, drinking, drugs, over eating, etc... I truly believe God was showing me something I needed to see; that the book I was writing, "It Started in the Dark," were the words He had given me to write and continue to live by. They are words to help in times of trouble, stress, depression, spiritual warfare, etc... I was taking my own "medicine," God's "medicine," and using it as prescribed. I was not being a hypocrite, which was one of Satan's lies, and God let me know that I should continue working on the book as Jim and I had been. I came down from the mountain the next day, ready to do battle and keep on keepin' on...

And now, you hold this book in your hands. This one will include the second six months of the first year of grief. I will begin the process again of sharing the things God has taught me and continues to teach me each day. I hope, and I pray, you will find yourself somewhere in these pages. Even if it's just a small thing that encourages you along the way. Just this morning my mom said that the part in the first book about wanting people to know, not only the sick Phil, but who he was when he was well, really struck her. My dad has had Parkinson's for almost 20 years, and he is a changed man. That can be very hard. I was glad she shared that with me—that the book spoke to her even though dad is still with her on this earth.

God's Word says we are not to hide His light under a bed, or in clay jars (in the NIV). Honestly, I am thankful, to once again be in my "cave" writing. Writing is a joy! Publishing is much more difficult. Without my husband, Jim, spearheading the entire process, there would be NO book to read. I would keep what I have written in simple email form, and it would go no further. He is the techie, and the wind beneath my wings, that God knew was needed to get it all out from underneath the "bed."

Thank you for joining me on this journey. We will find, together in these pages, that life is not always easy, but it can be blessed with Jesus Christ as our Lord and Savior. I'm not saying I have all the answers. But I have some experience under my belt that may be useful to help another travel their own journey through brokenness and beyond with God's power.

So let's begin with the story containing Me, Myself, and The Great I AM.

Me
2001

Myself
2014

"You cannot see
my face, for
no one may see
me and live."

Exodus 33:20 (NIV)

**The Great
I AM**

PREFACE

Before we start this story, I need to bring you up to date. This is the second book I have written about our son, Phil, leaving this earth for Heaven. He was diagnosed with Leukemia at the age of 10½. One month after his 16th birthday, Phil lost that battle. He was in his own bed, and we were by his side. It was the beginning of a journey that is beyond words, both his and ours. His was into his eternal Home with Jesus. Ours was into a darkness that can barely be expressed in words, although I try.

In my first book, "It Started in the Dark," I take you with me through the complete devastation of living without our child each day. It is me, in the depths of despair, barely able to breathe. It is not an easy read, but it is an honest one about the difficulty I faced each day in the darkest hours of the soul. In this book, I am coming up for air, just a bit. I am starting to see the healing power of The Great I AM take hold of my heart. I am starting to see a way through what once seemed so impossible. It might be an easier read than my first book, but it is no less honest. The Me parts were written as part of the healing process. They were sent out as emails on the dates shown. The Myself parts are who I am now, looking back over the last almost 14 years. The Great I AM parts speak for themselves. God's Word never changes. He is the Rock we stand on that will never be shaken.

My sister said that she basically saw four themes repeated many times in this book. They are: 1) Surrender completely to God. 2) God is our only source of healing. 3) Don't turn to alcohol, shopping, drugs, food, etc...to fill our needs. 4) We are lost for all of eternity without Jesus. I believe she is right. I was pleased that those were the messages she found conveyed in the stories I share with you here. The Bible tells us these same things many times over. I'm thankful God has led me to share the same Truth.

Today, almost 14 years later, sharing Phil's story about his Homegoing is such a privilege. My husband, Jim, and I have grown in our walk with Jesus to a place of trusting that God *does* work all things together for good to those that love Him and are called according to His purpose. (Romans 8:28) Even when we don't understand what God is doing, we can trust Him through it all. We are a family that endures many of the same trials other families face today. Our two older sons, Jimm and Chris, have given us six grandchildren to enjoy. They are in their thirties now, and have their own challenges in life. Ours is not a perfect family. But we are a family that seeks to serve our Lord each day.

This book picks up in May of 2002, six months after we have said, "Good-bye" to Phil. I have grown a bit more resigned to Phil being gone, and somewhat more focused on what God might being doing in and through so much pain and missing. Fourteen years later, in 2015, I am now much more able to rest in what is. My heart no longer hurts, although I miss Phil every day. These stories tell how God has brought me to this point. I hope they will speak to your heart on your own journey, whatever it might be. We all have pain and suffering to endure in this life. It doesn't have to be grief for you, but it has to be the same Lord and Savior to see us all through.

Maranatha! Come, Lord Jesus!

CHAPTER ONE

As the heavens are higher than the earth,
so are my ways higher than your ways
and my thoughts than your thoughts.
Isaiah 55:8-9 (NIV)

<u>Me</u>

Moving

Friday, 24 May 2002

When we were getting ready to move overseas to England in 1989, I remember sitting in my living room in Fremont, California and looking around. I remember thinking, "Why are we moving? I'm perfectly happy right here." Eight years later when we moved back to California from Germany, I remember thinking that moving overseas was one of the best things we could have ever done because of all the things we experienced while we were there. We made many wonderful friends, and learned many things. It felt good to be moving home to the U.S. in the end, but we were leaving so many memories behind in Europe. Now, when I see the movie, "The Sound of Music," my heart yearns for the Alps, the green meadows, and the sights and sounds of Bavaria. Oh, how beautiful it was there!

As I was driving home from work today, looking at the hills, the beautiful trees, and the wind blowing through them, I thought of Heaven and what Phil must be experiencing there. He didn't want to go. He was "perfectly happy here," just as I was in Fremont. Phil didn't really know what to expect, although we tried to prepare him as much as possible for the destination of Heaven. But how could we do that, really, when we have never been there ourselves? So much of it is trust...trust in God, and His promises about the place He has prepared for us.

If we had the choice and could tell God exactly how we would like it to be, we might think that that would be a good idea. I would probably request a place with white sandy beaches and aqua-blue lagoons—palm trees and sunshine, forever and ever... But what does God have planned? If my mind can imagine a place that I think is "perfect," I know it falls way short of all that God is preparing for us. If we were given the choice between our wildest imaginings, and what God would prepare, I would have to go with God's preparation because my thinking is so limited. If I were able to choose, I have a feeling I would be sadly disappointed compared to what others ended up with by letting God choose their preparations.

If Phil had been able to choose, he would have chosen to stay in this world with all of us. But I'll bet when he got to Heaven, he was not disappointed, and he was glad that the choice was not his to make. He lives in a perfect world now...a world without sickness, sorrow, pain, and disappointment...a world full of peace and joy, forever and ever in the presence of the very One who created him. Phil is not disappointed. I was not disappointed when we moved overseas. I was delighted! Everything was new and different and so interesting. It was the best move we ever made! We loved it! And Phil is loving Heaven now!

Phil said shortly before he died, "I just wish we could all go together." He knew that he would probably soon be leaving. He also knew, as much as is humanly possible, that he was going to a great place. But he didn't want to go alone. I wouldn't have wanted to move overseas without my family. We shared in that experience. We still talk about it a lot today; it is part of our past, and will always be part of our lives. Our son, Chris, recently went back to Fremont with his girlfriend, Holly. She grew up there. Holly showed him her old neighborhood and her old schools, and then they went to the neighborhood we lived in. But it did not satisfy Chris. It was not his home for very long, and so it didn't hold all the great memories he had from living overseas. Chris looks forward to the day when he can go back to Europe and show Holly where he spent his time, the places he hung out, the restaurants, the schools, and the sights he enjoyed.

How could we ever regret the experience of living overseas, even though I wondered why we would ever choose it in the first place when we were so happy right where we were in Fremont? I realize now, that our world was limited then, and we had no idea what was available, having not experienced yet all that we did living in England and Germany. By going overseas, we found out how small the world really is. We can get on a plane and travel around our world in hours, or perhaps a couple of days. The people there are not that different than the people here; they just speak different languages. They still have the same joys and the same sorrows.

I remember walking around the farm where one of our German friends grew up during World War II. As my friend, Renate, gave me a tour of the farm, she explained how the top of the barn was newer than the rest of the house because it had been partially destroyed during the war! Oh no, I thought, probably by Americans. And yet there we stood on that day side by side, good friends with one another.

We would not have experienced all these things had we not chosen to step out and try something new. We had taken that step of faith, so to speak, not so unlike the step of faith we take when we give *our hearts to the Lord...not really knowing all there is to know, not really knowing what we will experience, but trusting that it could be good—that it might be all that it's promised to be, and we may come away from it a totally new person. We could experience a fuller, more satisfying life than ever before. I've certainly found that to be true. Life is different when Jesus Christ has given you the Hope you so desire. When you take that step of faith and say **I believe**, my life is Yours Jesus, forgive me for my sinful ways, and help me to follow You the rest of my days, life, as we know it, changes!*

Phil didn't have many days to live this life. His life was seemingly cut so short. But I'm sure he doesn't mind now. He minded while he was here, just as I mind while I am here that he is not here. It hurts every day, and I long for the pain to subside. It will in time...

How wonderful it is though, to think of all that he is experiencing now. It is so far above what I can even comprehend—I long to see it also. I look forward to joining him there for all of eternity. Wouldn't it be wonderful if, "We could all go together"? Yes, there are days like today when I am driving to work, and I hope that this is the day that Jesus will come back...that this will be the last day I will have to walk this earth without Phil...that this will be the last day I will have to feel this pain. Sometimes that helps me to keep putting one foot in front of the other—the thought that I might only have to do this just one more day.

I'm ready for Jesus to come back. More than ready! Then there will be no more suffering and no more missing...just JOY! JOY! JOY! And we can all be there together experiencing all that God has prepared for us!

Oh Lord, help me to think about such things. Such good things!

Finally, brothers, whatever is true, whatever is noble, whatever is right, whatever is pure, whatever is lovely, whatever is admirable - if anything is excellent or praiseworthy - think about such things.
Philippians 4:8 (NIV)

That is what I have to do. If I don't...if I don't....I would choose to stay in bed with the covers pulled up over my head. If I didn't have the Hope of Christ, I would have no hope at all. If I didn't know that Phil loved being where he is now, I could not stand the missing him. I have to think about such things, and I have to believe that Phil is happier than he has ever been before—even if he would have chosen to stay here with all of us. Sometimes, the choice is taken out of our hands. But sometimes we are given a choice like moving to Germany or England. Sometimes, there is no time to make that choice—it is made for us before we have time to think about it.

*Now is the time, if you have not made that choice. Don't wait. Think about it today. You may think you are "perfectly happy here," and you don't need to think about such things, but think again. Tomorrow may be too late, and you don't want to miss out on all that the Lord is preparing for you in Heaven. Don't get too satisfied with "here," because **here** will pass away. Heaven won't. It will always be there. Will you?*

I don't know if Jesus will come back tonight. The day is ending, and so far, He's a no show! So as we head into the three-day weekend, we will enjoy the restful days. I hope you all do, too.

Have a great weekend!
Love, Diane

Myself

Phil didn't really know what to expect, although we tried to prepare him as much as possible for the destination of Heaven. But how could we do that really, when we have never been there ourselves?

How do we prepare someone to leave this earth? I believe the best way is to read to them out of God's Word about where they are going. I have done this more than once since doing it with Phil, and it seems to be the most calming thing we can do for a person.

God's Word is anointed; it speaks **volumes** when we have little to say. It does take some courage to walk into a hospital, or someone's home, carrying a Bible. We can feel like Bible thumpers. But we are not. We are just bringing them the Good News they are so longing to hear. I have had nurses poke their heads into a hospital room asking, "Is that the Bible you are reading?" Yes, it can be heard out in the halls. Who knows who might be touched by the Truth we are sharing.

But what does God have planned? If my mind can imagine a place that I think is "perfect," I know it falls way short of all that God is preparing for us.

Isn't that good to know? That we can't even truly imagine how awesome our eternal life in Heaven is going to be! But the sad side of that is, we also can't imagine how horrible eternal torment in Hell will be for those who don't believe, and neither can they. Too many think the party will be in Hell, and the boredom will be in Heaven. Nothing could be farther from the Truth! There will be no relationships in Hell, no comfort, no light, and no water, to name just a few of the things that will be missing. But what will be missing even more than that is God. He will not be there. He is present with us here today reading this. If you are not a believer, He does not live inside of you in the form of the Holy Spirit. But that doesn't mean God is completely removed from you. Feel that cool breeze? It comes from God. Hear that bird singing? It sings with God's melody. Hear that voice in the other room? That is a relationship provided by God. Everything good on this earth will be removed in Hell. And everything good on this earth will be even better in Heaven.

If Phil had been able to choose, he would have chosen to stay in this world with all of us. But I'll bet when he got to Heaven, he was not disappointed, and he was glad that the choice was not his to make.

We all want to stay here when we focus on here and the people we love and care about. But I have to tell you, and I will share more about this in an upcoming chapter, Phil got a glimpse of Heaven before he left here. And then he wanted nothing more than to be finished with this place. It amazed me that just one tiny glimpse of what awaits on the other side is better than everything that surrounded him here. I wasn't hurt by this; that he'd want Heaven more than even being with his mom—I was encouraged by it. It encourages me more than almost anything else to this day. I know what awaits us is good, very, very good, not only because of what God's Word says about it, but because of what Phil said about it!

Phil said shortly before he died, "I just wish we could all go together." He knew that he would probably soon be leaving.

Phil hated leaving all of us…not because he wasn't ready to be done with the suffering, but mainly, I think, because he knew how much we would hurt after he was gone. He was a very sensitive, caring young man. He loved us all so much. He wanted to be sure that I told everyone that he said, "Good-bye." I know of a few people in the hospital as I write this very paragraph…they may not be coming home, and their families sit at their bedsides. I know they are tired, and maybe they would really just like to move on Home to Heaven, but leaving is so hard. They don't want those left behind to hurt like they have hurt when they have been left by others. It is very normal, and it is very important for us to have a good perspective on where the dying are going. We can help them leave in peace, assuring them that we will be fine after a time; with God's help.

How could we ever regret the experience of living overseas, even though I wondered why we would ever choose it in the first place when we were so happy right where we were in Fremont?

Change is hard. Not many people like it. Most of us would just like things to stay the same, even when, a lot of time, same contains pain. We usually aren't ready to make a change until the pain becomes so great, we just can't stand it anymore. My friend, Michella, is probably having surgery soon. The pain in her neck is to a point that she is ready—ready to be done with it, no matter what it takes. To make a choice to change something, like moving overseas just "because," is very difficult. It's easier when our hand is forced sometimes. The same may be said for getting to know Jesus. Foxholes make it easy to call out to Jesus for help and reassurance. Good, beautiful, wonderful days make it harder. The need doesn't seem as great. But it is as great because we are not promised tomorrow. But we **are** promised an eternity with our Savior, if we so choose it.

Phil didn't have many days to live this life. His life was seemingly cut so short... It hurts every day, and I long for the pain to subside. It will in time...

The pain is gone today. It really is! It wasn't when I wrote the chapter about "Moving" six months into my grief. The pain was huge then! It seemed beyond repair. I had no idea where I was going, or how it would look when I arrived. Today, life is different, very different. The boys are in their 30's, and they have given us six grandchildren. We do have one grandchild in Heaven also; one who died in the womb at four months. I look forward to one day seeing the grandchild I have never met. Lives are sometimes cut seemingly short, and we don't have most of the answers for *why*. What we do have is the Hope for *what now*. What now is that God provides, and He is faithful, and we can depend on His promises. It is so good to now be writing the second half of this story, the second half of the first year that leads out of the dark and into the light and seeing more of those promises become a reality. Not that the second half of that first year ended the pain, but it was a continued part of the process of getting there. Tears today don't equate to the pain of that time. Tears today are more tender and infrequent, but not unheard of. That's okay. That's normal. That's the way life and death are. But as I read an email from a friend recently about grief, it reminded me that I'd rather have the memories, and a few tears sometimes, than to have the memories wiped from my mind. I said, "It's hard to remember, but how much harder it would be to forget!" I don't want to ever forget Phil. I just want to be able to remember him in a healthy, Hope-filled way. That is the goal. Not to forget, but to remember well!

Yes, there are days like today when I am driving to work, and I hope that this is the day that Jesus will come back...that this will be the last day I will have to walk this earth without Phil. Sometimes that helps me to keep putting one foot in front of the other—the thought that I might only have to do this just one more day.

We can do almost anything one day at a time. If we look a week, a month, or a year ahead, then it can seem like too big of a mountain to "climb." In the beginning of grief, it is one minute at a time. And then the moments between devastation start to lengthen. The darkness lifts briefly in the beginning, and for longer periods later on. Now, almost 13 years later, I can say that most days are filled with the light of God. The devastation is a long-ago memory, one that I don't dwell on. What I do dwell on is the Hope of Jesus. That makes for a much better day!

That is what I have to do. If I don't...if I don't...I would choose to stay in bed with the covers pulled up over my head. If I didn't have the Hope of Christ, I would have no hope at all. If I didn't know that Phil loved being where he is now, I could not stand the missing him.

So true! Even to this day! And it is much easier on this day, I must say. Many years ago I had to work very hard at not staying in bed with the covers pulled over my head. Today, I look forward to getting up each morning and spending those first precious moments of the day in the Word—reconnecting to what is true, and right and honorable. I used to be a late sleeper, but no longer. Mornings are the best part of the day for me now. I'm not sure exactly why, except for God's transformational power!

*But sometimes we are given a choice like moving to Germany or England. Sometimes, there is no time to make that choice—it is made for us before we have time to think about it. Don't get too satisfied with "here," because **here** will pass away. Heaven won't. It will always be there. Will you?*

When I spoke at the women's tea the day before Mother's Day, just a few weeks ago, I talked about Jesus coming back. I told the ladies that Jesus could come back in 10, 20, or 30 years, but He could also come back in 10, 20, or 30 minutes. I talked to them about their chairs, and whether they would be empty or full should Jesus return before I finished speaking that day. We prayed about saying, "Yes," to Jesus right at the beginning of the talk I gave. I knew there was no time to waste. The worst thing on that day would have been if Jesus had come back, and some of those ladies were still sitting in their chairs while the rest of us got taken Home to Heaven. That is true devastation! The devastation of this earth is temporary. But the devastation of not being a child of God, and not being taken Home to Heaven when Jesus returns for us is eternal devastation. I don't wish that upon anyone, and I will do my best to teach and encourage all I meet how to not let that happen! As we continue on in this second part of "It Started in the Dark," travelling into "It Ended in the Light," I know that is the purpose of sharing all that I am here. **It is all for naught, if it is not for Jesus!** He is the way, the truth, and the life we are all looking for. Let Jesus know that you need His love, His forgiveness, and His shed blood to wash you clean. Then we can travel on through these pages together on the same "page," looking forward to all that He has waiting for us. It is a blessed Hope!

Gift #1 – A blessed Hope comes with Jesus!

Is Jesus your Savior? If not, take some time to ask yourself why? And decide what you would like to do about it.

If Jesus is your Savior, take some time to thank Him for all that He has provided.

Record today's date and other notes you'd like to make:

The Great

<u>I AM</u>

*"Do not let your hearts be troubled. You believe
in God; believe also in me. My Father's house
has many rooms; if that were not so, would I have
told you that I am going there to prepare a place
for you? And if I go and prepare a place for you, I
will come back and take you to be with me that
you also may be where I am."*
John 14:1-4 (NIV)

CHAPTER TWO

When darkness overtakes the godly, light will come bursting in.
Psalm 112:4 (NLT)

<u>Me</u>

God's Healing

Thursday, 30 May 2002

I want to be healed. I crave it! I pray for it! I earnestly seek it every day. I don't want to feel this pain. I want my heart to stop bleeding. I want my energy to be restored. I want, I want, I want, to the point of working so hard at it that "it" exhausts me. What am I doing? Sometimes, I wonder.

I felt God asking me to write tonight but I didn't know what it would be about. I felt God telling me it would be something I would rather stay silent about. That I would be vulnerable, and it would be difficult. Would I be willing to share? Here I am...and already I feel vulnerable. And yet, if I don't share, then what's it all for anyway? I am not the first person, nor will I be the last, to feel any of these feelings. Probably some of you have already felt this way in your life, and you'll breathe a sigh of relief to know that you are not alone. Perhaps...

I want to work at this, this grief process. I want to work HARD at it. I want to get it "right." I want to turn over every dark and dirty rock and see what it says on the underneath side. I don't want anything to be hidden that might be kicked over later and revealed, causing pain five, ten, or twenty years from now that wasn't dealt with when it should have been. I want to "go there" if I need to and deal with it. And yet, at the same time, there are so many places I don't want to go physically because it hurts too much— because of the memories. What a strange mixture of emotions! I guess I want to go to all the places in my mind emotionally that need tending to; but I don't want to go to the mall, for instance, because that hurts too much. But I did, I went to the mall today, and guess what? It didn't hurt that bad. Sure, I thought of Phil. But it was easier today. Jim and I were there having lunch and then we walked around a bit. I was telling him, as we were having lunch, that I want to go, go, go, to so many places, but then I don't want to go because I know it will hurt. Like when you tell your doctor that it hurts when you do this...and he says, "Well then don't do that!" Well, it hurts when I go to the mall, so I won't do that. Wrong! I can't stay in my comfortable "cage" and avoid the pain. I have to eventually go out and face it...even if it hurts.

But you know what I am finding is the most important thing of all? The most important thing of all is to submit to God—to let the Healer heal me in His own way and in His own timing. I just read in my latest Bible study that it is more important to "know the Healer, than to be healed." Isn't that true? If my heart is never completely healed, but I know the Healer/God, I will be fine. All my work, all my ambition, will get me nowhere except exhausted, and I have plenty of that already. But to know God better is never a waste of time!

I am a "just do it" person. The more I talk with my mom on their travels (my parents travel full time), the more I see where I got part of that from. The other day I was talking with my mom and she is telling me that they are planning on buying a raft, an inflatable raft so when they get to Lake Louise in Canada, they will be able to go out onto the lake, and other lakes they come across in the future. My mom can't even swim! I told her she better have a life preserver because if the raft should tip over, she will drown! We laugh, but it is the truth. Now, my parents are edging up there towards 70, but they are adventurous. They decide on something, they make plans, and they follow through with it. It's a great quality, I believe! Even if they seem a little crazy at times, they know how to live life to the fullest! Everywhere they go, they go to have a good time, and they come away having had a good time!

So here I am, trying to "just do it" through grief, and it just isn't the way it's done. I wish it were. If determination was the way "through," I would be halfway there by now. Instead, there are days when it seems I have only just begun. Even though Phil has been gone 6½ months, it seems like yesterday at times. Determination is not what will get me through this. Perseverance will, but not the kind that I am accustomed to. The perseverance I need is to keep asking God for help...again, and again, and again.

*I thought about it this way. If my heart was bleeding all over the place and I was being taken into the operating room for the Physician to fix my wound, what would I be doing? I would not be telling him how to do it. I would not be assisting him in the operation. I would not even be awake. I would be lying back on the gurney, sleeping. I would hope. I would have no part in how **he** was going to fix it. I wouldn't even know how that would be possible having never gone to medical school. I would simply have to trust him, shut my eyes, lie back, and let him repair the wound.*

That seems simple enough when I look at it that way, so why does it not seem so simple when it is an emotional wound that only God can repair? Why am I not always willing to let Him fix me up, and trust Him for what I need...to lie back and rest in His arms until He stops the bleeding? It seems simple enough. But my "just do it" attitude keeps me from fully doing that until about now...until about 6½ months into grief when the wound is still bleeding profusely, and there is nothing I can do to stop it on my own. I go out for walk, after walk, after walk, and tell God how broken I am on that day. And then I go out again and tell Him the next time that I am really broken now...as compared to what? Yesterday? It's craziness! And the only way out of the craziness is to submit to His tender care. Oh, I think I have, until I submit the next time, and the next time—until God keeps calling me back to Him once again.

But the Lord still waits for you to come to
him so he can show you his love
and compassion. For the Lord is a faithful God.
Blessed are those who wait for
him to help them.
Isaiah 30:18 (NLT)

And so why is it so hard to wait for Him to help me? Because in the back of my mind, I still think I can do it myself! Somehow, I will find the energy, the reserves, and the determination to heal myself.

*I don't think so...not anymore. I believe God is showing me that I can only go so far on my own. Oh sure, I could look healed, act healed, and go on with my life. But I want more than that! I want **His** healing. I don't want to be left empty, hurting, and missing Phil all the days of my life. I want to be left with God's peace, His joy, and His love embedded so deep in my life that God will get the glory for what **He has done**. Not what I've done, not on my own strength for a half-done job that is just a messy patch over my wound—maybe one that the world is used to seeing, and it seems fine... Oh look at Diane, isn't she doing great? No! I want God's healing, so that when I am alone at night and the enemy comes to torture me with thoughts that can destroy me, I will not be destroyed by them. I will have the Victory that comes from knowing Jesus Christ and the power of His Resurrection. What Victory is that, you might ask? The Victory that comes with the Hope we are promised. I am stubborn. But God already knew that about me! Maybe that is why He chose me for this assignment. I do want to get this right; but not my right! **God's** right!*

O people of Zion, who live in
Jerusalem, you will weep no more.
He will be gracious if you ask for help.
He will respond instantly
to the sound of your cries.
Isaiah 30:19 (NLT)

I don't want to muffle my own cries. I want God to dry my tears!

Though the Lord gave you adversity
for food and affliction for drink,
he will still be with you to teach you.
You will see your teacher with your
own eyes, and you will hear a voice say,
"This is the way; turn around and walk here."
Isaiah 30:20-21 (NLT)

I don't want to find my own way through this. How crazy would
that be when God has already provided the way and He tells us,
"This is the way; turn around and walk here."

When I go for my walks and talk with God, I look up at the hills
and think of the verse:

"Though the mountains be shaken
and the hills be removed,
yet my unfailing love for you will not be shaken
nor my convent of peace be removed,"
says the Lord, who has compassion on you.
Isaiah 54:10 (NIV)

I know that no matter what I am feeling, God's love will always be.
Always! His peace will always be. Always! And He is the Great
Physician who can heal any pain, no matter how deep, no matter
how dark, no matter what!

I expect to be completely healed from this wound. Some may say I
am crazy. Some say that you can't recover fully from the loss of a

child. I am not talking about forgetting Phil, or acting like he never existed. Quite the opposite! I will always remember Phil and share with others what has happened. But I know the Great Healer, and I know He can do miracles! I know that if I stay out of His way and let Him do His work, He will fix me up better than new! Yes, better than new, because I will not be the same, I will be changed for the better! I'll be more willing, and more able to do what I was put on this earth to do—and if that is simply to love God with all my heart, with all my soul, with all my mind, and with all my strength, then that will be fine. Just fine! If that is all that I will be capable of when all this is said and done, then I will have accomplished what He asked in Matthew 22:36-40 (NLT):

> *"Teacher, which is the most important commandment in the law of Moses?" Jesus replied, "You must love the Lord your God with all your heart, all your soul, and all your mind." This is the first and greatest commandment. A second is equally important: 'Love your neighbor as yourself.' All the other commandments and all the demands of the prophets are based on these two commandments."*

I don't have to conquer the whole world. I just have to love God with everything I have. I will start there, and let Him do the rest. He is willing.

> *The Sovereign Lord, the Holy One of Israel says, "Only in returning to me and waiting for me will you be saved. In quietness and confidence is your strength." Isaiah 30:15 (NLT)*

That is where my strength is found on those quiet walks with God, looking up at the hills He created and asking Him to help me. I can't do it on my own, in my strength, if I am to be completely healed. It is more than this "just do it" person can accomplish. It is a large task, and I am not able. But with God, it is possible, because He is able!

It is good to know that this will not go on forever—although at times it seems to be forever already. It helps me, more than you know, to pour my heart out, my struggles out, and yes to even be vulnerable to all of you with what I am going through. It is one of the ways that God heals this wound. It is an amazing thing that I don't even fully understand. But I am grateful for it.

Thank you to those of you who take the time to read these e-mails, and even to those of you who don't read them but also don't send me e-mails back saying, "Cancel any further correspondence. You have gone off the deep end." I know I have gone off the deep end. But with God's help, I won't drown!

God was right; this is a difficult one to share tonight. I'd rather hit "delete" and go to bed. But I won't. I will pray, and then I will hit "send" because He asks me to, hoping this makes some sense to you.

All this, simply to say, I need to submit to the Healer.
You can't say I'm short on words—just patience.

Good night!
Diane

<u>Myself</u>

What am I doing? Sometimes, I wonder.

When I read back through this now, I know on one hand, I had no idea what I was doing. On the other hand, I was doing exactly what I should have been doing…walking it out with God, one day at a time. That's what we do when we don't have any answers—we cling to the only One who does. We seek the Lord, we find the Lord, and the Lord heals us in His own way and in His own timing.

I felt God telling me it would be something I would rather stay silent about. That I would be vulnerable, and it would be difficult. Would I be willing to share?

It really was hard to share some of these things. Honestly, it was hard to share a lot of these things. They were my deepest thoughts and struggles through grief. I wrote because it seemed I was asked to, and because it helped me sort through everything. But it was like taking my heart out of my chest, laying it on the table, and waiting for anyone that might want to, to take a sludge hammer to it. That's how vulnerable it felt. Yet, most were so kind. There were a few that unsubscribed along the way, but most didn't. I appreciate all of you to this day for being kind to me as I "bled" all over the place.

I want to work at this, this grief process. I want to work HARD at it. I want to get it "right." I want to turn over every dark and dirty rock and see what it says on the underneath side.

This is still very much a part of my walk…turning over every dark and dirty rock. But these days, the rocks are a lot smoother, easier, and usually underneath them I find blessings. I write much more about the goodness I see in God and His ways each day than the pain that my heart was feeling. Oh, there are still things from time to time that catch me off guard, that need some work concerning Phil. But mostly, I am blessed beyond measure. Did I get it "right?" through the years? I say, "**God** got it right." The hardest thing I had to do along the way was cooperate with God. Give up myself—my ways, my timing, my wants, to Him and let the Healer do His thing. He will, but we have to *let* Him. That's the hardest part, relinquishing control of our own lives into His loving hands. Let's face it; we want what we want when we want it. I wanted to be healed! We are bratty children. But God is our Father. He knows best. We have to trust that.

I can't stay in my comfortable "cage" and avoid the pain. I have to eventually go out and face it…even if it hurts.

26

I so remember wanting to stay on familiar paths so as to avoid painful moments. I liked the drive to work. I had been down that road before. I like the drive to church—which was the same road since I worked at the church. I got used to the grocery store. Ok, I can do that now. But I remember when the day came I had jury duty. OH NO! I have to get on the freeway and drive past things I haven't seen yet without Phil in the car with me…it scared me, I knew the pain was waiting there. But little by little, we do face all those things, and little by little they hurt less and less. It's all a part of the process of healing—one that we can't avoid if we truly want to live again. Jesus will make a way, He will be with us. He felt His own pain, and His compassion is there for us.

The most important thing of all is to submit to God—to let the Healer heal me in His own way and in His own timing.

Submit. There is a verse in James that talks about resisting the devil, and he will flee from us. But it starts with "submission." We can't fight these battles on our own. We need the power of God, both in us and around us, to be victorious. Our own strength will only last for a period of time, and then it will fail. That's not to be pessimistic, it is simply the truth. But God's strength is always the same, it never fails, and we can depend on it. I can't resist temptation on my own. But when I submit to God, He can provide a way of escape so that I will be able to endure it. We may think it doesn't work. But what doesn't work, is that we don't even want to ask for help…because we know God will give it to us, and we want that "chocolate chip cookie"! So we think to ourselves, "I'm not going to ask God to help me not eat it." The battle is lost before we even begin, because we aren't willing to begin with God. I know, because I love chocolate chip cookies!

Determination is not what will get me through this. Perseverance will, but not the kind that I am accustomed to. The perseverance I need is to keep asking God for help…again, and again, and again.

Yes, chocolate chip cookies are not going away—no temptation is! We live in a fallen world! I was just out to lunch yesterday at a place that makes delicious cookies—almost as good as homemade. I didn't buy one…why? Because the friend I was with said, if she gets started, she can't stop. And I remembered the verse about not causing someone else to stumble. So, I didn't buy one. But I still wanted a cookie yesterday, and they give samples away there, so I had a couple of those. If we are waiting for the temptations to be gone, or our own determination to take the problem/pain away, it's not going to happen. We can't be "determined" enough to make it through each temptation, each problem, or each painful circumstance of life. But God is with us each day to see us through it all, and He will. Again and again! Ask, and you shall receive. That is why we were given the Holy Spirit when Jesus ascended back into Heaven. Jesus told His disciples not to leave Jerusalem until they received this gift from the Father. Jesus knew they were NOT capable of living this life, or even doing Kingdom work, on their own without His power within. The same is true of us today. It's just that simple. Like it or not!

And so why is it so hard to wait for Him to help me? Because in the back of my mind, I still think I can do it myself! Somehow, I will find the energy, the reserves, and the determination to heal myself.

Do you see my struggle here, which is everyone's struggle? We want to do it our "own selves"! Thank you very much, God! I've got this! That will always be our battle. Satan wants us to think we are in control. The enemy is out to kill, steal, and destroy everything good that God has for us. Satan will lie to us and tell us we are strong enough to battle grief, loneliness, heartache, temptations, etc…on our own. And then when we find we aren't, our enemy, Satan, will accuse us of being weak. And he will be the very one to beat us up for falling for the temptation he bombarded us with in the first place. And God, our most loving Savior, Jesus Christ, waits patiently for us to turn to Him. The Holy Spirit is more than willing to use His power to bring us through. But will we let Him? That is the question.

I believe God is showing me that I can only go so far on my own.

I saw how far I could go on my own, and it wasn't far. But I'm here all these years later, to share the Good News with everyone who is willing to "listen." When we come to the end of ourselves, we find Jesus was there waiting for us all along. And He is most willing. And He is most able! If we don't get to that point of surrender, we miss the greatest moment of our lives, finding out just Who Jesus really is—a Savior that can be trusted, depended on, and willing to do it all. I was reading in Matthew 19 yesterday, about the man who asked what he must do to gain eternal life? I read it, and thought of it as I never have before. This man felt he had done everything right, and he told Jesus that. But then he asks, "What else must I do?" Jesus answered him by saying, "If you want to be perfect…" The word "perfect" caught my attention. It seemed that Jesus understood what this man was trying to do. He was trying to "earn" his way into Heaven, so Jesus then gave him an impossible assignment—be perfect, sell everything and follow Me, which Jesus knew the man would never be able to do. Jesus told His disciples after they had asked Him, "who in the world can be saved?"—that what is not humanly possible, is possible with God. Jesus wanted this man to let **Him** do it for him instead of trying to be perfect. Are we willing to let **Jesus** do it for us?

I want God's healing so that when I am alone at night, and the enemy comes to torture me with thoughts that can destroy me, I will not be destroyed by them.

The days can be so much easier than the nights. Just like when we are sick, we can make it through the days okay, but aren't the nighttimes just sooo long! We wait for the sun to come back up so that we won't be alone in our misery. But night does come, and being alone does come, and what do we do then? We can't always cover our pain with busyness, trips, fun, food, and all the rest. And those alone times are when the enemy is most vicious, attacking our thoughts, shooting arrows at our hearts, and making us feel like life isn't worth living. What do we do then? We have to find Jesus' healing power during our daylight hours, so when the darkness does come, there's leftover "light" to see us through until morning. The world's "cover-ups" don't work. We need the deep down healing that comes from the Holy Spirit living inside of us.

I know that if I stay out of His way and let Him do His work, He will fix me up better than new! Yes, better than new; because I will not be the same, but I will be changed for the better!

I'm not the same today. I never will be, and I never want to be. Jesus transforms us for the better, through the good days and the bad. He has a plan for our good, not to harm us, but to bring us hope and a future. My husband, Jim, always says we are to show up and stay out of God's way. It's simple, but true. Even when I am asked to speak certain places, I can prepare all I want and need to. But when the time actually comes, I need to show up, and then stay out of God's way. When I do, I have experienced amazing times of God just doing His thing, and I'm seemingly just the tool standing there being used by Him. That's when powerful Kingdom work is going on. Not when we are clever and wise on our own. In 1 Corinthians 1:19 (NLT) it says, "I will destroy human wisdom and discard their most brilliant ideas."

...and if that is simply to love God with all my heart, with all my soul, with all my mind, and with all my strength, then that will be fine. Just fine! If that is all that I will be capable of when all this is said and done, then I will have accomplished what He asked in Matthew 22:36-40 (NLT):

I didn't know what I would be capable of when all was said and done. I'm not sure that all is said and done even yet…how could it be with so much Kingdom work left to do on this earth? But, I do hope that my first priority each day is to love God with all my heart, and be devoted to His ways. From there, it's all gravy! This thought did take the pressure off though—if nothing else could. I would just focus on learning to love God more and more…and wait for Jesus to come back! That's what you call tying a knot in the end of the rope, and holding on for dear life. That's what I did, until Jesus gave me my life back. I'm still waiting for His return!

It is good to know that this will not go on forever, although at times it seems to be forever already.

I can barely remember those forever moments now. I know they were there, and I know how painful they were. But my mind can't quite comprehend just how horrible it was anymore. And that is a good thing. I know enough to know and share, but I don't have to relive it every day. Maybe that's the way Heaven will be…we will know enough to know, so we know how good we have it. But we won't have to relive the painful days on this earth? Just thinking out loud there…

I know I have gone off the deep end, but with God's help, I won't drown!

I went off the deep end with Jesus. I became a Jesus Freak, some may say. And I'm SO THANKFUL that I love Jesus freakishly! I have become so Heavenly minded that I can now be of some earthly good! That's what makes life worth living. My desire is to follow Jesus every day. I don't do it perfectly…like the man was asked by Jesus, "If you want to be perfect…" No, I have a lot of learning yet to do. But I do know now that I can follow the One who is perfect. When we walk in His footsteps, we are assured we are at least heading in the right direction!

All this, simply to say I need to submit to the Healer.
You can't say I'm short on words, just patience!

Short on words is not my gift—maybe as a child, when I was shy—but then again, it's not that I didn't have the words; I just couldn't get them out. My friend, Ann, explained it to me this way, "You didn't have a voice." Somewhere along the way, God has given me a voice, and I want to use it to shout His praises! If you have not given your life to the Lord, you are missing out on the very best this life has to offer. No riches, no beautiful homes, no fancy cars, not even good health can substitute for what Jesus offers to each and every one of us who will call upon His name! It starts deep, with a surrendered heart, and builds from there.

When I was baptized years ago, with Phil sitting in the audience watching, I stepped into the tub. Right then, they decided to do a song. They played, *I Surrender All*. "Really, God?" I thought. It seemed all too appropriate. I was willing to be dunked for Jesus. But was I willing to surrender, not only my life, but what was most precious to me, my children? I didn't have the answer on that day. But I had the question to ponder…and now I have found the answer. This is what I can say on this day. "Yes, Lord, you can have my son. You first gave him to me, and He belongs to You. Whether he is here on this earth with me, or in Heaven with You, he is Yours, and has always been Yours. I will continue to love You and serve You. No matter what. Thank You for letting me be his mom for 16 years here. And thank You for providing a way to be with Phil again when this earthly life is done. I love You, Lord Jesus. Thank You for Your sacrifice on the Cross. I surrender all to You—every day, one day at a time, **with Your help**!"

<u>Gift #2</u> – Finding that surrender is the only way to win the battle.

Have you come to a point of surrender in your own life with Christ?

What are you trying to do on your own that only Jesus can do in and through you?

Record today's date and other notes you'd like to make:

The Great

<u>I AM</u>

O people of Zion, who live in Jerusalem, you will weep no more. He will be gracious if you ask for help. He will respond instantly to the sound of your cries.
Isaiah 30:19 (NLT)

CHAPTER THREE

*But Stephen, full of the Holy Spirit, gazed steadily upward into
heaven and saw the glory of God...*
Act 7:55 (NLT).

Me

"I See The Heavens..."

Wednesday, 12 Jun 2002

*I was reading Acts 7 this afternoon. I had asked God where I
should go in the Bible, and this came to me, so I turned there. I
wondered what I would find. This chapter is about Stephen. In Acts
6 it says that Stephen was a man full of God's grace and power. He
doesn't get many pages in the Bible, but he got enough to make an
impact. As I was reading along, I came to the end of Acts 7, where
Stephen's life came to an abrupt end. He was stoned to death.*

*You might think this was his worst day, but I doubt it. Since it talks
about Stephen gazing upward into Heaven and seeing the glory of
God, and seeing Jesus standing at God's right hand, I think that
would be the best day of my life!*

You might think he would be angry at those who stoned him. But he wasn't. It says his last words were, "Lord, don't charge them with this sin!" Wow, why would anyone say that to a group of people who were stoning them to death?

You might think that those around him would never believe in Jesus. But at least one did. Saul was there. He was later known as, Paul, and he was transformed by the resurrected Christ and spent the rest of his life spreading the Good News.

I asked God why He was having me read this today. As I read, I started remembering Phil's vision of Heaven. I thought that I had told this part of Phil's story, but many seem surprised when it comes up, so maybe I haven't shared it with you. It is an awesome experience that I will never forget. It happened on Monday night, two nights before Phil went home. This is what happened...

I was lying with Phil on his bed. He was on his back, and I was on my stomach next to him. I was reading to him out of the Bible, and he started to cry. He said, "Mom, everything you are reading to me answers every question I have in my head." He said something to the effect that he didn't read the Bible much before, but now he sees why you need to.

After awhile, he said, "Mom, I see a light."
(I had asked Phil that if he ever saw a light, would he please tell me.)
I said, "Phil, go toward the light!"
I remember looking at his closed eyes, at his eye lids, and thinking, I don't see anything.
Then he was quiet. I'm not sure how long he was quiet. I'm not sure if he continued breathing, or if his heart continued beating. I'm not even sure what I did during those moments. But after some time had passed, Phil sort of gasped and he jerked back a bit. And then when he spoke, his words had an angry tone to them.

He said, "I THOUGHT I was finished! Oh, I don't want to be here!"

He seemed disturbed, which was so unlike Phil. To hear an angry tone come out of him was foreign most of the time. So, being the weird mother that I am, I asked him some questions, because I WANTED to know. (My mom has said she doesn't want me next to her bed when she is dying. I tell her I will send people into her room, and they will come out and tell me.) Hey, you don't get to talk with someone every day who has seen Heaven.

Phil then said, "Mom, I saw Heaven. There were a lot of people there." I asked him what it looked like, and if he recognized anyone? I asked him if he saw Jesus? He didn't see Jesus, and he didn't recognize anyone. He said it looked sort of like a picture of Heaven that he had in his wallet. He said it was so beautiful! He still seemed disturbed, so I thanked him. Yes, I thanked him for coming back and telling me about seeing Heaven. I told him that God knew I needed to hear about it—and then he quieted down. His peace returned, and he told me something else; he told me that the devil had been lying to him. He said that the devil had told him that it hurts to die, and it doesn't. He said his lungs stung a bit because he had stopped breathing. But dying didn't hurt. And he said he felt bad because he didn't want to breathe anymore, but he didn't want God to be mad at him, so he thought he should try to breathe again.

*This is what he told me, and please keep in mind, Phil was **not** a person who told stories. He didn't make things up, or even elaborate on the truth a bit. He was usually just very straight forward and honest with whatever he said. He was one to be believed when he told you something.*

I don't know why Phil was given a glimpse of Heaven before going Home—but I'm glad he was able to. I'm glad he was able to share it with me, and it comforts me to know he is happy now. Phil rarely got mad, and he loved being here, and he loved us. As sick as he was, it was difficult for him to want to leave. But one glimpse of Heaven was all it took. After one short experience of feeling the peace that awaited him, he wanted nothing to do with this world anymore. I bet that's the way Stephen must have felt.

But Stephen, full of the Holy Spirit,
gazed steadily upward into heaven and saw the
glory of God, and he saw Jesus
standing in the place of honor at God's right hand.
And he told them, "Look, I see the heavens opened and the Son of
Man standing in the place of honor at God's right hand!"
Acts 7:55-56 (NLT)

I'm not saying Phil is like Stephen. Please don't get me wrong.
Stephen was a great man of God who is honored to have his story
in the Bible. But I am saying that Stephen's story helped me to
remember Phil's experience, and how awesome it will be to see
Heaven some day.

And as they stoned him, Stephen prayed, "Lord Jesus, receive my
spirit." And he fell to his knees, shouting, "Lord, don't charge
them with this sin!" And with that, he died.
Acts 7:59 (NLT)

Stephen didn't have much time between when he saw Heaven, and
when he arrived there. Phil had about 48 hours between when he
saw Heaven and when he went Home to Heaven. During that time,
his memories of that experience had a chance to fade. In fact, at
one point when he needed to know about God's promises and
God's grace, I reminded him of his Heavenly vision. He said that it
was getting harder to remember it. I have to take into
consideration how sick he was, and how his body was failing him.
But that was in less than 48 hours.

How quickly we forget God's provisions for us, and this is not to
put Phil down in any way. I am just being honest with you here
about his experience and the things that he told me. I am so
grateful for all that he shared with me, and I know because he has
arrived in his Heavenly Home already, he would want me to share
whatever might be useful and help others know of God's goodness.
But it does make me think about how quickly we can forget how
good God is to us. He answers our prayers, and we are so grateful.
We say we will trust Him with all we have! Then the next day, a

*new "storm" arises and there we are again, back to stressing about whether God will provide in this new situation. It is our human fleshly way of thinking. I forget also. I panic and get worried about tomorrow even after all that God has shown me. That's why I keep going back to God's Word and spending time with Him. It is the only way that I am able to rest in God completely. I need to know God more and more, so I don't forget. The only way **through** this grief is to **not** forget, and to learn to trust. When God's Word is fresh on my mind, when I have just spent time with God, then I don't forget so easily; and I am not so easily swayed by the strong winds in a storm. Then my "house" is built on solid rock, not shifting sands.*

"Anyone who listens to my teaching and obeys me is wise, like a person who builds a house on solid rock. Though the rain comes in torrents and the floodwaters rise and the winds beat against that house, it won't collapse, because it is built on rock. But anyone who hears my teaching and ignores it is foolish, like a person who builds a house on sand. When the rains and the floods come and the winds beat against that house, it will fall with a mighty crash."
Matthew 7:24-27 (NLT)

I have taken that mighty crash, and I don't like it at all! I have forgotten God's promises at times, and those are the hardest times. I have learned to depend on God's Word like never before in my life. I have learned the importance of quiet time, being still and knowing that He is God. I have learned that there is only one way through this and that is God's way. And I continue to learn. I don't think for a moment that I have arrived...no way, no how. This is a journey, and I am somewhere in the middle of it. But I couldn't tell you where. I just know that when it is finished, the Victory is mine because Jesus has already secured that.

I have likened dying to being born. When Phil was in his final hours, we coached him and wiped the sweat from his brow. We brought him cool water and encouraged him. When he left this world, it was literally like watching him being born into Heaven, and his room looked like a delivery room when he was gone.

I guess it's sort of backwards though. Phil was born into Heaven, and now I labor.
Before, I labored, and Phil was born on earth.
Now I have the pains. Now I have to focus and relax and breathe. (Like with Lamaze.)

I aced my Lamaze classes. I really did! I had all three of my boys with no drugs. That was in the days when they told us how much it would hurt the baby to take any sort of pain medication. Well, we wouldn't want to do that now, would we?! What was I thinking?

But God knew, because God knew that those three labors and deliveries would in some strange way prepare me for now. I think about it so often; how I focused. How I relaxed with each contraction. Once in a while, Jim would see my brow furl and he would know I wasn't relaxing, so he would remind me to relax and breathe. I'D LIKE TO REMIND HIM! He would bring me ice chips and coach me each step of the way.

Now, God is coaching me through this grief with His Word. God is reminding me to unfurl my brow and relax...to lay back and rest...to not fight against the pain in my heart, but let God deliver me from it. You may think it is crazy, but it is the truth! When panic starts to rise in my chest, and I think I can't stand one more minute without Phil, I relax, I breathe, I pray, and I remember that I don't have to do this. God will do it for me. He will get me through this, like He has every day so far.

It's not easy. But it is possible. Tonight as I arrived at church, I greeted some friends in the lobby. One of my friends was there with her teenage son, and it was a sweet scene as he stood with his arm around his mom. It was a sweet scene to see his love for her, and it was a sweet scene for me personally because I saw a glimpse of Phil. He would have had his arm around me—no embarrassment, just sweet love. My heart skipped a beat as I walked up to them, and I took a breath. God comforted my heart once again. Easy? NO WAY! Possible? With God, yes! Peace reigned in me because God filled the hole in my heart with His love.

I am up to one day at a time now. I feel like in this last week, I can truly say that. What that means is, I know that when I wake in the morning, God will get me through the day. It used to be just minutes at a time.

In the last week or so, there have been days when I woke up and my first thought has not been about Phil not being here. This is progress. I remember the first morning it happened, a couple of minutes had passed and I was shocked when it dawned on me that I hadn't thought about Phil yet. Now it seems to be happening more often.

Changes are taking place. Progress is being made in these almost seven months without Phil being here. The journey is still difficult and the pain is still intense, but there will be a delivery here one day. That, I know. The more I get to know God, the more I trust Him. The more time I spend in His Word, the more I am learning about the life He wants us all to have...not pain free...not trouble free...but FREE. TRULY FREE!

I'll leave you with my favorite verse right now. I repeat it often throughout the day...

> *You will keep in perfect peace*
> *him whose mind is steadfast*
> *because he trusts in you.*
> *Isaiah 26:3 (NIV)*

God keeps me in perfect peace when I keep my mind on Him and not on my troubles.
So amazing, but so true.

Have a wonderful day!
Love, Diane

__Myself__

I was reading Acts 7 this afternoon. I had asked God where I should go in the Bible, and this came to me, so I turned there.

Many wonder where to go in God's Word to find what's needed. There are all different methods. Sometimes, being in a Bible study helps. Then there are certain assignments that get us moving around in the Bible. Sometimes, we can just open up to any random page, and we will find what we need. Sometimes, we can systematically read through a book. I am doing that right now with Matthew. Then I will read Mark. I am going through the Gospels presently because I am interested in knowing what Jesus had to say, personally. If you have a red-letter edition Bible, it can be helpful in getting to know Jesus because everything He said will be in red. As I read through Matthew, I am seeing Jesus in a new light, once again, just as I saw Mary Poppins in a new light just recently. As a child, I thought Mary Poppins was the nicest lady ever! When I watched her as an adult, I saw that she was very straight forward, no messing around, and no excuses. She always had everyone's best interest at heart, but it didn't always look warm, loving, and kind. I am seeing that Jesus is much like that. He minces no words. He makes his point. He is not a people pleaser, but He has everyone's best interest at heart. I read this verse recently, which sort of sums up what I am saying here, *"Teacher," they said, "we know how honest you are. You teach the way of God truthfully. You are impartial and don't play favorites."* Matthew 22:16 (NLT)

Phil's vision of Heaven. It is an awesome experience that I will never forget.

When I wrote these words, Phil had only been gone seven months. It is now 12 ½ years later and I have to say this experience with Phil is one of the most profound memories that I have. The reason being, it is the one that has kept me going when nothing else could have calmed my fears, eased my aching heart, or helped me see a Hope in the future. I don't know why some get to see Heaven ahead of time, and get to come back and tell us. And I know that many of those stories are probably not true. But many of them are true. And this one is. And what I do know about it is that God knew I needed to hear it, and He gave it to me as a gift that I will treasure forever. Phil didn't expect this to happen. I didn't expect this to happen. But it did happen. And it was a HUGE help to me, to know that Phil is exactly where he wants to be on this day, and that I will see him again.

He said, "Mom, everything you are reading to me answers every question I have in my head."

This was an interesting remark by Phil. I didn't really know what to read to him, I only knew that it calmed him when I did. I would flip through the pages and try to read him the encouraging parts. Even once, when I stepped out of his room for a few minutes and his dad read to him, I suggested that he read only the encouraging stuff to him. But whatever it was God had us read, it helped Phil. He was listening. He was getting his questions answered, questions I didn't even know that he had. Thank you, Jesus, for always being there when we need You, and with all the answers we need.

I said, "Phil, go toward the light!"

I have thought about this statement many, many, many times since. I have questioned my own sanity in that moment, and the only answer I can come up with is that the Holy Spirit took control of my words. What mother, in her right mind, would encourage her child to go towards the light, knowing he might not come back? Honestly, I don't know what I was thinking, so I can't explain it to you here. I won't even try. But I did say it, he did do it, and now I am thankful!

I'm not sure how long he was quiet. I'm not sure if he continued breathing, or if his heart continued beating. I'm not even sure what I did during those moments.

I have thought about this too, and I now think I must have been in a sort of trance for those moments he was gone. Not a spooky trance, but a godly "pause" so that Phil could be undisturbed while he was seeing things that we can only imagine. It would have seemed normal that I would have reached over to see if his heart was still beating. But I didn't. It would have seemed normal to have checked his breathing. But I didn't. The only thing I knew was that I had told him to go toward the light, and then the next thing I remember was his head was going back into his pillow as he took a breath of air. Then he said this:

He said, "I THOUGHT I was finished! Oh, I don't want to be here!"
He seemed disturbed, which was so unlike Phil.

Phil was not easily angered. Ask his brothers who teased him as most big brothers do. They would try to get a fight out of him, but he would brush it off, laugh it off, or walk away. Fighting didn't interest Phil. His temper hadn't been a problem since he was two! But in this moment, I heard anger. I heard frustration. He voiced it! He had seen beyond his room, beyond this world, and he LIKED IT! And in thinking about that just now, I'm sure he felt healthy, light, and energetic…all things he hadn't felt in a while. He once told me he couldn't ever remember feeling good. One time Phil was sitting in the living room chair, and he was so happy about something, he said, "I'd get up and jump up and down if I could. But I can't!" I don't know how he felt in Heaven, but I'm sure it was a whole lot better than he was feeling on earth at that time. What a relief it must have been, and then he came back…and he was NOT happy!

So, being the weird mother that I am, I asked him some questions, because I WANTED to know.

I wasn't doing the writing then that I did after Phil was gone, but it must have always been in me…the desire to ask questions and then write it down. God placed it in me so that I can sit here today and type out these stories. I love sharing them with you. I am asked

quite often if it bothers me to talk about Phil, and all of this.
Absolutely not! I am very comfortable with it, and enjoy sharing
all that God has done concerning Phil's illness and Homegoing.
Once, I met my sister's birth mom. She was adopted into our
family when she was under a year. She met her birth mom when
she was about 40. I had the privilege of spending some time at my
sister's house when she was there, and I asked her so many
questions that she got suspicious of me. After I left, she asked my
sister why I questioned her so much. My sister explained to her
that I liked to write. Yes, I like a good story…a true story! And
that is why I tell this story about Phil's trip to Heaven. What better
story is there than that, other than that Jesus is coming back one
day soon! I love that story in the Bible the most!

*He said it looked sort of like a picture of Heaven that he had in his
wallet. He said it was so beautiful!*

I still have Phil's wallet, and the card inside with the picture of a
person being welcomed into Heaven. At first I was a bit
disappointed, thinking that maybe Phil had just seen what he had
imagined in his head because of the picture on the card. But in later
years I realized the truth. He said it "sort" of looked like that
picture. Why wouldn't it? Heaven is a real, physical place, a place
of purity, and love. He said it was beautiful! That is what that card
depicts. It's not that his view of Heaven was a *copy* of the
card…it's that the card is a *copy* of what Heaven really is! He and
others have seen it. Who knows, maybe even the person who
painted the picture on the card copied it from a personal view like
Phil had? I have no idea…just a thought there. What we do know
is that living here on earth is a shadow of what is to come. The
card in Phil's wallet couldn't capture exactly what he saw, but it
gave him a good reference to give to me in that moment—God
knew that the day Phil was given that card and he placed it in his
wallet. Maybe God was thinking on that day, "Just wait Phil. I'm
going to show you the real thing before you leave. And then I'm
going to take you there to be with Me!"

I thanked him for coming back and telling me about seeing Heaven. I told him that God knew I needed to hear about it, and then he quieted down.

Phil had such a kind and giving heart. He very quickly put his needs away, and thought about what I had said to him—that I needed to hear what he was telling me, and that I needed him to come back to earth to do that. He came back into his very sick body, and comforted me, his mom. And I hope, with all my heart, that in some way what he did comforts you on this day, too. If you are struggling with what lies beyond, if you have loved ones who have gone ahead, who knew and loved Jesus, and this brings you peace knowing how happy they are to be there, then "mission accomplished." This gift wasn't just for me, or I wouldn't be sharing it here today, and you wouldn't be reading these words. It is for you, too, because Jesus loves you that much! Jesus came and died on a Cross for You. He rose again for you. He wants you to be with Him where He is. I hope you are prepared to meet Jesus one day, because you will. But, and this is VERY important, you must "meet" Jesus here first, before your final breath, so that when you meet Him on the other side, you are prepared. Otherwise you will not be welcomed into Jesus' Home. And please know this; no one knows the heart of anyone who has gone ahead. We can't make those judgment calls. So be at peace with where your loved ones are. God gave them every opportunity, just as He is giving you on this day. God does not play favorites. Everyone is given a fair shot at Heaven. Some do say "No," but we won't know who said what until we get there, so we can't spend our days worrying about it once they are gone. All we can do is spread the Good News while we are all still here, agreeing with our Father that we want none to perish! Just this morning in reading Matthew, I read how Jesus talked about the Kingdom of Heaven. He said that all those who were ready went in with Him to the marriage feast. And then the door was locked. The five bridesmaids returned later, they hadn't been prepared for His coming. They stood outside calling, "Sir, open the door for us!" But He called back, "I don't know you!" So stay awake and be prepared, because you do not know the day or hour of my return." Matthew 25:12 (NLT) Are you prepared on this day? If not, welcome Jesus into your heart in this very moment, give your life to Him, and follow Him each day, so when the day of His return comes, Jesus will know you because you have known Him here.

He told me that the devil had been lying to him. He said that the devil had told him that it hurts to die, and it doesn't.

I have had times when I have been able to share this with the dying. I haven't been there myself, in that place of wondering as my death drew near…what will it feel like? I honestly didn't know that Phil was concerned about that until he told me this. How awesome of God to ease that fear for him in his final days. Yes, living is painful, the dying process can be very painful, but the actual dying moment is a good moment for all those who do believe. What a testimony Phil gave me to share with all of you here today. It doesn't hurt to die!

…he didn't want God to be mad at him, so he thought he should try to breathe again.

God might have used Phil's good boy personality in this moment to urge him to take a breath. When he took that breath, that was the moment I realized he was back—though I hadn't realized he was gone after I told him to go toward the light. He came back into this world for two more days. And still, it was unreal that he would really be leaving us. I was just talking to my daughter-in-law, Holly, yesterday about this. When we are given 3 months, as her dad was, or just weeks as Jim's aunt has been, or as in Phil's case just 48 more hours till he took his last breath, it still does not seem possible that this person will be leaving us soon. The morning of Phil's Homegoing, I sat on the edge of my bed asking God for strength, telling Him I didn't know how much longer this would go on, but I needed His help in doing it. It should seem obvious. But we were not designed to die; we were designed in the Garden of Eden to live forever. Our spirits will live on, even though our present physical bodies won't.

Phil had about 48 hours between when he saw Heaven and when he went Home to Heaven. During that time, his memories of that experience had a chance to fade.

This surprised me. The fear started to build in him again. The devil is ruthless, and in those final days when Satan knows he won't be able to get his "claws" into us much longer, I think he really pours it on. That is why reading God's Word to those during the end days is SOOO important! God's Word ushers the devil out, and Jesus in! The devil does not like God's Word, and when it is read out loud, he really doesn't like it. As it says in James, when we *submit* to God, then we are to resist the devil, and he will flee from us! But, Satan is like a pesky flea, he will come back again and again and again. That is why we need the Word, ALWAYS!

The only way through this grief is to not forget, and to trust. When God's Word is fresh on my mind, when I have just spent time with God, then I don't forget so easily and I am not so easily swayed by the strong winds in a storm.

Continuing to read God's Word, to this day, still calms the storm that can creep in. Everything, and I mean EVERYTHING, will get in the way of opening up God's Word. Try it! You will find that Facebook calls to you, your friends text you, or you text them, the dishes suddenly need to be done, you need to clip that nail, where are the clippers?...and so on… Anything that can get in the way, will. It takes perseverance to open the Word of God. Sometimes I tell people, just lay the Bible open and leave it that way. Then when you are walking by doing those thousand other things that seem to creep in ahead of reading the Word, you can just glance at it and read at least one line. Once you do that, it can draw you in, and you will learn many things about the way of our Lord.

This is a journey, and I am somewhere in the middle of it. But I couldn't tell you where. I just know that when it is finished, the Victory is mine because Jesus has already secured that.

I knew the victory had been won, but I had to continue to walk it out, daily, to see it for myself. I am thankful that Jesus fought this battle over 2,000 years ago. The devil knows he is on borrowed time. I am not in the middle of this particular battle any more. I am in the middle of others, but not this one. I know where I am, now, in my grief...I am securely in the healing arms of Christ Jesus! And I am grateful. Amen!!

When he left this world, it was literally like watching him being born into Heaven, and his room looked like a delivery room when he was gone.

Towels, ice chips, medication, rumpled sheets, etc...they were all there—left behind when the men in the van took Phil's empty body away in the middle of that dark, cold, foggy November night. Memories that no parent wants to have, but have them we do. I kissed him on his forehead before they wheeled him out our front door. How could I not? The body they wheeled away used to contain my son. He now lived in the Heaven he came back to tell me about. I knew that, but emotionally, and spiritually, I had a long, long, long way to go. Thankfully, I didn't know what I had just stepped into on that night. As foggy as the night was, my mind and emotions were foggier. The sadness on the night only increased in future weeks and months. Healing would come in time. But the battle to truly BELIEVE all that Jesus died to give me was just beginning.

God is reminding me to unfurl my brow and relax...to lay back and rest...to not fight against the pain in my heart, but let God deliver me from it.

When I would lean into my grief, it hurt even more, if that is possible. Yes, like not relaxing in the middle of a contraction. When I was in labor with all of our boys, focus and concentration were my friends. This routine didn't stop the birth pains from coming, but it helped me endure them while it was there. My husband would watch the monitor, and say, "Here comes another one." I thanked him politely! NOT! Grief lasts a lot longer than contractions do, but God never gives up on us, and He never leaves us to do it on our own. My husband always likes to tell the story of the "ice chips." I was in labor with Phil when I asked my husband to please (and I'm sure I used the word "Please") get me some ice chips. He headed for the door, but I told him not to leave me! He didn't know what to do…to go get what I had asked for, or stay with me? So he stood in the doorway and called for ice chips! What a devoted husband he was. God is even more devoted to His children. He will help us when we are hurting, and He is able to even be with us while also giving us Living Water/ice chips. He can be trusted to see us through, if we will concentrate on His promises and focus on His love each day. It's not easy. It takes work. God's grace is free. Living in it is the challenge.

I am up to one day at a time now.

One day at a time. Wow, that was an accomplishment at that time. What I meant by this was, I knew I wouldn't die of the pain for just one day—that I could survive longer than a minute, or until lunch—that God had seen me through a lot of yesterdays up to this point, so I was pretty sure He would get me through this *one* day. I wasn't counting on the whole week just yet, I might die before it was through. But on this day, I was pretty sure I would live to see the sun go down. If you've been there, you know what I mean. If you haven't…you don't want to be.

The more time I spend in His Word, the more I am learning about the life He wants us all to have. Not pain free. Not trouble free. But free. Truly free!

I am free of grief pains today. The "contractions" have stopped. I get twinges from time to time of what once was, and what might have been, but focusing on those things does NOT help! Those thoughts must be moved through, and **today** must be lived in. Just today I went to my granddaughter, Laila's, kindergarten graduation. That is my focus for today, celebrating with her, and all the rest of the family as these days come now. Being set free from grief through the power and Hope we have in Jesus Christ allows for this, and encourages this. Jesus died to conquer death. Let's live in that victory until we meet Him face to face, and frustrate our enemy, Satan, in doing so. Thank You, Jesus, for the eternal life You promised to all those who will believe!

Gift #3 – Heaven. Pure Heaven. Forever, and ever, and ever. Amen!

What blocks your view of Heaven?

What would it look like to focus on something other than your grief today?

Record today's date and other notes you'd like to make:

The Great

<u>I AM</u>

*You will keep in perfect peace
him whose mind is steadfast
because he trusts in you.*
Isaiah 26:3 (NIV)

CHAPTER FOUR

Let everything that has breath praise the Lord.
Psalm 150:6 (NIV)

<u>Me</u>

The Pruning Season

Tuesday, 02 Jul 2002

Thank God for this minute...just this minute. That is all we have at one time. In the next minute the phone could ring. What might the news be? In the next minute we could have discovered a lump that will change the path of our lives. In the next minute the plane we are on could develop engine problems that would quickly change our thinking about the small bag of peanuts we just received, to meeting God face to face. I don't mean to be morbid here, but most of us have experienced something that changed the minute we are in now, to the last minute that we felt that way for a long time, if ever again.

We did. You probably have. It might not mean your life is over. But it will mean that how you will experience this life will change forever. Why do we even think that we are the only ones this will not happen to? Why do we think that when it does happen to us, it shouldn't have? Why? Because we are human beings, with a limited view of God's plan for our lives. We think about the small little space of time that our lives encompass as being something much larger. We think that we are invincible, that we will never actually die, or that death is so far off in the future, it really is not worth thinking about. Or maybe we do think about it, and then it causes such fear, we can't think about it. So many reasons why we do the things we do. There is no single answer for any of it. Or is there?

What is the single most important answer that we need to know? "Let everything that has breath praise the Lord." Praise the One who made us. Praise the One who knows us inside and out. Praise the One who knows what lies behind, and already knows what's up ahead. There is One who knows who we will need to come alongside us in this life, and what lessons we will need in this life to help us learn what is important. Do we want to know what tomorrow holds, really? Our Father in Heaven knows. And Jesus knew when He walked this earth.

Something I heard recently, which I had never thought about, was that Jesus could read about His future in the Old Testament. He could pull out a scroll and read about His life, and about His death. Why had I never thought about that? It seems a simple conclusion, but one that had slipped past my thinking. I don't want to be able to do that. I would not have wanted to know when Phil was born, that 10½ years later he would get Leukemia, and then 5½ years later that he would die from it. We don't want to know things like that; at least, I don't.

It may seem strange, but when I walk through the parks and I see the young families pushing their children on the swings, or in their strollers, and holding them up to get a drink from the water fountain, I think about what lies ahead in their future. I remember being in the park with our boys, especially Phil, because he loved playgrounds so much. Being the youngest, the memories are fresher. I remember him going down the slides, drinking from the fountains, and running with the other children. He didn't have a care in the world. And as his mother, I never thought how precious that time was, because I didn't know he would be sick one day soon and those days would end. Of course I didn't think about that, and of course these families in the parks don't think about that. That would be crazy. They never think that those years with their children might someday be all that they have. But I do think about it, unfortunately. And I watch them, and I hope that they never have to deal with losing one of their children. They look so young and so innocent. And now, I am not.

Jim and I were driving to Fresno a few months ago and we drove through fields and fields of grapes. Jim likes to take a more back road to Fresno, instead of the freeway. As we drove through those grape vineyards, I looked at the different ages of the vines that were growing. Some branches were on vines that were straight as an arrow, thin, without a gnarl. Some were a bit thicker and starting to twist and turn a bit, a gnarl here and there, having been around a bit longer. Then there were the "old timers" as I thought of them. They were very thick, with many twists and turns in the vine, and there were gnarls and crevices and signs of having been through many types of weather condition, perhaps...so mature looking, and yet so strong looking, too. It seemed a strong wind would blow the thin new vines and branches right over, but it looked as if nothing could move the more mature ones—not even a mighty wind.

Being the strange person that I am, of course, I brought this up in our discussion as we drove along. I said, "Jim, if you were one of these grape vines, which one would you be? Which one do you relate to the most?" Now Jim, knowing me well, was kind and understanding with such a strange question, and instead of saying, "What are you talking about? What could you possibly be thinking?" he asked me which one I thought I related to. Good answer Jim! He was figuring out what the little woman is driving at before jumping in and getting all wet!

Anyway, we talked about the different levels of maturity in the vines and branches, and I could see my Grandma in the very mature ones—with the life she had led, the things she had experienced that made her the person she was when I knew her best, in her final years. Joy and peace would be a good way to describe what I saw in her. She had been through so much, and there was not much that would move in a strong wind at that point. I know she probably looked forward to going "Home" and seeing those she had lost. But she lived a joyous life waiting to get there.

Then I looked at the thin, straight ones, and I thought of our boys, just starting out their lives—having not experienced a whole lot, although with Phil they have experienced things that most young people have not. Those branches were so fresh, so young, and so innocent looking. Their whole fruit bearing lives were still ahead of them.

And of course, I felt like the branches that had grown a bit thicker (no pun intended), with some twists and turns, some gnarls and cracks, and with many days of the fruit bearing already in the past. But really, maybe they were right in the midst of fruit bearing years. (Spiritual Fruit bearing, not child-bearing! HA) I know enough to know better, and yet I still don't know enough.

But the truth is, the Bible talks about Jesus being the Vine, and we are the branches.

> *"I am the vine; you are the branches. If you remain in me and I in you, you will bear much fruit; apart from me you can do nothing." John 15:5 (NIV)*

That's really good to know, because if there were a vine that represented Jesus out in that field, it would be the most mature, all-knowing, wise, gnarled, "been there" type of vine around. It would truly stand out in any vineyard. My Grandma's branch wouldn't even compare to the Vine of Jesus! And all we are asked to do is to remain in Him, and to stay attached to His Vine. We are to let the energy and experience of God flow through us. If we don't, we're not going to make it.

> "If anyone does not remain in me, he is like a branch that is thrown away and withers; such branches are picked up, thrown away into the fire and burned." John 15:6 (NIV)

I know that feeling of withering. I know what it feels like to disconnect myself from the True Vine and try to breathe on my own. It doesn't work. I start to wither and feel the breath being sucked right out of me. I feel tired, worn, and in need of nourishment. I feel the need for God in my life!

Jesus is the Vine. Jesus is the nourishment. Jesus is the answer to what I need. Nothing else! Nothing! Other things can help, other people can help, other sources of information can help, even our Grief Share group can help, but only God can heal! The rest just helps me keep my focus on the Vine.

If this experience with Phil being sick, and then losing him, doesn't give me a breakthrough with God, perhaps nothing ever will. I think that's why I feel such a strong desire to not let Phil's life be wasted—not only because I want his life to have counted for something, something eternal, but because this is what God had planned for my life. For some reason it was necessary. If I turn my back on it and walk away from God because I don't fully understand it, I will probably be missing out on the most important thing in my life. God did not make Phil sick. He did not make Phil die. That comes from the fallen world we live in. But God allowed it, knowing that no matter how terrible it was, good could come out of it. God could use it for His Kingdom work. And He could use me also...if I am willing. I am willing.

I just want to be a branch, connected to the Vine that is Jesus. I don't want to have to be the vine that feels the weight of the world on my shoulders. I want to be held up there in the sunshine and let Him flow into me, giving me life. As a branch, I understand that there will be "pruning," and that it will hurt. But because of that *pruning, I will grow stronger. I will be more productive. I will accomplish what I was put here to do.*

Snip, snip, snip...as they come down the row of grapes cutting away what needs to be cut away, bracing up what seems to have slipped a bit, getting the branches ready for their "work." The Vine is set, strong and steady. It's the branches that need the constant work, the constant pruning—and we complain, "Ouch! That hurts! I don't like that! Why does that have to happen? Why can't I just be left alone? Why here? Why now? Why not later, or never? Do I deserve this treatment? Couldn't I have lived without it?" Yes, we moan and complain!

Could we have lived without the pruning? Or would we have withered and died, and then been thrown into the fire and burned? Hmmm, what does that remind you of? A place I never want to end up!

I don't like this pruning any more than anyone else. It hurts!
I don't like that I walk through parks now and think of young children in terms of what is in their future, and what their parents will do if such a tragedy strikes them.
I don't like that I need a grief group on Monday night, because I have lost someone most precious to me.
I don't like that the simple question, "How many children do you have?" becomes a complicated emotional answer.
I don't like that fun seems wrong, and sadness seems right.
I don't like that Phil hasn't seen the yearbook that sits on his bed because his picture is in the back of it...in the memorial section.
I don't like a lot of things about this. But there are things I do like.

I do like that I will never be the same again, because I can use this crisis as a breakthrough.
I do like that Phil is safe and secure, and there are so many things in this world that he will never have to deal with.
I do like that God is my refuge, and I don't have to do this alone.
I do like that my perspective on this world has totally changed, making it possible to have peace in the midst of trials.

I do like that God gave me a precious gift in my son, and He knows the reason why He had to leave, even if I don't.
I do like that I can trust God completely, because He loves me more than anyone ever will.
I do like that the pruning season doesn't last forever, but it is an opportunity for great growth!
I do like that God let's me write about all of this!

Breathe in, breathe out—only possible with God!
Truly living again after losing your child—only possible with God!

To Be a Branch

This pruning isn't easy Lord, it hurts, each snip You take
I don't really care for this season, of my life, but what's at stake
Is learning to lean on You, or going it on my own
Learning that You only, hold the power for what is sown
Will I rest in Your care, and seek Your will in this
Or will I follow my own path, fight against instead of with
You and all You're offering, it seems an easy choice
But no choice is that easy, when we hear the enemy's voice
Help me focus on You Lord, and the promises You gave
Never let me veer away, thinking I know a better way
You are the one true Gardener, knowing which branch to cut
Or prune back just a little, You alone know just how much
Each and everyone of us, can bear each day we live
Keep a watch over me, tend to me as I give
My life completely to You, in You I will remain
You are the Vine, I am the branch, I will call upon Your name

As the Scripture says, "Anyone who trusts in him will never be put to shame." For there is no difference between the Jew and Gentile - the same Lord is Lord of all and richly blesses all who call on him, for, "Everyone who calls on the name of the Lord will be saved." Romans 10:11-13 (NIV)

Have a great day!
Love, Diane

Myself

In the next minute the phone could ring. What might the news be?

We recently got the news that Jim's Aunt Morna has cancer. What kind? Where? How much? Those are the questions we all ask. She is 81 years old now, and has had a couple of strokes. But she had just been to the doctor the month before. She said she had never felt better. She got a clean bill of health that day. Three weeks later, she had trouble breathing. When we found out what she had, I called it Stage 4 Everything Cancer. Morna never ended up getting any sort of treatment. The cancer was too far gone. She started eating less and less, and sleeping more and more. It wasn't much more than a few weeks after her initial diagnosis that Morna left this world for a better one. How many of us have these stories to tell? We all do.

Why do we even think that we are the only ones this will not happen to? Why do we think that when it does happen to us, it shouldn't have?

God is God, no matter what. But for some, He seems to change when life suddenly changes. This is understandable. We think about who God is when what *is*, no longer *is*—when life gets harder, the questions get bigger, and the doubts start to rise more. We have to prepare for these moments in time. We need to be prepared for these phone calls that come—because they will come, that is guaranteed. We didn't know our phone call would be about Jim's aunt, but we knew the day would come when our phone would ring about someone we love. I remember well our phone call to the states to tell our parents that Phil was sick. Of course there were tears, questions, and doubts. The difference now is, we have gotten to know that God is God, no matter what comes our way. Grief can give you that gift to be used in the future.

What is the single most important answer that we need to know? "Let everything that has breath praise the Lord."

We don't have an answer for most things, only God does. And most times, He doesn't tell us. Where we are can seem like a dark place to be, and it is, granted. But God is light, and in Him there is no darkness at all. We can praise Him for that, and trust Him in that. Blind faith? Not really. It's a faith in what is True, and that is why we can cling to it. Anything else in this world can, and usually does, fail us. Yes, even our family, our friends, our jobs, and our own health fail at times. But God never changes. He is steadfast through the good times and the bad. We can look back and see that He has always been there. How can we know that? Because, we are still here on this day, sharing this moment together. We have come through things we thought we would never live through, but we have. We can take courage from that, and know that we will live through this moment, too…and the next. And hopefully, we will come out of all of it, with more of God's wisdom, after whatever battle we are presently in has passed on by. Because it will, eventually, pass on by.

Do we want to know what tomorrow holds, really? But our Father in Heaven does know. And Jesus knew when He walked this earth.

Jesus was so confident. We can read His words in the gospels, and they are amazing. No one could throw Him for a loop. No one could confound Him. No one could catch Him off guard. Jesus walked with confidence, spoke with confidence, and fought the devil with complete confidence. How many times did Jesus remove demons from people who came to Him for healing? I am reading it over, and over, and over in Matthew, Mark, etc…and the demons feared Him, as they should. If the demons fear Jesus, should we fear anything with Him as our Savior and our King? I know we still do at times. But it is a good question to ask. We should not fear! Jesus can be trusted. Even when the disciples were out in the middle of the lake in a huge storm, Jesus slept. He had it all under control! And He still does. We can be confident in this life, because we are in the hands of the One who controls all things. Let's work on really believing that Truth!

I said, "Jim, if you were one of these grape vines, which one would you be? Which one do you relate to the most?"

My poor husband…he is married to someone who looks at things a bit differently than most. Maybe I'm always looking for the story in it? You have to understand, my mind was always on grief at first, and for a very long time. I was always looking for a way through, a way out, or just a way. I didn't view the world the same at all anymore. Most of the time, there was no getting away from difficult thoughts wherever I went, except when I dove into the Word and thought about the Hope we have in Jesus.

I could see my Grandma in the very mature ones...

The grape vineyards were very interesting that day, because we saw so many different ones at different stages of their development. I could appreciate that some had been around the block a few seasons, like a grandparent has. They had weathered some storms, and some hot sun. They had produced some good fruit. We hope we can say the same when we are the age of grandparents. If there's no spiritual fruit in our lives by then, we haven't been focusing on the right things in life. And by fruit, I mean the things of God that have been passed on to others. I had a dream the other night about a bowl of fruit. It came right before I was to have a difficult conversation with a friend. I thought about the Fruit of the Spirit—love, joy, peace, patience, kindness, goodness, faithfulness, gentleness and self-control. I knew that should be my focus during our conversation. It was, and it went well.

Then I looked at the thin, straight ones and I thought of our boys, just starting out their lives.

Our boys were younger then, not married, and no children. They have a few more gnarls to their credit now. That's not a bad thing; it is just a maturity thing. I remember the night our first grandson was born. We arrived at the hospital all excited for his delivery. Everything was going great. His head made its arrival just fine, but then his shoulders decided to be stubborn. I was standing in the hallway when Holly's mom, Karyl, came out of the room. The look on her face said it all. Things were not going well. The operating room doors were opened up across the hall, and we waited those few long moments to see what would come next. Chris was about to have a son, and his son wasn't making it easy. That matures a person very quickly! The story ended well, with nurses on top of Holly pushing, and lots of pushing from Holly, Jackson finally made his *full* appearance in the world. He is eight now, and the sweetest boy. But I cut his dad's hair, and there's a lot more gray up there than there used to be!

And of course, I felt like the branch that had grown a bit thicker (no pun intended), with some twists and turns, some gnarls and cracks.

Ok, I probably have more grey hair from that night with Jackson, also! But when we get into our 50's, there are a lot of reasons to have gray hair. It comes with the territory. The 50's are good though, because they do contain wisdom that is God-given, if we have been focusing our attention on His Word, and His plan for our lives. There is an up side to that and a down side. The up side is that we are hopefully not making some of the same mistakes we used to make. The down side is that we see those younger than us making some of our old mistakes, and try as we might to warn them against it, they rarely listen. Would we have? Of course not, but we can at least try to tell them, just like our parents did for us.

I know enough to know better, and yet I still don't know enough.

In the fifties, we know better than to think we know it all. There is a bumper sticker that says if we need to know something, ask a teenager, they know everything. I should design one that says if you need to know something, don't ask a person in their fifties; they are just realizing they will never know it all. It is a good place to be though, because we can rest in what we have learned so far, and enjoy the next forty years, God willing, slowly adding to it.

We do start to slow down, and that is okay. We want to stop and smell the roses with the little ones God adds to our lives. It is time.

...if there were a vine that represented Jesus out in that field, it would be the most mature, all-knowing, wise, gnarled, "been there" type of vine around.

All this to say, there is only One who knows it all. Jesus! The all-wise, all-knowing Lord of all. He may have only been 33, but He was here when the world was created, and He will be here when it is made new. And Jesus' brief stop here in human flesh changed all of eternity for the better. He left us with Hope. What more do we need, when all hope in this world is lost? What more do we need in our grief? My brother, Rick, was telling me the other day about some struggles with his job. He was putting it all into perspective though. He said a family near where he lived recently had to make the decision to stop life-support on their little three year old. Rick said that nothing he is dealing with would even matter in their world right now. I had to agree. Bills, jobs, family problems, home repairs, etc...are all weightless compared to letting that little person go and rest in the arms of Jesus.

I know that feeling of withering. I know what it feels like to disconnect myself from the True Vine and try to breathe on my own. It doesn't work.

I pray those parents of that little three year old are attached to the Vine, and feel Jesus' life blood coursing through their veins. It might seem like a trickle in the beginning, because the thirst is SO great, but in time it will be the only thing, the **very** thing, that brings them through. Anytime I got distracted, and felt disconnected, I started to sink—just like Peter when he took his eyes off Jesus after he got out of the boat to try walking on the water. Those who are grieving have just been thrown overboard in the midst of a terrible storm. Jesus is reaching out His hand to all that will take it. Slowly, but SURELY, He will get us all walking on the water, above the sadness, the guilt, the pain, the anger, and whatever else our enemy, Satan, would like to pull us under with!

Jesus removes demons! If you don't believe that, pick up a copy of the Bible and read through the gospels. Demons abound, but even more so, Jesus is there! He is more powerful than all the demons combined!

If this experience with Phil being sick, and then losing him, doesn't give me a breakthrough with God, perhaps nothing ever will. If I turn my back on it and walk away from God because I don't fully understand it, I will probably be missing out on the most important thing in my life.

I don't know what could have affected my life more than this. But my life isn't over yet, and maybe there are more books in the making? I'm just going with what is right now, doing whatever it is God is asking me to do. I'm not trying to be an expert; I'm just trying to stay attached to the Expert so when God whispers His Truths, in this chaotic noisy world, I don't miss hearing Him. Maybe that's why the shower is always a good place to connect with our Lord...the running water drowns out the clamoring world, and we can hear Him better in there.

I just want to be a branch, connected to the Vine that is Jesus. The Vine is set, strong and steady. It's the branches that need the constant work, the constant pruning...

I don't pretend to know much about gardening, or agriculture. My dad has helped us plant some flowers in the backyard. I do my best to keep them watered, and still sometimes they wither and die. I don't have a green thumb, but I did find those grape vineyards interesting as we drove by them that day—seeing them as the different stages of life we go through, processing where Jim and I were at that time in our grief, and knowing that if we stay attached to the Vine, Jesus, we will be supplied with all we need each day.

Could we have lived without the pruning?

Not being a gardener, pruning is not my business. But being in the hair business, I know how a shaft of hair works. I know that trimming hair keeps it healthy. I know that when we get split ends, it can travel up the shaft and break the hair off. Hair will actually grow longer if we trim off the split ends regularly. It seems wrong. It seems we should just let it grow and not touch it so it can grow longer. It also seems wrong when God prunes us, cutting off pieces of our lives when it seems most inappropriate. "Hey, I needed that job!" Or, "What? I'm not ready to move right now!" "Don't touch that dial! I'm in the middle of that program." We do have our own plan for our own lives, and sometimes it seems all God does is mess things up. But, we have to trust! One of my longtime clients, Brad, was just in yesterday getting his hair cut. We greeted each other with pleasantries, as is normally done. "How are you?" "Fine." "How are you?" "Fine." But we know one another well enough to move past that. Once he sat down, he admitted it all hasn't been fine. I admitted the same. We discussed. Brad and his wife had to move, and they run a day care in their home. It seemed things were going from bad to worse. But in the end, God placed them in a nice home, newly remodeled, that works well for the children. In the midst of it all, it all seemed like the wrong pruning, in the wrong place, at the wrong time. But God can be trusted. Brad and I both agreed on that. And Brad trusted me with his haircut, too!

I don't like...

I will share a couple of the ones that really still stand out to me. I'm sure you have your own.

I don't like that the simple question, "How many children do you have?" becomes a complicated emotional answer.

Like most things, this has become so much easier. So if it's still hard for you, hang in there. You will get more comfortable answering this question. It will even give you an avenue for sharing the Good News of Jesus Christ a lot of the time! At first, I didn't know whether to say, "Two," or "Three." I found that perplexing, and difficult. But then I realized after some time, that I have three children. Of course I have three children. I will **always** have three children. They just live in different places. I have a

66

child in California, a child in Oregon, and a child in Heaven. Now, that last location will get varied responses, and that's what can open up interesting discussions. But I must admit, there are times when I still avoid the long response, and just say, "Yes. I have three boys." It depends on the "audience," and the amount of time given. But I never say "two boys." I know the right answer now!

I don't like that Phil hasn't seen the yearbook that sits on his bed because his picture is in the back of it...in the memorial section.

This is something no parent ever wants to experience. I mean, we were in High School, we know what the memorial pages represent...classmates that didn't make it to get their yearbook. But our child? Never! That will not be. But it was for us, and it may be for you. I remember the day I went to the high school to get Phil's yearbook. Some of the kids had signed it for him. It was tough, tough, tough. But it wasn't the toughest thing to come. The day a letter arrived in the mail, addressed *to* Phil, *from* Phil, was AWFUL!! What the school had done was have each child write their "Obituary" in their sophomore year, so that it could be mailed to them after they graduated from their senior year. I know—kind of a strange idea. The school mailed out the envelopes, and Phil's was in the stack to be mailed. I got the mail out of our box that day, walked into the house, and saw his writing, and opened the letter, and WAILED! Talk about painful! Those are moments along the way that are never forgotten. Things like that happen. Nobody means any harm by it, but harm happens anyway. It's all just part of the process, and the living in this life. I still have the letter. I love that Phil wrote it, that it's in his handwriting, and I'm fine with it now. Many years later, I walked back onto that high school campus to attend our granddaughter, Denell's, soccer game. There was a flood of memories and emotions, but I was fine. God, and years, had eased the pain, and I still enjoy attending many of her games at that school, as I will the other grandkids as the years go by. As I said, it's just part of the process. Things can't and shouldn't be avoided for too long. They must be lived and learned through.

I do like...

There are many things to be thankful for.

I do like that God gave me a precious gift in my son, and He knows the reason why He had to leave, even if I don't.

Phil was our first unplanned child. We planned baby number one, and baby number two. Baby number three was all God's idea! We had given away all our baby things, and taken down the crib. But along came Phil four and a half years after Chris. He was such a good baby, and we loved him so much. Of course, after God gave him to us, we couldn't imagine life without our third son. Who would any of us be today if Phil's life hadn't touched ours, even if it was just for a moment? Our daughter-in-law, Holly, got to meet Phil. She worked in the restaurant where Chris worked. That is where they met. We went in for dinner one night after Chris had moved back from San Diego. She said she came to our table that night. We were all introduced to her, including Phil. Sadly, we met many people Chris had worked with that night, so I don't specifically remember meeting Holly. I tell her now, I wish she had told us that she was going to be our future daughter-in-law. I would have paid more attention! Phil met many people, and many people met him through his 16 years of life. He experienced those years to the fullest. On his program, the day of his memorial service, I listed most of what he had done through the years in a little write up I did. I almost just changed the word "little" there, because it wasn't little, it was three pages long! I'm not short on words, as you can tell. But it was comforting to list all the things that Phil had done, accomplished, enjoyed, and all the rest, in his sixteen years. They were not wasted years, I can tell you that—from swimming with a Manatee, going up in a hot air balloon, traveling Europe when we lived there…the list goes on and on. Phil was a blessing, such a gift, and I wouldn't have wanted to miss what we enjoyed with him, no matter how much it hurt to say good-bye so soon.

I do like that God let's me write about all of this!

And here we are, as my fingers fly, and I enjoy writing. If you are
willing to read this, and it speaks to you, I am thankful. Thankful
that God uses all of this for you and others. Maybe it's just a good
read on a quiet afternoon. Maybe it draws you closer to God.
Maybe it heals something that you didn't even realize needed to be
considered. Maybe you're ready to put this book down, or maybe
you like it so much you're ready to buy a copy for someone else.
Whatever purpose God has in this, I thank Him for it, and trust that
as I sit quiet on this day, looking back, and sharing all this with all
of you, it will be all that God intends for it to be. Thank You,
Jesus!

Gift #4 – Beginning to know that God is God, no matter what comes our way.

What are the things you really don't like about what you're experiencing?

What are the things that perhaps you do like?

Record today's date and other notes you'd like to make:

The Great

<u>I AM</u>

"I am the vine; you are the branches.
If you remain in me and I in you,
you will bear much fruit;
apart from me you can do nothing."
John 15:5 (NIV)

CHAPTER FIVE

God is not human, that he should lie,
not a human being, that he should change his mind.
Numbers 23:19 (NIV)

Me

Do You Wonder?

Sunday, 14 Jul 2002

Do you wonder what they're going to say about you after you're gone? Don't we all kind of think of that from time to time? What will our "eulogy" be like? Will they speak kindly about us? Will the group gathered snicker because they know what we were really like, or will they nod their heads in agreement about how much we actually did touch their lives? Will our children stand and say we loved them, no matter what—that we were there for them, no matter what, that we showed them how much God loves them by how much we loved them? Will those gathered, who may not have known us well, wish they had? Will they come away wanting to be a better person, wanting to have faith like we had? Or will those that have gathered leave the service unimpressed?

You may think you are too young to think about your own mortality. But just from reading my e-mails, you know that you are never too young. Phil was only 16. Today, the friend we said good-bye to was only 46. I hope Lynn wouldn't mind that I share her age, but I'm struck by her age because she was born exactly two days after Jim, in March, of 1956. She was young—too young to be leaving this earth and her friends and family behind—but she did. They all spoke about her today, and from what they said, the hole that will be left is a BIG one!—one that will not quickly be filled in by time and life. The life she lived will affect the rest of their lives, my life, and all our days on this earth.

I had the enormous privilege of sitting with Lynn for an hour on Tuesday, June 4, 2002. I say an enormous privilege because it was a very meaningful hour that I feel was a gift from God—and within about 36 hours, Lynn left for "Home." The phone rang in our house on Thursday morning, June 6 at 7:00 a.m. Jim came into our bedroom and said that Dave, Lynn's husband, just called. I looked at him and said, "Lynn died, didn't she?" He said she had.

I can't say I was shocked, because I wasn't. But what I can say is that I felt so blessed and thankful to have just sat with her, and to have just learned a little bit more about this wonderful woman. I got to hear about her life. She shared about her step-children, her husband, her hobbies, her garden, and many other things. I felt it was a tremendous blessing that God brought our lives together at all, let alone to bring us together in her final days so that we could connect that one last time before she went Home.

Lynn and I were not close friends. We were new friends, brought together by our love for the Lord, her illness, and Phil's. She and her husband have prayed for us through our trials, and we have prayed for them. They watched as Phil suffered through his fight with cancer. We watched as Lynn struggled with hers. They watched as Phil moved from walking into church, to riding into church in his wheelchair. We watched as Lynn moved from riding in her wheelchair into church, to walking, and back to her wheelchair. We watched one another, hugged one another, prayed for one another, and we will continue to do so now that Lynn and Phil have left us. Lynn could tell Phil she had just seen his mom, and that I am doing fine. I feel like God gave me the gift of spending that time with Lynn, to help comfort me in my grief. And maybe, just maybe, God gave Lynn a gift, too. I don't know what she felt as we visited; I don't know what she was thinking, or why God called me to her house on that day. But someday, I will. And someday I will find out if my visit perhaps helped her to make that final journey. Was she watching me more closely on that day? Was she being comforted to see me smile, to see me continue on living my life after having lost Phil, knowing that, soon, her husband, Dave, might have to continue living on without her? I don't know. But I will never forget my final visit. It will always be one of the greatest blessings in my life. To have met Lynn, and then to listen to those that knew her best at her service, made me want to be a better person. They quoted Proverbs 31 in describing her:

Who can find a virtuous and capable wife?
She is worth more than precious rubies.
Her husband can trust her, and she will greatly enrich his life...
She is energetic and strong, a hard worker... She watches for bargains; her lights burn late into the night... She extends a helping hand to the poor and opens her arms to the needy...
She is clothed with strength and dignity, and she laughs with no fear of the future...
Proverbs 31:10-11, 17-18, 20, 25 (NLT)

There is much more written there, but that will give you an idea for now. Does this sound too good to be true? For most of us it does. But that is how Lynn was described, today, by those who knew her best. Lynn was not a woman without trials in her life. We learned that today. She had plenty of reasons to complain and turn away from God because life was perhaps "too hard" and she had been dealt a bad hand. But she never did that.

*Lynn's battle and faith comforts me in another way—and I hope it is okay if I share that with you here. For so many years, we prayed for Phil to be healed, believing that God **can** heal. Lynn also* *prayed for God's healing, and she believed that she **would be** healed. She never gave up the fight, and she never gave up her hope in God's healing power. Well, as you all know, Phil went Home even after all the prayers that were said for him, and that is TOUGH. It bothers me. I wanted to see Phil healed on this earth! But that was not to be, and I sometimes question if my faith was not enough...if Jim's was not enough...if Phil's was not enough? So I watched Lynn, and I prayed for Lynn, and I watched Lynn's faith never waver. I knew that if anyone's faith could bring about an earthly healing, Lynn's could. But it didn't. God took her Home. And honestly, as much as I am saddened by that, I am comforted. I know that God has a perfect plan, a reason for all things, and I trust in Him all the more having known Lynn. Her faith reassured me that we don't always know why, and we can't, but that trusting God is what's most important. Some people are miraculously healed on this earth—like my sister-in-law, Cindy's, best friend was healed from Lupus. But some people are not. It's not always a matter of not having enough faith. It's more a matter of trusting God, no matter what.*

*An interesting thing was said, at the service today, by a friend of Lynn's. She said something to this effect, "Lynn not only believed in God, she **believed** God." Now think about that, because there is a big difference in those statements. Many of us believe in God, but do we believe all that God says and all that God promises us? If we don't, how would we ever really trust Him?*

Everything we read in God's Book is true. When it says God is my refuge, then I have to believe that He is. When it says that I can come to Him when I am burdened and heavy laden, and He will lift my load, I have to believe He can. I have to ask Him for it. When it says that God is my shelter, and that He will never leave me, I have to depend on it. I'm never disappointed, although sometimes I might have to cry for a while, and call out to Him to find relief. But I believe that is more for my benefit than anything. Tears are healthy, and there are times when they are needed to make us feel better.

Let me share, if I may....HA! Of course I will!

The other day, I had a problem. To me, it was big problem! So what did I do? I went to climb a hill and talk to God. It dawned on me today, that that is just what Jesus would do. There were many times He would withdraw from the crowds and go up on a mountain and pray.

> *About eight days after Jesus said this,*
> *he took Peter, John and James*
> *with him and went up*
> *onto a mountain to pray.*
> *Luke 9:28 (NIV)*

*I hiked, and hiked, and talked with God, and questioned things that were happening. I asked for help, and all the usual things you do in a conversation with God. About a half hour into my climb, as I was looking up at the sky, I told God that I knew He was there, and I knew He could hear me, but I wasn't hearing anything back. I wasn't getting anything from Him. And just then, I looked to my left, and there was a sign that said, "Please stay on trail." I laughed, as I know that God will speak to us in so many different ways. I knew that He was telling me to keep on keepin' on—follow the path that leads to Him. I was to keep climbing that hill, keep talking to Him, and I would eventually find what I was looking for. What I found at the top of the hill was not an answer to my problem. It was not a solution as to what needed to be done. But I found that I could trust God with whatever it was, and have my peace restored even in the midst of it all. I found that God really was the One in control. I had forgotten that for part of the hike up the hill. I needed to **believe** God, not just believe **in** Him. I needed to trust Him with this, and every situation that happens in my life. Our Father has all the answers before we even have all the questions!*

Friends like Lynn can teach us that by how they live. That is what her family and friends were telling us all today. She trusted God completely, and she stayed on the trail until it took her "Home" where she will never be confused or disappointed again. Her step-children stood and blessed her today. Her husband praised her. Her friends spoke of her deeds publicly, and rewarded her with kind words. Is there any greater tribute?

> *Therefore we do not lose heart.*
> *Though outwardly we are wasting away,*
> *yet inwardly we are being renewed day by day.*
> *2 Corinthians 4:16 (NIV)*

Lynn and Phil were physically wasting away, yet they were being renewed inwardly day by day. They showed that in their eyes, and in their smiles, because what was inside of them could not die. God's eternal glory shined through both of them. That is what I saw when I was with them.

This life sometimes seems long, and it seems hard, but there are people that will come across our path that will help it all make sense. Phil was one of those for me; and Lynn was another. To the world, they were stricken down, died too young, and their troubles seemed immense. But they did not fix their eyes on what we all saw happening to their bodies. Their eyes were fixed on what was eternal.

*The other day, once again, I questioned how I could possibly just go on with my life? It seems so wrong—like Phil might not have mattered if I can continue to enjoy life, smile, laugh, go to the fair, to the movies, and on vacation. Then it came to me, we are not just "going on with our lives" as if nothing happened—as if Phil was never a part of our lives—we are going on with our lives **forever changed** for the **better**.*

Even if life is short, 16 years, or 46 years, make it count for something BIG! The example has been set by these two, and many others. Let's follow in their footsteps and "stay on the trail" that leads us "Home."

Lynn loved the Lord with all of her heart. She lived fully. When Lynn arrived Home, I hope she said:

"Phil, I just saw your mom, and she's doing fine."

Yes! I hope that's what Lynn told him!

Love, Diane

<u>Myself</u>

What will our "eulogy" be like? Will they speak kindly about us? Will the group gathered snicker because they know what we were really like, or will they nod their heads in agreement about how much we actually did touch their lives?

A friend was just telling me a few weeks back about a service she went to. She knew the lady quite well because of doing business with her. She said that the woman described at the service was nothing like the woman she knew. She found it quite odd—was she two different people, depending on who she was with? My friend didn't know. Having spent that last hour with Lynn, and then hearing who she was at her service, I experienced the same exact person. I was inspired, and encouraged. And little did I know then the impact just being there at her service would have on my ultimate healing process! There are certain points along the way through sorrow that we will always remember—for the good, and sometimes for the bad—some are huge steps forward, some can be steps backwards. But we remember them, and we can choose to go with them, or ignore them if they are not good for us. When I heard that Lynn not only believed *in* God, but that she *believed* God, it became a cornerstone of sorts in my healing process. I knew that I needed to believe what God's Word said, even if I couldn't fully grasp it yet. One day I sat with a friend, and I asked her the question, "Do you know how you don't doubt?" She said, "No, how?" I said, "You don't." It took her a bit by surprise. Really? It can be that simple? I had read it in a book, and I had never forgotten it. I realized when I read it, that doubting was a choice I could make, or not make. Which path would I chose? Would I believe or doubt? The more I chose to believe God's promises, the more I healed. And when I chose to doubt, it did me no good. It just caused me nothing but fear and anguish. **Believe**. That is what I had to do. And I'm still here, almost 13 years later now, still believing. And it works! Because it is God's Truth that I am believing.

I had the enormous privilege of sitting with Lynn for an hour on Tuesday, June 4, 2002. I say an enormous privilege because it was a very meaningful hour that I feel was a gift from God—and within about 36 hours, Lynn left for "Home."

I still remember that day. I was in downtown Pleasanton having lunch with my friend, Lilia. We stood out in front of the restaurant when we were finished, and I said to her, "I think I'm supposed to go see Lynn." I made a phone call, and headed off toward Livermore. Dave met me at the door, and led me into Lynn's room. She was very ill, but quite able to converse for a full hour. At the end of the hour she needed to make a trip to the bathroom, so I stepped out of her room while Dave helped her. When I entered back into her room, she was exhausted and sweating. I knew it was time to leave. As I drove home and entered the freeway onramp, God whispered to my heart, "That is the last time you will see Lynn." It was a gentle whisper, and not one that astounded me in that moment. But that is why, when the phone rang on Thursday morning, I was not surprised that Lynn was gone. And I was so thankful that I had listened to the prompting of the Holy Spirit to make a visit to her house that day. What a treasure I would have missed had I not gone!

She could tell Phil she had just seen his mom, and she is doing fine. I feel like God gave me the gift of spending that time with her, to help comfort me in my grief.

I didn't know as I sat by Lynn's bed that she would soon be leaving, just as I didn't know that about Phil. But there have been others I have been with, whose departure seemed more eminent.

One gentleman, J.D., was a special man to me. I met him at church when he came in looking for some help. I was the receptionist at the time. What a sweet guy he was. He found help in our church, and became very involved in the men's ministry for years. When Phil went Home, J.D. brought us a spiral ham. I don't know why that sticks with me like it does, but we sure enjoyed that ham. He always had a smile on his face, and a genuine warmth about him. I got word that J.D. had cancer. I had not known, and I immediately wanted to go see him, which I did. When J.D. opened the door I barely recognized him, he was so thin. When he smiled, I then saw him behind the narrow face. He invited me in and, once again, we sat for about an hour and talked. He had so much to share with me about God, and the comfort God had given him through one particular moment in the I.C.U. God met him there in a special way, and J.D. said that since that moment, he had not been afraid. He also said he wished he had lived his whole life as he had the last few months, resting in God with such complete peace. His eyes lit up as we talked. I said very little, more listening and enjoying his stories than anything. It was then time for me to get back to work, so he walked me to the door. I gave him a hug, and told him what I have told just a few others, "If you get to Heaven before me, please give Phil a hug for me." He assured me he would. Two weeks later, J.D. was gone. I got one last hug from J.D. on this earth, and Phil got one more hug in Heaven, via a friend, from me.

Was she watching me more closely on that day? Was she being comforted to see me smile, to see me continue on living my life after having lost Phil, knowing that soon her husband, Dave, might have to continue living on without her?

"No one can know a person's thoughts except that person's own spirit…" 1 Cor. 2:11 (NLT) Sometimes we can't even know our own thoughts, or our own needs. In just writing that, I wonder if Lynn had been praying and asking God to bring her some comfort about her husband? Theirs was a new marriage, I don't think a first for either one of them, but a marriage that was founded on Jesus. I'm sure she was concerned about how Dave would do, and God knew that. I hope that I was some help to her on that day—maybe that's why at the end of our visit, she started to leave for Home. Dave said she never really recovered from that last trip to the bathroom. Later that day, she went to the hospital, and then 36 hours later she was gone. Maybe I was just what the "doctor" ordered to give her peace and help her to let go? Dave missed her so, and I'm sure he still does, although I trust that God has brought him through his sorrow and into the rest of his life by now. I don't see Dave anymore, but I will always remember after Lynn was gone, seeing how he had their wedding rings made into the most beautiful Cross that he wore around his neck. I'd never seen that done before.

I will never forget my final visit. It will always be one of the greatest blessings in my life.

We think that those we have known for the greatest amount of time will have the biggest impact on our lives, and many times they do—but here I sit writing about Lynn all these years later. I barely knew Lynn and Dave. We had prayed together a few times, and had seen each other coming and going. Why would I be her last visitor? She had a ton of friends. They both did. Yet God called me, and said, "Go." And I went. The reason for my visit is one of the mysteries of God. We can't know why He asks us to do certain things, but we need to still do them. It may take decades, and maybe even a lifetime to see what God is doing, but obedience does bring a special kind of joy.

To have met Lynn, and then listen to those that knew her best at her service, made me want to be a better person.

I didn't want to be Lynn. But what I wanted was to be a woman of God like she was. I wanted my children to one day be able to describe me as they did her, a woman after God's own heart, like King David. Recently, our son has been going through some hard things. We are not normally what I call, "everyday" people. Some parents talk to their grown children every day, but we don't. We call from time to time. We connect when we need to, and in between, we are at peace with each other. But because of the tribulations of late, our son Jimm and I have been talking, or texting, daily. And it is an interesting time to be there for him. I don't like what he is having to go through, but I like that he trusts me to pray for him, and encourage him as he goes through it. I certainly don't have all the answers, but I can pray for them along the way, and do what I can. He said to me, "Mom, you're the most godly person I know." I just stopped typing after I wrote that, even now. I don't say that to brag, so I hesitate to even include it here. But I share it because maybe Lynn has helped me be that "better person" that I wanted to be; the godly woman she was. And I am thankful for Lynn, and others, who propel me and hold me accountable—the ones who don't let me off easy, don't give me easy answers, but help me in my walk with Jesus. Those are the people I want around me. Not "Yes" people, who think I'm wonderful, but people who say, "You might want to rethink that decision." This is the second book, now, about the first year of grief. The first one took a whole TEAM of people to finish up after the original words were put on paper. I can't begin to express how much I appreciate those who drew my attention to things that needed changing, fixing, and rewording, etc… I want that, not only in my writings, but in my daily life. It's not easy to take "criticism." But when it comes from a brother, or sister, or son in Christ, it can be good and helpful! We have to be open to it, and I pray that I am, more and more each day I live. Help me Jesus!

*For so many years, we prayed for Phil to be healed, believing that God **can** heal. Lynn also prayed for God's healing, and she believed that she **would be** healed.*

We all can pray for healing, but we doubt, don't we? I did. Jim did. Phil did. I'm sure Lynn even did, but that's not what I saw and heard from her, and I appreciated that. I hadn't read the book about how to stop doubting when I knew Lynn. So I prayed, and I prayed for God to help me in my unbelief as the father did in Mark 9:24. I was thankful to read that in the Bible, and not feel so alone. But I knew, with Lynn, that she was really walking out her faith. That helped me, because when she still died, as we all will eventually, I could accept whatever God decided with Phil. She LOVED God, she TRUSTED Him, and she still went Home. So, okay, then I will be okay. Because it will all be okay, one day. And it is. I realized that it's not that I needed more faith in my prayers for Phil to be healed—God wanted me to have a strong faith for sure, and He still does, because, "The effective, fervent prayer of a righteous man avails much." James 5:16 (NKJV) But even when we utter up weak, doubt-filled prayers, God knows our hearts, and He knows we are doing the best with what we have learned so far in our walk with Jesus. So I am able to do better today. I am more able to curb the doubts when they enter into my head, and say "No" to them. I do it all the time, because doubts plague us all, still. They don't go away, they can lessen when we listen to them less, but they still come at every human being on this earth. I just choose to not let them stay attached to me when they invade my thinking.

Right now, as I type this, I am waiting for the first shipment of "It Started in the Dark." They are due in next Wednesday—one week from today. They will arrive just days before our Book Gala party, where everyone will be coming to get the very first ones available. I'm so thankful to Lilia and Lynn for throwing this shin-dig. Some even want me to sign their books? I don't know why, but I will comply, and give God the Glory as we proceed through that exercise. But why I include this part of the story here is, I am battling the doubts of, WHAT IF THE BOOKS GET DELAYED? Even if it's two days late, then we will be onto Saturday, and there is no UPS delivery on Saturday, and then Sunday night is the party, and I will show up empty handed, and....blah, blah, blah, blah, blah! WAIT!! Stop doubting, and BELIEVE that God is in control. So I choose to trust, today, and tomorrow, and the next day. And if the books do get delayed, we will praise Jesus anyway! And the books will arrive when they arrive. (You'll probably read later on in this book when they did arrive.) As I prayed about this, this very morning, once again giving the timing to God, He reminded me of the other side of that timing, and His perfect help along the way. With all the work that needed to be done, and watching Jim work tirelessly at the end of his day job to publish the book, and all the corrections that needed to be done by my editor, Connie, and me, and then the proof-readers, and the redoing of the cover, and on and on, we got it done and ordered, in time for the party! We did not dilly-dally at all. It took three months, and it is arriving not a day too soon. God is in all that, too, lest I forget! He brought us to this moment, and instead of worrying, I am thanking Him for helping us to complete it just in time! And today, I am enjoying the continuing work on, "It Ended in the Light"—sitting here writing in my PJ's, and loving just being back in my "cave" doing the easy part. Book publishing is hard work, with many spiritual attacks included. It is not for the faint of heart. The writing is easy in comparison. So, I will let you know in future chapters about the books at the Book Gala. I have heard that God is a drama King. He likes last minute endings! Once again, He is probably enjoying Himself, knowing how it all turns out, as He is building my faith.

*An interesting thing was said at the service today by a friend of Lynn's. She said something to this effect, "Lynn not only believed in God, she **believed** God."*

Psalm 91 is one of my first reads every morning right now. I'd like to say I have memorized it, and I am trying, but I haven't gotten more than halfway through it. The reason why I like it is because it covers all the fears in life. It talks about plagues, terrors of the night, evils, traps, etc... And it starts with, "Those who live in the shelter of the Most High will find rest in the shadow of the Almighty." (NLT) I could stop right at that first verse for quite a long time. With it, I picture standing under a roof. For me, it's wooden, and I'm standing in the shadow it makes. I feel covered by God in that spot. And I feel safe. But to feel safe there, we have to **believe**. That's what the last 12 plus years have brought me to. I believe that God's Word is true. I have been rescued so many times, from so many dark places, by focusing on the things of God, and His promises, that God has proven His faithfulness to me. Maybe it takes all those times of needing to be rescued, to finally understand that we will be.

Everything we read in His Book is true. When it says God is my refuge, then I have to believe that He is.

This thought continues on with what I have been saying above. Psalm 91:2 says, "This I declare of the Lord: He alone is my

refuge, my place of safety; he is my God, and I am trusting him."
(NLT) The other day as I searched again to be rescued from the
darkness this life can inflict upon us, I felt so secure in knowing
that I can turn to my Savior for help. Where else can we find that
kind of help in this world? What else do we have that offers us
what Jesus does? Other things can dull the pain for a time. But they
don't offer the help we really need. Unhealthy pain relievers
eventually cause us more pain. But Jesus, and the Hope He gives
us, builds in our lives. Each time we turn to Jesus for the answers
to our problems, He builds our faith in Him. That gives us
confidence to continue on. When the waves hit, and we have
chosen unhealthy remedies, the waves can knock us flat because
we have been weakened. But when we have made the choice for
Jesus, those waves may rock our world a bit, but they can't smash
to smithereens the Rock we stand on. Our Rock is steady and true,
always. Our pastor gave us an illustration of Satan's power against
God's one day. He made the motion like he was flicking a flea off
his arm. What a great picture of how small our adversary really is
compared to God.

*The other day I had a problem. To me, it was big problem! So what
did I do? I went to climb a hill and talk to God.*

That problem has long since passed, but I still remember what it
was. We don't literally have to go to a mountain when life presses
in on us, but sometimes it is good to. Like the story I shared in the
Introduction, mountain retreats can help us clear out what the
"valley" is crowding us with. Mainly, we just need to get alone and
seek our Father's advice, find our Savior's Hope, and listen
intently for the Holy Spirit's encouragement in our situation.

*I looked to my left and there was a sign that said, "Please stay on
trail."*

God's directions won't always be in the form of a sign! God has
many ways of speaking to us. But getting away, getting quiet, and
seeking His face is helpful in hearing from Him. The other day I
was sitting at the counter, here in our home, with my

granddaughter, Kylie. She is 9. She had been spending two weeks with us, and her time was just about finished. The two weeks had been filled with fun and activities. For just a moment, it was like everything stopped. She was doing something on her phone, and I was working on something beside her, and the house was totally silent. She looked at me and said, "I'm bored." I said, "You're bored? Why? Because it's quiet?" She answered, "Yes." I told her, "This is the way it normally is here." Her response surprised me. She said, "I feel bad for you." I laughed, "Bad?" I said, "I like it. We can hear God better when it's quiet. Even in the shower, that's a good place to hear God because the noise is drowned out." I don't know quite what she thought about all that, but it is a conversation that I will long remember.

What I found at the top of the hill was not an answer to my problem. But I found that I could trust God with whatever it was.

All my problems did not go away when I got to the top of the mountain. And even at Denise's mountain retreat, things were still brewing when I headed back down to the valley. But there was a peace that I brought home with me. That is what I needed...not for the problems to be fixed, but for our Lord's peace to reign. Jesus said in John 14:27, "Peace I leave with you." When problems come, we have to call on Jesus. We may get tired of having to make that choice over and over. We just want things to be better, to be easier in life, and not so stressful. But if we look at it from the other angle, what if we didn't have Jesus to run to? What if our Father in Heaven wasn't waiting for us to calm our fears? What if the Holy Spirit fled for His own mountain when our world was crashing all around us? What then? It would not be good; that I know. So instead of getting tired because we have to seek God all the time, let's be super thankful He is there for us to seek at all!

Lynn and Phil were physically wasting away, yet they were being renewed inwardly day by day. They showed that in their eyes, and in their smiles, because what was inside of them could not die.

There are people we know, that are walking around dead inside. They are not physically dying, as Lynn and Phil were, but what they have is much worse. It appears fine from the outside, but their insides are being eaten up with anger, hate, unforgiveness, lust, addictions…the list is endless. We wonder why they are so mean, so rude, or so unkind? How can they act that way toward others? If we really understood their pain, we would want to love them. But it is HARD! We want to be mean back. But we are called to love. The Bible says it is easy to love a friend, but we are called to love our enemies in Matthew 5:44. Sometimes, our "enemies" seem to live in our homes. They are our spouse, or child, or parent. Even in our homes, and sometimes especially in our homes, we need the Holy Spirit to be fully alive and active in our lives. If someone isn't shining on the outside, they need our love and prayers shining from the inside.

This life sometimes seems long, and it seems hard, but there are people that will come across our path that will help it all make sense.

I'm so thankful for Lynn, and for Phil, and for so many others that have changed my life. I'm thankful for friends and family that are still with me, too, that keep encouraging me. When we are on a roller coaster of emotions due to life's happenings, we need those who are able to ride alongside of us on a steady train. It's like the swimmers in a lake that I recently experienced. When they can look up between strokes and see the guide boat beside them, they know they are swimming straight. We need someone beside us, keeping us on the straight and narrow path. We need to have Jesus as our number One Guide, and then spend time with those that know Jesus, those that will speak His words of Truth into our messy lives.

*…we are not just "going on with our lives" as if nothing happened—as if Phil were never a part of our lives—we are going on with our lives **forever changed** for the **better**.*

How true this was, is, and has become! Our lives never just went on, they went on totally changed because Phil was with us for 16 years. I will be forever grateful for the gift God gave us through his life. Some may say our story didn't end well. But our story isn't finished yet. Case in point, I'm still writing it, right here, right now. I'm still living it out each day, and growing each day in my relationship with God. I love learning new things in the Word, finding new gems to hold on to, and new pieces of wisdom that might be good for me and those I know. When we meet Jesus by saying, yes, to His saving Grace, we also can't just go on with our lives as if nothing happened. We need to be going on with our lives forever changed for the better. If we're not, we need to ask ourselves if we are spending enough time with Jesus each day? The thing I love about our pastors at church is their personal interaction with God. They share it with us each week from the pulpit. We hear it in their prayers, and in their sermons. It's personal to them. They are not speaking of a God they don't know. They heard from Him during the week. They share their struggles, and their challenges, and how God is growing them in their faith. Their faith is alive and active, as should be ours!

"Phil, I just saw your mom and she's doing fine."

Yes! I hope that's what Lynn told him!

It's greedy of me, to want personal messengers going on to Heaven and seeing Phil, and telling him I'm fine. But maybe God allows me that little bit of indulgence. I'm not trying to communicate with the dead, which the Bible forbids. I'm just sending a bit of my earthly love into Phil's Heavenly Home. One day, I hope to do the same for someone else.

Gift #5 – Learning to believe!

What's your greatest challenge in walking this life out with Jesus?

Do you open up God's Word each day looking for answers along the way?

Record today's date and other notes you'd like to make:

The Great

<u>I AM</u>

Her children stand and bless her.
Her husband praises her:
"There are many virtuous
and capable women in the world,
but you surpass them all!"
Charm is deceptive, and beauty
does not last; but a woman
who fears the Lord will be greatly
praised. Reward her for all she has done.
Let her deeds publicly declare her praise.
Proverbs 31:28-31 (NLT)

CHAPTER SIX

*And may the Lord our God show us his approval and make
our efforts successful. Yes, make our efforts successful.*
Psalm 90:17 (NLT)

Me

The Lie

Friday, 19 Jul 2002

*I felt like a failure, but I didn't know it. I just knew that something
was very wrong. God gave me a clue early in the week that I
laughed at. Later, I wasn't laughing... God knew what was in store.
I didn't. But He would show me when the week was over.*

*I write this on Friday night after working 4½ days this week at the
church. My job-share partner at the receptionist's desk went on
vacation and I was filling in for her during the three days she was
gone, and then I was to do my normal Thursday/Friday duty, too.
No problem, I thought. I'm up for this. In fact, I'm feeling pretty
good these days. I feel some healing beginning in my heart, so I
thought this should be fine. I had already planned on taking a full*

hour for lunch each day so that I could leave the church and go to a park. There I could be by myself, refill my tanks with some prayer time, and then come back ready to take on the afternoon. Monday was good. Tuesday, I think, was the day God gave me the clue, which I mentioned above. Wednesday was getting a little bit more difficult, but with only two more days to go, it seemed to be okay. Thursday, I was getting more depleted, and by Friday morning, I told my manager, Kim, that I wouldn't be able to stay for the whole day. It was a clear signal this morning with the deep breaths I was having to take that I was trying to fill the emptiness growing inside. My heart was starting to hurt as in days past, and I felt physically shaky by Friday morning.

What was up with this? Didn't I have the perfect plan of long lunches with God to get me through this week? Hadn't I prayed and spent time with Him in the evening to refuel my spiritual tank? Why was I faltering towards the end of the five days?

I came home early on my last day a bit confused and worn out. I felt that I could probably work on my computer, though, since it would be quiet work. But that didn't even go well. I had to stop because my heart was hurting again. I got quiet for a while, read my Bible, and then I watched a program I like. I was searching and seeking God because something seemed so amiss. I was disturbed inside and it seemed to be more than a regular tired. It felt so uncomfortable, and I knew there was a missing piece to how I felt. I asked God to help me know what was missing. I talked with Him, and waited for an answer...

Maybe I needed to write? So I tried that. It felt like it was more work than normal. Normally, work is not even a word I would use when I write—pure pleasure is what I would call it. But I was searching and searching for that missing piece. As I was writing on my computer, it shut down. It turned completely off. You could say it was the heat today. I don't know how computers work really, but I think it was God putting a stop to my writing. It wasn't time yet. I didn't have the missing piece that was causing my unease.

I went out and had some dinner, watched a little baseball, and then went for my walk. It was a beautiful evening, but I wasn't even able to do my usual pace. I was dragging. The music didn't even help me pick up my step. I sat on a bench and just listened to a song. I laughed when I got up to walk again because the song that started said, "You know when I sit and when I rise." As always, it was God's perfect timing. I think He has quite a sense of humor!

When I was about three quarters of the way through my walk, it finally came to me...I felt like a failure. I had failed to complete a full five days at work. I didn't make it—with all my planning, praying, and determination, it still didn't sustain me. What a failure I was. What a wimp! Other people work five days a week— even others who have lost loved ones are able to keep a full time job. I know many of them—but not me. I couldn't even get through one week...a failure. I was weak and just not all that I should be. The tears sprang to the surface and I knew I had my "key." I knew why I felt such unease. I am a person who likes challenges, and I looked upon this as a new challenge. I like to succeed. Don't we all?

Wow! That just reminded me of what I was reading this afternoon in the Psalms:

> *And may the Lord our God show us his*
> *approval and make our efforts successful.*
> *Yes, make our efforts successful. Psalm 90:17 (NLT)*

I had underlined it and written next to it, "We all want to be successful."

On my walk, I sat on another bench and thought about this feeling of failure that I had. I knew it was a lie from the evil one to take me down, to make me feel bad. But that didn't change the fact that I felt bad. I needed to examine this lie and see what the truth really was. What was God's view on this situation? Did He think I was a failure? I mean, it has been 8 months and 5 days since Phil went Home. Does He think that I should have recovered enough to work a full week by now? Was I falling short somehow in not having the strength to do that? When I told Pastor Dave I was going home today, he commented about my progress—I had made it 4½ days, when in the past, two was beyond my limit—that was a good thought.

This verse came to me:
For I can do everything through Christ, who gives me strength.
Philippians 4:13 (NLT)

*I continued to walk and kept repeating, "I can do all things through Christ, who gives me strength." But I was wondering what had happened? Then I knew... Christ **had** given me the strength to do exactly what He wanted me to do, and no more. By Friday, around noon, most things that needed doing had been done, and I could leave work without much fuss. God had given me the strength up to that point. But then it was time to go. My job at that point was to realize that, and leave...go home, find Jesus, search for what He wanted me to learn, and then write about it, because that is what I do.*

So what do I do with the lies that go through my head that I am weak because others can do what I cannot? Others can complete a full week of work, week after week, and I cannot.

How silly of me! I haven't had to work a full week, week after week, since I was 20 years old. I have always been a stay-at-home mom and maybe that's exactly what God had called me to be those many years ago. Having not worked outside the home while raising our boys, I was able to be home with Phil through his long illness. We had not gotten used to that second paycheck. I was there when Phil would call from school saying he was having a hard day, that he wasn't feeling well. It made me so grateful that I could quickly be there for him. Having not worked outside the home, when I took this job at the church a little over a year ago, the news of it received raised eyebrows from Phil as he exclaimed, "But you've always been my stay-at-home-mom!" It made me wonder what in the world I was doing taking a job at that time? It was only because I felt it was what God was asking me to do, that I did it. I know why now, although then I didn't. Now I know that my two days a week are part of my healing process.

A failure? I don't think so. I know not!

We are all called to do different things in this life, and if we try to match up our abilities or callings with what others are doing, we will feel like a failure. God has made each one of us unique, and no matter what it looks like to those around us, if we are right with God, if our heart is where it should be, we are answering to the right Person—our Father in Heaven.

Sometimes when I read books or articles, and I think, "I should write more like that." Then I remember—if I alter what I do, to be like someone else, I am missing the calling of God on my life. I am not to be like another, but unique. If it is what God is asking of me, and I am obedient, He will be happy with me even if no one else is.

As far as working full-time, it is a temptation for me, now, because I do not have children at home to take care of anymore. It would make perfect sense for me to get a full-time job and bring in some extra money. Wouldn't it? Or would it? What if I did work outside the home full time, and I ended up missing the real call on my life? And what if that call is to write? It may seem a small thing, but maybe somewhere out there, there is someone who needs to read this. Maybe there is a hurting heart that is locked in those chains that the evil one would like to put us in to keep us down—chains like the lie that we are a failure because we are not the same as others, not as good as others, or not as productive as others?

*Maybe this week was exactly what it was supposed to be, and I was not a failure at all. I was starting to spread my wings, and felt some healing and some energy returning. But what if I took those feelings and went the wrong direction with them and missed God's calling on my life because I started working on my own strength and not His? Maybe this week was to show me that I can do all things **through Christ** who strengthens me, and no more. We try to* *work so hard at it, when it is not supposed to be by our strength at all, but Christ's in us. When God was done with what He wanted, I was on my own.*

Don't get me wrong, I love the job I do at the church. I love everything about it—the people, the work, even the constant phone ringing. I think that is what confuses me so much—how can something I love so much, be so emotionally exhausting? By Wednesday, I came home and hung my body over the chair in the dining room and said to Jim, "I love my job, but I'm so tired." We laughed! The more hours I put in, the more I loved it. The longer I worked with everyone there, the more I wanted to be with them. It was all good. And the temptation to work there full time, if a position became available, and I was accepted for it, would be great. But I truly believe that God let me know this week that it is not the time. If I am to fulfill His call on my life, I am to take life slowly right now. I am to spend as much time as possible with God, and allow Him to heal my heart. My Father has a great future planned for me. If I wait on Him, He will renew my strength when the time is right. There is ministry work that definitely needs to get done, but by those God chooses to do it.

Jim has always worked full time, and although it has helped him to work from home a lot in this past year, he has had to continue to work through his grieving period. He chose many years ago to marry, and have a family, and support that family to the best of his ability. He continues to do so. I am so grateful for all he has done through the years to take care of the boys and me. He would tell you that there are times that it is difficult to get through the day when his heart is breaking, but God has given him the strength to do it. I, on the other hand, have led a different life at home with the boys, and for now God is keeping me home a bit longer. I will continue to listen for God's leading and learn from Him by being quiet and prayerful. I know that if I did not, I would probably not write half as much as I do, if at all—I would be "too busy."

People ask me what I will do in Kansas City next week. Jim is travelling there on business. I am accompanying him there, for

R&R. Those that know me best know I do R&R quite well. I am not one to get lonely, although I love being with people. Being alone refreshes my soul. Being alone is where I find God most easily. And then I am able to feel His joy and peace in this busy and sometimes painful world we live in. Living for Jesus is what makes life most exciting. Writing for Him is what I love to do. It's what I feel called to do, during this season in my life, as well as working only TWO DAYS A WEEK!

Would you like to know what the clue was about my week ahead that God gave me in the beginning of the week? He reminded me of it on my walk tonight. It was a license plate frame I saw that said, "Life is too short to work full-time."

It made me laugh when I saw it, and by tonight, it made me remember what an awesome God we serve, because He is so ahead of us, and so completely involved in every aspect of our lives. The pieces are all there if we will just look for them and acknowledge that God is the One who puts all things in place. Nothing is an accident; nothing is a surprise to our Father in Heaven. I think He enjoys surprising us though, and is happy when we realize He is the One watching over our every step. Though we may stumble, He will catch us when we fall.

I felt like I was stumbling along tonight when I left for my walk. But I can tell you honestly, when God revealed what was keeping me bound, the lie that I was a failure, I was free once again! The evil one wants to keep us in the chains that should no longer hold us. If we take it to God, and ask Him to help us, He WILL help us! I could still be there in that lie—but I would not give up because I knew there was something wrong, and I knew that God had the answer. I walked back home lighter than air because the truth had set me free!

This I declare of the Lord:
He alone is my refuge, my place of safety;
he is my God, and I am trusting him.

*For he will rescue you from every trap and protect
you from the fatal plague. Psalm 91:2-3 (NLT)*

Good night,
Diane

<u>Myself</u>

*What was up with this? Didn't I have the perfect plan of long
lunches with God to get me through this week? Hadn't I prayed
and spent time with Him in the evening to refuel my spiritual tank?
Why was I faltering towards the end of the five days?*

I was rushing it. I can see that now, looking back, but I couldn't
see it then, looking forward. I knew I had to prepare as best I could
to accomplish "my goal," for the week. I wanted to be of help at
work, and to fill in where necessary. But it was a lot for my broken
heart to endure. In reading this again, though, I see God had good
lessons in it for me. If He had given me the strength to complete
that entire week, I might not be here today writing this. I may have
missed this calling, or at least delayed it, by answering another one
that wasn't from Him. That's the thing about trying to figure out
how we are to serve God. We want to serve; He puts that desire in
our heart when Jesus becomes our Savior. Jesus said, "If any of
you wants to be my follower, you must turn from your selfish
ways, take up your cross daily, and follow me." Luke 9:23 (NLT) I
wanted to, but I still needed to find out what my "selfish ways"
were, and learn how to follow Jesus in the footsteps He had
designed for me. If I had had a "successful" full week at work, I
might have gone down a good path of working full time at the
church, but not *thee* path my Father had for me. Taking on full
time work outside of our home might have been a "detour" instead
of a direct path. I don't like detours; they waste precious time.

*I sat on a bench and just listened to a song. I laughed when I got
up to walk again because the song that started said, "You know
when I sit and when I rise."*

It's funny how most times I can't remember what I had for dinner last night, or where I put my keys, but I can remember this moment in time from over 12 years ago. I can remember that walk, and getting up from that bench with those words playing in my ears. I walked most every day early on in grief. Other than being in my room for times of prayer and being in the Word, walking was probably one of the most helpful pain relievers I had at that time. I would put my portable CD player on, put my headphones in, and go out walking. (This was before having all our music on our iPhones.) I had two CD's that I listened to, over and over and over. They helped me keep my sanity as I listened to words of inspiration. Still to this day, when I hear those songs, I am amazed at how each one had a special encouraging message.

When I was about three quarters of the way through my walk it finally came to me...I felt like a failure.

Obviously, reading this, it reminds me how much I prayed on those walks, and cried out to God. Jesus would meet me out walking, and comfort my hurting heart. On that day, He removed the lie that was trying to destroy me, for truth that would keep me on the right path to healing. Jesus helped me carry on. Isn't it terrible, how, when we are doing the very best we can, the enemy will still try to take us down?! I even saw his attacks on Phil, a sweet, very ill child, just trying to make a peaceful journey Home. The lies would come in and Phil would grow fearful. Only with the Truth of God poured into him could his peace be restored. Who isn't fearful in those moments, during those finals weeks and days? We wouldn't be human if we weren't afraid to some degree. We all have questions as we head into unknown territory. Phil told me that the devil had been lying to him—he had been given the idea, from Satan, that it hurts to die. When Phil got a glimpse of Heaven, two days before he actually travelled Home, he was comforted in that experience to know that the actual dying part, moving from this life to the next, wasn't painful. The process of cancer and many other diseases can be painful, that's for sure; but when we are released from these bodies, the pain stops if we are headed to Heaven. There is no pain in Heaven. That's why we need a Bible very, very handy at the bedside of those leaving us! Not only to comfort them through some of their last thoughts on this earth, but to help them find their way Home to Heaven if they haven't found it as yet. For those who trust in the saving Grace of Jesus Christ, this earth is as close to Hell as we will ever get!

I was weak. And just not all that I should be.

Who's to say what we should be? We put expectations on ourselves that God never places there. It is said, "If God brings us to it, He will bring us through it." I believe that is true. God saw me through what He was asking me to do that week. He had given me His strength to complete what needed to be done. I have learned through the years, to better recognize God's calls on my life, compared to those I put on myself. Our Lord doesn't always make His calls easy on us, but He does make them possible.

What was God's view on this situation? Did He think I was a failure? I mean, it has been 8 months and 5 days since Phil went Home.

I sort of chuckle at this. If I was still counting months and DAYS, I was early on in grief. I had not yet come to that point in my walk through the darkness to be able to say, "I am 8 months *closer* to seeing Phil again," which is how I count out the time now. Instead I was counting how long I had been *without* him. That's such a painful way to count... This different counting "technique" came to light one day a couple of years ago when I attended an AA meeting with a friend of mine. When I witnessed the woman in the group getting a chip for six months, one year, and so on, of living without alcohol, it dawned on me, I am coming up on ten years of living without Phil. I wanted my Ten Year chip. Jim and I started a small business venture after that realization called *Closer Coins*. The goal with these coins is to be encouraged as we get closer to seeing our loved one again—or closer to many things—maybe it's someone returning from war, or someone who is 3 Years closer to getting their degree. Instead of counting how far we have to go, we focus on how far we have come. I'm coming up, soon, on needing a 13 Year Closer Coin. Praise God!

When I told Pastor Dave I was going home today, he commented about my progress—I had made it 4½ days, when in the past, two was beyond my limit—that was a good thought.

Words of encouragement can stick, just as words of discouragement can. Dave reacted perfectly on that day. He commented on the progress I had made, instead of the failure I felt. Thank you for that, Dave. It was a brief encounter that helped so much in that moment.

It made me wonder what in the world I was doing taking a job at that time? It was only because I felt it was what God was asking me to do, that I did it. I know why now, although then I didn't. Now I know that my two days a week are part of my healing process.

I love how reading about this reminds me of how it all happened. I was in the church one day, helping to get ready for a women's retreat. The receptionist at the time, Debbie, was leaving soon. Her job had been posted for a couple of months. I had not taken notice. I wasn't looking for a job. We talked on that day about her job, and I looked at her clothing. Casual wear. I remember thinking, I can dress like that since jeans are my favorite attire. (It was casual Friday.) The office manager, Kim, came to the top of the stairs above where I was working on the retreat stuff. I said, "I think I'm supposed to apply for Debbie's job." Kim went and got me the application. I filled it out. It was easy. I had little to no real previous job experience. Filling in my name and address was about it. I had worked as a Medical Transcriber when I was twenty, so I did remember to fill in that I did know how to type! Needless to say, I got the job. But still, I wondered why I was supposed to go to work? Was it because Phil would be leaving us, and I'd need something to do? Or was it because God was going to heal Phil, and I'd need something to do? I know the answer to that now… The front desk at CrossWinds Church in Dublin, CA became a place where, for a period of time, I was stretched and healed. For just two days a week, I had to leave my comfort zone at home, and feel some of the sting of rejoining the world when I would have rather not. It was hard as I cried all the way to work, and cried all the way home. It was hard when I had to escape to the shelter of a bathroom stall to catch my breath. It was hard because I had to face many things that I could have hidden from at home in my quiet place. But God knew it was a safe place for me, as He surrounded me with people who knew my loss, and who cared—pastors, administrators, and worship leaders, etc… And God knew it was just enough, at two days a week, to not be too much, and not be too little. God is good, and He knows, as He challenges us to keep putting one foot in front of the other even when we would rather not.

"But you've always been my stay-at-home-mom!"

And, yes, Phil was stretched too. He depended on me, a lot! But we both needed some time away from each other—for me to learn that I had a life outside of his illness, and for him, to learn that others could be there for him, as well as God. I could not be his God, he needed Jesus for that. And since Jim worked from home two days a week, God provided those days for dad and son to spend time together. It was good to get me out of the way a bit. The day did come, as Phil's illness progressed, that God let me know it was time to go home. I remember that day… I was at the copy machine downstairs, right where I had been when I first talked to Debbie about the job. How do I describe it—there was a quickening in my spirit that made the job not make much sense anymore compared to being with Phil. God impressed it upon my heart that being with Phil full time was where I needed to be. I talked with Kim about it, and she totally understood. My job-share partner picked up my two days a week, if I remember right, and I returned home to care for Phil. I don't remember, now, how long this was before his departure for Heaven, but I have a perfect peace about the time I spent with Phil before he went Home. God is so amazing, and it's so important to be listening when He whispers His instructions to us.

It would make perfect sense for me to get a full-time job and bring in some extra money. Wouldn't it? Or would it? What if I did work outside the home full time, and I ended up missing the real call on my life? And what if that call is to write?

Uh…I still don't work full time. I should say, I don't work full time outside of the home. I keep more than busy, especially when I get to write. And stay-at-home moms work full time, as well as moms outside of the home. That I know! Even though we don't have children at home right now, we do have my dad living with us part time. And it's not that my husband is not a big help, always, but still…the house can fall apart very quickly when I'm not walking through it picking up things constantly. I know when our boys were at home, I would clear out all the remnants from the evening before when the boys went off to school. If I didn't do it, daily, we wouldn't have been able to walk through our house!

I did get called to a new job venture about six years ago. I went to beauty school when I was 50. I didn't drop out, I got a job, and I could be working full time. But instead, I'm working two days a week again. There were times early on when I worked more, but right now, two days a week seems right. We all just have to work that out with God, and see what it is He would have us do with our days. I don't know if what I write here will be of help to a large group of people, but what if it just helps you? I wouldn't want to be cutting hair six days a week, and writing zero days a week. Then we would have missed out on this time together. I'd like to share the story of how I ended up in beauty school. It was one of the God things that I marvel at. I'll try to keep it brief…

I called my sister, Karen, over six years ago, and asked her to meet me for coffee—just to catch up, nothing in particular. In our conversation I told her that maybe I should get a job now that we are empty nesters. (The job at the church had ended a few years back.) I told Karen that I wasn't interested in working in an office again. She asked me what I like to do? I said, "I like to cut hair." (I had cut our boys' hair for years, as well as others'.) Karen said, "Well, why don't you do that?" I replied, "What a concept!" I called a local beauty school, and within a few days I was not only signed up, I had gotten a super deal that was only going on for two months. I sensed that God was urging me not to waste time in applying for school—then I knew why. Beauty school cost me $850, and I made $1,100 in tips while I was there. Talk about a gift from God! The school that I attended in Castro Valley, CA was purchased while I was there and now charges over $20,000 to attend! That's why I love this story—God not only led me into a career that I enjoy, He helped me do it for free! I had just about enough tip money left over at the end to pay for my state board exam. How do I know exactly how much I made in tips? Well, each day when the young girls I attended school with would spend their tip money for lunch, I would save mine and eat my peanut butter sandwich from home. I probably ate a peanut butter sandwich almost every day for the nine months and two weeks it took me to complete school. It was a fun nine months, and I got to meet many young ladies just starting out their lives. Some of them even met Jesus because of the Bible study God led me to start with them while I was there. God opened the doors for me to go to beauty school, and He also opened the door for introductions to Jesus.

Jim has always worked full time, and although it has helped him to work from home a lot in this past year, he has had to continue to work through his grieving period.

I am thankful for the strength that God fills Jim with. He did work full time through all the grief he felt. He continued to support us, and he continues to do so. Now he not only works full time, he helps me get these pages into a book. And he does it with such a willing and excited heart. I pray God blesses him for his faithfulness not only to God, but to me through the years.

"Life is too short to work full-time."

The truth is, we all work full time at something. Is it to serve God, or man? Is it to serve others, or ourselves? Do we even know? As believers, "A spiritual gift is given to each of us so we can help each other." 1 Corinthians 12:7 (NLT) When we discover what gift we have been given, we will find great joy using it in God's Kingdom work.

"God in heaven appoints each person's work." John 3:27 (NLT)

Gift #6 – Discovering the call(s) of God on our lives.

Have you ever taken a spiritual gifts test? If so, what is/are yours?

Have you prayed about your career, and sought God's guidance concerning your calling?

Record today's date and other notes you'd like to make:

The Great

<u>I AM</u>

The steps of the godly are directed by the Lord.
He delights in every detail of their lives.
Though they stumble, they will not fall,
for the Lord holds them by the hand.
Psalm 37:23-24 (NLT)

CHAPTER SEVEN

*Brothers, I do not consider myself yet to
have taken hold of it. But one thing I do:
Forgetting what is behind and
straining toward what is ahead.
I press on toward the goal to win the
prize for which God has called
me heavenward in Christ Jesus.*
Philippians 3:13-14 (NIV)

<u>Me</u>

New Beginnings

Friday, 19 Jul 2002

*My brother, Steve, calls it "Heaventown." He says that Phil has
moved a little north of Pleasanton, where we live, to Heaventown. I
like that! It makes me smile. It brings into perspective the thought
that Phil has actually just moved a little north, and we will be
joining him there later.*

My thoughts these last few days are ones of moving on. I hesitate to say what I'm about to say, but I feel God has called me to be honest in my writings—to share what is on my heart, because if it is on my heart, it may very well be on the hearts of others in the same situation and they may need to know they are not alone. Maybe they will then be able to say what I'm about to say...

I'm sick of it!

What? That's right! I'm sick of feeling so very sad. I'm sick of mourning. I want to turn my mourning into dancing! I want to take off the sackcloth and ashes and have them replaced with garments of praise. I want to move ahead, to "press on toward the goal to win the prize for which God has called me heavenward in Christ Jesus." Philippians 3:14 (NIV)

Phil loved prizes! He was not competitive, so to speak, but he loved trophies sitting on his shelves. He liked it when he won his first patch in sharpshooting. Don't we all love prizes? Don't we all love to be rewarded for a job well done, or a race run well? Phil told me when he was younger that he never liked baseball or basketball, but that he only played those sports because he wanted what his brothers had...a trophy.

He must have loved his arrival in Heaven where his true reward awaited him. He pressed on toward the goal to the end, and now he has his prize.

*Rejoice and be glad, because great is your reward in heaven –
Matthew 5:12 (NIV)*

*For the Son of Man is going to come in his Father's glory
with his angels, and then he will reward each person
according to what he has done.
Matthew 16:27 (NIV)*

"May the LORD repay you for what you have done. May you be richly rewarded by the LORD, the God of Israel, under whose wings you have come to take refuge." Ruth 2:12 (NIV)

Why would God put these verses in the Bible if He didn't think they would be important to us—if it didn't matter that there was a reward or a prize at the end of our journey? And who can imagine what the prize might be? We can't even come close, I'm sure. It is beyond our wildest imaginations!

I believe there comes a time in the journey of grief where we get sick of the valley—where the darkness is not so inviting anymore, even though in the beginning we really just wanted to stay there. It felt right at first. The world didn't understand anyway, and we would rather just stay under our covers and not have to face anything or anyone.

I believe there also comes a time in the journey of grief where the valley becomes tiresome, and we want to be done with feeling that way. We get exhausted with running the same thoughts over and over in our heads about how it all was, what we said, what they said, what anyone said—a time when we realize that honoring those we have lost has nothing to do with feeling sad and grieving for them, but it has everything to do with getting on with our lives as they would want us to do...as we are called to do!

I read a verse the other day that said:

"But for you who fear my name, the Sun of Righteousness will rise with healing in his wings. And you will go free, leaping with joy like calves let out to pasture." Malachi 4:2 (NV)

Can't you just see it? I can! I can see Phil arriving in Heaven leaping with joy like calves let out to pasture. Oh what joy, for Phil to be truly free of the bondage of this earth, and the bondage of his sick body at last! As Martin Luther King said: "Free at last!" That must have been the way Phil felt!

And if he can feel that way, I can, too. I want to. The Sun of Righteousness, Jesus Christ, came to heal the brokenhearted. He did not intend for us to live our lives in the bondage of grief. There is a time for mourning and a time to dance. My time for dancing seems to be coming, even though I know without a doubt that there will still be many days where my heart will ache, the tears will fall, and I will be back to square one for a period of time.

Some may say it's only been nine months, what are you thinking? Some may say it's been nine months, it's about time. It really doesn't matter what "some may say" because grief is an individual activity that has no time frame. It will never be the same twice, even for the same person. It is up to God and that person as to how long it will last. Mine is not over, but I feel a "straining toward what is ahead." It is a yearning that comes from deep inside, and this morning as I looked at Phil's picture beside my desk once again, I said to him, "Phil, you know how much I love you. I love you with every part of my being. But I am sick of feeling so sad." Yes, I talk to pictures, I talk to anything that moves, and even things that don't.

Phil would understand. He never wanted me to feel bad. He could tell the instant something was up with me and he would question me about it. He would be the very first one to say, "Get on with your life, Mom. I'm free. I'm running like never before! I'm leaping like never before! I won't be falling off any more porch steps because my legs are so weak they won't hold the weight of me. I won't need any more blood transfusions to boost my energy level and bring some color back into my face. I won't need your help putting on my shoes and socks so I will have the energy to walk out to the car. I'm free Mom, truly free of all of that, and you should be also! We ran our race together for as long as it lasted, and it is finished. I have my prize! Yours will be coming. But until that time, press on! Forget what lies behind except for what it has taught you. Look ahead. I'll be waiting at the finish line for you!"

...His name is Bryce Benjamin and he was born on August 15th, 2002, just nine months and one day after Phil went Home. He lives

next door, and he is the third boy born in that family, just as Phil was in ours.

Bryce Benjamin is a very special baby to me, because when I look at him, I see a new beginning. I see what God has created in the nine months since Phil has gone Home, and I marvel at what God can create in that amount of time. A tiny seed planted has grown into a fully developed human being who will one day walk and talk and live his very own life.

I've heard that prayers are like tiny seeds we can plant. For every prayer said, a seed is planted that God will water, nurture, and grow. And it has shown me how very important the simplest prayers can be. They don't have to be long or complicated, just simple and lovingly said by those that think about another long enough to say a prayer for them.

Seeds have been planted in my heart in the last nine months. Seeds of prayers said by all of you, and they have grown. They have grown to fill the empty spaces that were left when Phil left. They have grown to fill doubts that arise, and to steady a faith that may waver from time to time. They have grown to replace the weeds of hurt and pain into flowers of joy and warm memories. They will continue to grow, each at their own rate, each in their own way, until the garden in my heart will be one of beautiful wild flowers warmed by the Son—instead of a barren ice field that was slippery and dangerous to tread on for awhile.

This is all possible because God is the Gardener, and He tends to His children with the greatest of care. He watches over each seed that has been planted, from those that started as prayers, to those that are babies yet to be born. Our Father can see us. He created us. He loves us.

> *For you created my inmost being;*
> *you knit me together in my mother's womb.*
> *I praise you because I am fearfully and wonderfully made;*
> *your works are wonderful.*

I know that full well.
My frame was not hidden from you
when I was made in the secret place.
When I was woven together in the depths of the earth,
your eyes saw my unformed body.
All the days ordained for me were
written in your book
before one of them came to be.
Psalm 139:13-16 (NIV)

God saw Bryce from day one, just as He saw all of us. And Jesus will be waiting there for us on our last day, ready to welcome us Home. Our Father has a plan for our lives that we can't even imagine. There will be valleys, there will be mountain peaks, and there will be everything in between. But through it all, we will never be alone.

I don't want to be sick of this grief. I pray that if this mourning period continues, that God will give me the patience to endure it, the strength to continue to persevere through it until this race is run. I know that I am not finished yet. But that doesn't change the fact that I want to be. It is the human condition to want to get it done fast. It is not God's way. God's way is so much better. He has so many good things to teach us along the way. We should not want to miss out on any of the valuable lessons He has for us, no matter how painful it may be. It is worth it.

An example:
Almost two weeks ago, I had a night like none I have ever had before. It was a night when I was alone in the house and grief hit me like a ton of bricks, plus some. I went through the house closing the windows so as not to disturb the neighbors with my sobbing, wailing, and groaning. It was not a pretty sight.

In the midst of my agony, God spoke to me. He told me it was time to wash Phil's clothes—the ones that remained in his hamper from his last few days on this earth. I didn't want to. But I got up off the floor, where I was curled, and did just that.

Then I went back to the floor, when God spoke to me again. He told me it was time to clean out Phil's dresser. I didn't want to. But I got up, got the bag that said pick-up was on Thursday (the next day when I would thankfully be at work) and I started with his bottom drawer until I got to the top one, placing each article of his clothing into the bag, sparing just a few for those that I would like to give to certain people.

I have NEVER before in my life felt such agony! Never!

Where was God in the agony I felt? He was helping me heal. Instructing me and guiding me through what needed to be done, but what I never could have done without His help. It is a job much too terrible for any mother to have to do, but one that needs doing. What did I feel when it was over? Relief. Release. Gratitude. A sense of freedom. Healing had begun. The "shrine" needed to go, the memories needed to stay, and I needed to draw a line between the two—with God's help. God knew that, and He knew when the time was right. God had been preparing me for this moment. The ice in that cold winter field has been chipped away just a little bit more so that more of those beautiful wild flowers can bloom in my heart.

New beginnings...yes, for sure...every day, in every way, we're always carried by a God who loves us too much to leave us on our own. It hurts without question. But there is healing in the hurt, and there is a knowing in the hurt, that it will pass.

Just three days after going through Phil's things, I was sitting at a picnic spot on a hill overlooking a beautiful lake in Canada. Jim and I were on a trip there to see my parents. They were on vacation in Canada. As we sat at this picnic table taking in the beauty of God's creation, eating our salami sandwiches in the warm sunshine, I took in a deep breath and thanked God for His love. I wondered how it is possible to go from such agony three days before, to such peace and tranquility just three days later. Well, I guess we could ask Jesus since He rose in three days after His agony on the Cross and brought peace to all of us.

Yes, we are free in Jesus. But we will hurt, we will have loss, and we will heal and see new beginnings all the time if we just open our eyes and our hearts to all the Lord has planned for us.

"For I know the plans I have for you," declares the Lord, "plans to prosper you and not to harm you, plans to give you hope and a future.
Then you will call upon me and come and pray to me, and I will listen to you. You will seek me and find me when you seek me with all your heart. I will be found by you," declares the Lord, "and will bring you back from captivity."
Jeremiah 29:11-13 (NIV)

My Hope is in Him!

Love,
Diane

Myself

My brother, Steve, calls it "Heaventown."

Today is my brother, Steve's, birthday. He is 59 today, and I don't think he would mind me telling you his age. I haven't called him as yet, I'm writing this chapter, and then I will give him a call. I know what I will get on the other end of the phone. It will be, "Hey Sis, how ya doin?" And he will be his normal, cheerful, cowboy self. I will wish him a Happy Birthday, maybe tease him a bit about his age, and then we will talk. I already know what we will talk about…the things of God. It's what we always talk about and I like that.

Steve and Phil were good buddies. When Phil was first sick, he and I flew home from Germany for nine months of chemotherapy treatment. Jim had to remain in Germany, where we lived at that time, with our other two boys, Jimm and Chris. Jimm was just finishing up his Senior year in High School. Chris was in 10th grade. Phil and I lived with his Bedstemor (Grandma) because she was only fifteen minutes from Fresno Children's Hospital. My mother-in-law welcomed us in and blessed us so much by providing a place to be. Steve and his wife, Marlene, lived only ten minutes away from us while in Fresno. Steve took Phil under his wing, and they fished, camped, and did guy stuff together when Phil was up for it. They grew very close, and because of that, Steve risked a very broken heart. Whenever we reach out in love, we risk things. The day of Phil's Memorial Service was probably one of the hardest days of Steve's life. Even with a strong trust in God, and a knowing of where Phil was, his heart grieved deeply. I have always appreciated the love he showed to Phil during such a difficult time. Happy Birthday big brother! I love and appreciate you!

*My thoughts these last few days are ones of moving on. I hesitate to say what I'm about to say, but I feel God has called me to be honest in my writings—**I'm sick of it!***

I'm not one to waste a lot of time. My friends, who have watched me through the years, have seen that. I don't waste a trip through a room without grabbing something and taking it with me if it needs to be put away. I don't sit around twiddling my thumbs wondering what to do next. I'm more about organizing what I have before me in the day so as not to waste a minute in between one thing and the next. I probably have a bit of OCD, but don't ask Jim because he will tell you there is no "bit" about it, I HAVE IT!

When I wrote, "I'm sick of it," it was because I wanted the pain to be over, and life to get on with itself. But grief is not like that. I hate to say that it controls the griever, the griever doesn't control it, but it's probably more true than not. The only thing larger than the dark grief itself is the large light of Heaven—the pure Truth of God infiltrating into the dark caverns of the mind, the will, and the emotions.

My son, Jimm, said an interesting thing just this morning on the phone. He said that a person can see a beam of light from a flashlight a long time before the person holding the flashlight can see the person they are looking for. I had never really thought about that. The only exception to that rule might be when God is The Light that is shining towards us in our darkness. He can see us even in the dark. *God is light; in him there is no darkness at all.* 1 John 1:5 (NIV) When our Father comes looking for us, He already knows where we are and what state we are in. He comes to reveal our condition to **us**, not to Himself. When God asked Adam, "Where are you?" It wasn't because God didn't know where Adam was, or what condition he was in. God asked him, "Have you eaten the fruit I commanded you not to eat?" Genesis 3:11 (NLT) Can't you just see it?—a parent asking a child with chocolate all over their face if they've been into the ice cream? The child actually thinks the parent doesn't already know. It can be a great comfort to know that our Father in Heaven already knows all about us. He knows when we are sick of it. He knows when we need a break. He knows, and He provides; little by little, He brings us out of that dark place. He did for me, and He will for you, too.

He must have loved his arrival in Heaven where his true reward awaited him. He pressed on toward the goal to the end, and now he has his prize

When Phil was about 8 or so, he played basketball for one season. I asked him if he liked it? He said not really, he didn't like all the running! He is a child after his dad's heart. Jim sees no need for sore muscles. I, on the other hand, love the feeling of having been stretched beyond my limit, and the ache of sore muscles that follow. I can't say it is true with grief though; it didn't seem a "necessary" ache at the time. Now, almost 13 years later, I understand that it was. There are rewards that come, even in this lifetime. There is a peace and a contentment that accompanies a heart healed through sorrows of many kinds. When we press on through the sorrows, there is a prize that Jesus holds out to us, just like He held His hand out to Peter when he started to sink on the water. Jesus teaches us how to live above the circumstances of life like an eagle—to rise above the storms that swirl below us all the time on this earth. *But those who trust in the Lord will find new strength. They will soar high on wings like eagles.* Isaiah 40:31 (NLT)

I attended a women's retreat once many years ago. The woman who was speaking that weekend told the story of asking someone, "How are you doing?" They replied, "Fine, under the circumstances." The woman replied, "What are you doing under there?" I bought one of her books at the retreat and I still remember how she signed, it: "May you learn to live your life above the circumstances." Why? Because our rewards are not found under the circumstances in our lives, they are found when we soar on wings like eagles with the strength given to us by our Savior.

I believe there comes a time in the journey of grief where we get sick of the valley—where the darkness is not so inviting anymore, even though in the beginning we really just wanted to stay there. It felt right at first.

On a cold winter morning, curling up under our blankets is a most welcome place to be. I always feel blessed when the rain is falling outside to be warm and dry. I think of many who are out on the streets and hope they have found a dry place to be. My brother, Keith, spent three years living on the streets. He chose that way of life to simplify for a time. I don't know that he would recommend it to many, but he learned a great deal during that period in his life. One of the things he said when he was re-establishing his life was how easy it was to go onto the streets, but how extremely difficult it was to get back off of them. Those with no helping hand, job offer, place to clean up, transportation, or even current I.D., etc…have a very difficult time. Our son, Chris, was able to help Keith get a job as a chef in a restaurant where he worked, and that was Keith's start back. Keith tells the story of one day sleeping in a construction site near the restaurant. The workers came in early one morning and woke him up. He asked them what time it was? They told him, and he said he had to get to work. He said they looked a bit surprised! But homeless people have to start somewhere. Keith shared the Good News of Jesus Christ on the streets with many people. He talked to people that would scare me. I believe God used him in many ways that I would be of no use. It is not a world I would understand, as Keith would not understand some of mine. I find it all very interesting. At first it may have felt right for Keith to be on the streets. But there came a time to get things back in order—to crawl out from under the "blanket" that street life afforded him—to embrace all that God has waiting for those that know and love Him, as Keith and I both do.

We get exhausted with running the same thoughts over and over in our heads about how it all was, what we said, what they said, what anyone said—a time when we realize that honoring those we have lost has nothing to do with feeling sad and grieving for them, but it has everything to do with getting on with our lives as they would want us to do.

We honor those we love by remembering. Yesterday was 9/11/14. Our country remembered, and our country has moved on. There are new buildings on Ground Zero. I haven't visited it, but many I know have. I know of a young couple who had their picture taken at the top of the World Trade Center building just a few days before it was no longer. That is a memorable picture for them. They just posted it again on Facebook. Phil and I flew out of Boston on 9/9/01, out of the very airport that one of the planes that crashed flew out of. We were safely back home when disaster struck our country and planes were grounded everywhere. Phil and I watched together from home as fires burned. We watched a week later as another small plane crashed in New York somewhere. Phil said to me that day, "Maybe it's not such a bad time to be leaving." Two months later Phil left for Home. I remember all these things because I not only wrote about them, but I ran them over and over and over in my head, sorting through all the rubble to make some sense of it. We can't really make sense of most of it because we are not God. *As the heavens are higher than the earth, so are my ways higher than your ways and my thoughts than your thoughts.* Isaiah 55:9 (NIV) When we can **believe** that, we can rest in that, and put our thoughts to rest.

I can see Phil arriving in Heaven leaping with joy like calves let out to pasture. Oh what joy!

Phil was the playground kid! He loved to spot a playground and point it out. I played a lot of softball when we lived in Germany. Jim worked on a military base as a private contractor. The gym, tennis courts, baseball fields, etc…were all very much a part of military life, and we were able to use all of these facilities even though we didn't live on base. There was a playground right next to the field I played on, and Phil spent many hours there with his friends as Jim helped coach the team. I remember a time when we had traveled down to Venice, Italy (Yes, life overseas was rough.) I was playing in a baseball tournament in May of 1996. I was sitting on the bleachers and Phil was lying down on the bench with his head on my feet as a pillow. When we got up to leave, I noticed some children jumping and playing nearby and I remember having the thought, Phil doesn't do that any more. He was slowly, slowing down. His Leukemia had not been diagnosed as yet, but it was in full force. By the end of May, we found out why he was no longer leaping like a calf let out to pasture. I love that Phil is leaping in Heaven now—even though he would be 28 years old on earth, he is still our child.

My time for dancing seems to be coming, even though I know without a doubt that there will still be many days where my heart will ache, the tears will fall, and I will be back to square one for a period of time.

I was back at square one more times that I had any idea I would be. I was grasping for straws, hoping the pain would soon stop. I don't mean to be negative here, but real…the pain was a long way from gone. When I had surgery of the female type about six years ago, the doctor told me it would take at least two months for recovery. I sort of laughed inside, and thought, I'll give it two weeks. Well, the doctor got the last laugh there. Two months later, after being very restful, I was just getting back to somewhat normal. Once again, I wanted to rush the healing process. And once again, it could not be rushed. It would come, in time, as it did with grief. Rest, time, and God are our best friends as we heal. There is no other way around it!

It really doesn't matter what "some may say" because grief is an individual activity that has no time frame.

Yesterday I cut my client, John's, hair at work. He told me they would be putting their cat down that night. I'm not a cat lover, I'm not even an animal lover, but I know those who are. I told him I was sorry, and I was. Their cat is 18 years old, and today they are living without their beloved pet. It is a sad day for them. I won't see John again for another four to five weeks...he will then come in for his next haircut. The pain and loss will have lessened by then, it is a cat. But the memories of their cat will always be with them, and some of the pain will still be lingering, perhaps for a long time. No one can say when it is time for the pain to stop. But once again, with rest, time, and God, we can live fully again.

I looked at Phil's picture beside my desk once again, I said to him, "Phil, you know how much I love you. I love you with every part of my being, but I am sick of feeling so sad."

I have looked at Phil's picture that hangs in our bedroom, now, more of late. I think because my first book, *It Started in the Dark,* is finished and in the hands of people reading our story. It seems a long time in the coming. I am asked a lot, "How long did it take you to write it?" Once again, it's not an easy thing to answer. Do I just say, "A year"? Or do I explain that it started 18 years ago in Munich when Phil was diagnosed, or twelve and a half years ago when Phil went Home? Or did it start way back in grammar school? My friend, Ann, called me a storyteller the other day. I was a bit puzzled by that, and I said, "I just share what is happening." She said, "Yes, but you are a good storyteller." It reminded me of being about 9, and how the girls at school would gather around me in the bathroom and I would make up stories to tell them. I was entertaining them I think. When I look back on that now, I wonder what I was doing. I was a shy little girl, who rarely talked, and I was there telling them stories? I have to believe God was preparing me to tell His story one day—the story of Jesus, the Savior of the world. The reason we can have Hope in this troublesome world is Jesus. The reason I can even be here today continuing to tell stories that may do more than just entertain, but may encourage, is Jesus. The reason that I can now look at Phil's picture and say I'm not "so sad" anymore, but more grateful than anything, is Jesus. I do still love Phil with every part of my being, but God's healing power is greater than any pain his leaving has caused me.

I won't be falling off any more porch steps because my legs are so weak they won't hold the weight of me.

We were going out for ice cream one day, and Phil fell down the porch steps (only two of them), and into the bushes. He was very sick, and very weak. The bushes kept him from getting badly hurt. He sat on the steps while I cleaned up his scrapes, and then he, Chris, and I went on to have ice cream. I still walk down those very steps to take our grandkids out for ice cream. Chris and Holly own the house we lived in then. Phil shared something with me, and I'm trying to remember it here. I had told him a story about one day having to go out in my car and drive to a private place. I needed to be alone so that I could cry to my heart's content, which I did. But I also found the peace of God to my heart's content, too, after crying there that day. Phil's "porch falling" wasn't too long before he left this earth. And he cried a lot those last ten days or so as he worked through many different emotions. When I shared my "car crying" with him, he said he had experienced the same thing one day. He found that even after falling off the porch, it didn't matter, because he had found God's peace. I'm glad we could talk to each other about these things.

Bryce Benjamin is a very special baby to me, because when I look at him, I see a new beginning.

Bryce is now a very tall, very lanky young man. Bryce could ride a bike with two wheels when he was just over two years old! Bryce, his dad, and one of his older brothers ride motocross. They are very good at it. Many things have changed in the old neighborhood, but Bryce still lives with his family next door to

Chris and Holly. I see them out washing the mud off their motorcycles quite frequently.

They will continue to grow, each at their own rate, each in their own way, until the garden in my heart will be one of beautiful wild flowers warmed by the Son—instead of a barren ice field that was slippery and dangerous to tread on for awhile.

Once a year my friend, Lynn, and I, and whoever else would like to join us, make our way out to FILOLI. It is a garden estate here near the coast of California. FILOLI stands for Fight-Love-Live. It was the motto of the people who owned the estate. If you have ever seen the Warren Beatty movie, "Heaven Can Wait," part of it was filmed at FILOLI. Talk about a beautiful garden full of flowers. We usually try to go in April. We were told one time that it is close to being in Heaven when the place is in full bloom.

The prayers said on behalf of our family have taken root and bloomed through the years. I see the beauty of what God has done, and He's still doing it. I'm not saying that our family is perfect, or our life is perfect…that would not be life here on earth. We have the same troubles as any family does, sometimes more, sometimes less. But to think that if every prayer prayed for us bloomed into a flower, I have to believe it would fill the garden estate of FILOLI and then some. So thank you, if you are one of those who have prayed for us through the years.

I pray that if this mourning period continues that God will give me the patience to endure it, the strength to continue to persevere through it until this race is run.

And He has! And continues to do so. Thank You, Jesus!

In the midst of my agony, God spoke to me. He told me it was time to wash Phil's clothes—the ones that remained in his hamper from his last few days on this earth. I didn't want to... God spoke to me again. He told me it was time to clean out Phil's dresser. I didn't want to.

This needs some explanation. Why would a good and loving God do this? Why would He take a completely broken person and ask something like this at a time like this? I didn't know it at the time, but looking back, now I know why. Because no matter what day it would have been, no matter how good I might have felt going into the process of completing these humanly impossible tasks, I would have ended up on the floor sobbing. I believe God said, "Well, now is as good a time as any." I was already there emotionally, He just used that time of intense pain to get a job done that He knew I needed to eventually do. I would not have wanted anyone else to go through Phil's things, not even his dad. I was his main caretaker. I bought his clothes for him. I washed them. I put them away in his drawers. This was a personal task that I needed to do, and I didn't want to do it. EVER!!

I have NEVER before in my life felt such agony! Never!

I can't even explain to you how horrible this was, so I won't try. But anyone who still has a room intact, from a loved one that has been gone some time, knows what I am talking about. The thought of going in there and clearing out their things doesn't get easier, I don't think. Maybe it gets harder. I don't know when the perfect time to do this is; it's different for everyone. But I would venture to say, if it has been years, it's time. And there will be tears, and it will be hard. But:

What did I feel when it was over? Relief. Release. Gratitude. A sense of freedom. Healing had begun. The "shrine" needed to go, the memories needed to stay, and I needed to draw a line between the two—with God's help.

Taking care of our loved one's things is part of the healing process. *When Jesus saw him lying there and learned that he had been in this condition for a long time, he asked him, "Do you want to get well?"* John 5:6 (NIV) There is a time for all things, and we have to draw a line somewhere in the sands of time. It is the only way to move on and into what our loved ones would want for us. We have to not sit in the dark and grieve for the rest of our days... *Then*

Jesus said to him, "Get up! Pick up your mat and walk."
John 5:8 (NIV) We have to allow the Holy Spirit to pick us up
from within and we have to walk into our future with the Hope we
have been given through Jesus Christ. That is what He died to give
us! It is His gift to us so that we don't have to grieve as those
without Hope. (1 Thess. 4:13)

Just three days after going through Phil's things, I was sitting at a
picnic spot on a hill overlooking a beautiful lake in Canada... I
wondered how it is possible to go from such agony three days
before, to such peace and tranquility just three days later.

I just realized that God knew we would be in Canada three days
later. Some have asked me if writing all this helps me to continue
to heal. I have answered that I don't think so, most of the healing
has been completed. But yet, God is still showing me His loving
care during this time as I dissect all these writings and comment on
them. What if I had ignored His urging to go through Phil's things
before we left for Canada? They would have still been waiting
there for us when we got home. I still would have had to take care
of that horrific task. I wouldn't have had the peace of that moment
at the picnic spot to compare to the agony I had felt just three days
before. It was perfectly planned out by God so that He could show
me how He could take my mourning and turn it into
dancing…doing just what I had asked for in this writing. God had
heard my cry. He heard that I was SICK OF IT!! And He was
answering my prayer to help me move along out of it. All I can say
is:

My Hope is in Him!

And it will continue to be, until I meet my Savior face to face!

Gift #7 – Seeing new gifts from God showing up on the grief journey!

In all the pain and missing you have been feeling, has God asked something of you?

Have you listened and moved in the direction He is asking, or are you still a bit hesitant?

Record today's date and other notes you'd like to make:

The Great

<u>I AM</u>

*When Jesus saw him lying there
and learned that he had been in this
condition for a long time, he asked him,
"Do you want to get well?"*
John 5:6 (NIV)

CHAPTER EIGHT

"You have shown me the way of life,
and you will fill me with joy in your presence. "
Acts 2:28 (NLT)

<u>Me</u>

Something Has To Die...

Tuesday, 10 Sep 2002

As I sat in Florida, in my friend, Deb's, trailer at the beach, I
listened to a taped sermon given by a pastor here, one who has
become a friend over the years as I return to visit with Deb from
time to time. The words he spoke on the tape were words I could
relate to. He taught on the Israelite's wilderness wanderings and
their eventual entrance into the Promised Land. He talked about
their leaders, Moses and Aaron, and the faith that was required of
them to lead their people across the Jordan River when the
floodwaters were high. They needed to take that step of faith into
the river before God stopped the water from flowing downstream.
He talked about God's provisions as they wandered for 40 years,
and he talked about Moses and what he had done that had

displeased God. God had asked him to speak to the rock to bring forth water. But Moses hit the rock with his stick. The water was still supplied by God, but Moses would never enter the Promised Land because of what he had done. Some may feel that was harsh, but it's only because we can't see the whole picture. God knew that something must die before they could enter the Promised Land, and that something was to be Moses.

What is the "something" in our lives that must die before we can enter into our "Promised Land," before we can experience the fullness of God and all of His promises in our lives? Does it have to be a person, or can it be a plan that has passed its time, a relationship that is no longer healthy, or a habit that needs to be gotten rid of?

I relate to this story because part of it is very clear to me. The something that must die was my son. That may seem harsh, but only because we cannot see the whole picture yet. During Phil's illness, we were wandering around in the desert. We were lost a lot of the time and seeking God's direction like never before in our lives. We needed "water" from the rock and there were probably many times that we were beating the rock with the stick instead of just depending on God's timing for things. But just like the Israelites, we learned many things in our wanderings. We learned how to trust God, and that He can be trusted. We learned to pray to Him for answers, and wait on Him. We learned these things as some would say, in the school of hard knocks. And it hurt. It was not pleasant and we got tired. But we learned.

When it was time to leave the wilderness wanderings, something had to die. But it was not just Phil who died, although that is the obvious conclusion. What had to die were pride, stubbornness, self-sufficiency, and human wisdom. What had to be born were humbleness, a willing heart, dependency on God, and godly wisdom: things that are opposite of what the world would want, things that we hold onto with all our might for way too long, things that make life much more difficult than it needs to be.

This is not to say these things have been perfected in our lives, or in my life, but they are in the process of being refined and this will continue until the day I die. And during this process, our time can be spent in the "Promised Land" right here on earth, because we don't have to wait until we get to Heaven to experience and live in a lot of God's promises.

Some may ask, what is the "Promised Land"? It is a place of knowing who God is, knowing how awesome are His deeds, and trusting when trust is the last thing we would want to do. It is the place where true rest is found in the midst of difficult trials in our lives. It is the place where peace will reign when there is nothing peaceful to be found. It is knowing that God is with us when we can't feel Him, when we can't see Him, and when the world tells us we're crazy. It is where we are all meant to live our lives. But it is the place that most of us miss on our journey through this life because we are so lost in the wilderness of what we think life is.

Jesus is our Friend. He wants the best for us. He does not want us to be unhappy, worried, or stressed. He wants us to relax and enjoy all that He has to offer us, if we will only receive it.

It's like me being in Florida right now spending time with my best friend. Deb is at work, just as God is, and yet Deb and her husband, Alan, set me up here in their vacation trailer at the beach with everything I might need to be able to relax and enjoy my visit. They know the ups and downs in my life right now and especially how broken my heart is during this season of grief. They cannot mend my heart, but they can nurture my soul and help me to heal if I will accept their kindness and generosity. God is the only One who can heal my heart, and He is doing so. He will nurture my soul and offer me His peace and love if I will accept it from Him. Sometimes our Father in Heaven uses another person to let His love shine into our lives, like He is with me right now. And what is my job in that? It is to be open, trusting, and to enter into His "Promised Land" with a surrendered heart, willing to let Him lead me where I need to go. Unfortunately, for surrender to happen, usually something must die. Did it take the death of our son to surrender? I don't know if it did. But I have. I do, every day—I surrender.

I don't know if there was an easier way, but this is the way that God chose for me at this time in my life. And because of that, I will not live my life in the wilderness of stress and confusion. I don't have the strength for that anymore. My strength comes from God, and my Hope rests in Jesus, and it is good.

God has shown me how to live my life. He has given me a taste of what the "Promised Land" here on earth has to offer. Will I now go back to the wilderness and rejoin that craziness? Or will I stay here in what the world calls "craziness," and live in peace? I choose to stay in the promised land of peace.

God knew our lives would be difficult. He didn't plan it this way in the Garden, but He knew it would happen. Our Father knew we would be a stubborn lot, too. He knew we would be just like children, His children, wanting our own way. But He also provided a way that we could grow up. Some don't want to. Some just want to do it themselves, and they will fuss and fume and turn their back on God, refusing His helping hand. That would be like me telling Deb, here in Florida, that I know she wants to help me during this difficult time in my life—thank you very much...but NO! And Deb would step back and let me go it on my own because she loves me that much, and she would probably be there waiting for the time when I would turn back to her and ask, "Would you please help me?" That's what God is waiting for, and even more so. Some friends might dessert us in our hour of need, but God never will. Acts 3:19-20 (NIV) says:

Now turn from your sins and turn to God, so you can be cleansed of your sins.
Then wonderful times of refreshment will come from the presence of the Lord.

I like that word refreshment, especially being here in Florida in September. A big cold glass of lemonade is delicious in this heat! I'm thankful this trailer has air-conditioning.

But what is it to be refreshed by God? It is to be washed with His peace when nothing in this world even comes close. It is to feel a pain so intensely from missing someone you have lost, wondering if it might make you go insane, and then taking that pain to God and asking Him, "Will You help me?" It is crying out those tears that can no longer be contained, and knowing that God is collecting each and every one of them for us in His bottle.

You keep track of all my sorrows.
You have collected all my tears in your bottle.
You have recorded each one in your book.
Psalm 56:8 (NLT)

God sees our pain. God knows our pain, and God helps us through our pain by refreshing us with His Holy Spirit of comfort. Jesus said, when He left us, that He would be sending us a Comforter. Are you going to refuse that on a cold, chilly night of pain? I'm not. I need it! The world is harsh. I think I'll stay under thee Comforter!

When doubts filled my mind, your comfort gave me
renewed hope and cheer. Psalm 94:19 NLT)

Something must die, but that does not always mean that someone must die physically. What we must die to is ourselves if we want to enter the "Promised Land." We must say "Yes" to God and "No" to the parts of us that will eventually make us miserable. We need to ask God for His wisdom as to what those things are. Sometimes we just cannot see them and we think everything is fine. How can we not realize when we are miserable? That's a good question.

If we are not talking to someone because we are mad, and our pride won't let us reconcile with them, are we really happy and at peace, or just stuck in our pride? If we are not taking time for God each day and seeking His direction in our lives, do we even realize that we are wandering around lost and confused, or do we think all is well? If our jobs have us stressed, if our families have us stressed, if we have no time to stop and smell the roses that God has provided for our enjoyment, are we really living the life God has called us to live?

It reminds me of the day I spent later in this same week with Deb. We were pool side at a hotel on the beach, south of where she lives, and we were just spending the day doing nothing. We were napping, laughing, and eating, having watched the sun rise in the wee morning hours. We were talking, people watching, and enjoying all that God provides in this beautiful world. As I sat with my feet dangling in the pool water, it seemed like God was pleased. Pleased that we had stopped long enough to enjoy the world He had created. We had stopped long enough to notice our surroundings, to rest in them, and in Him. I believe God is glad when we simply listen to the waves crashing on the sand—the sand that He spoke to Abraham about in Genesis 22:17 (NLT), "I will surely bless you and make your descendants as numerous as the stars in the sky and as the sand on the seashore." But we have to stop long enough to do this—to enjoy God's creation, to breathe in the sea air and not just drive by it on our way to get somewhere that we think we need to be because time is money...so to speak.

God is time. So He owns all the time in the world. He never hurries. He never has to. Do we? Do we trust God enough to rest in His time frame for our lives? Do we trust Him enough to put it into His hands and not take it back because we think we know better?

On the way home from the airport after this trip, Jim informed me that the appraiser would be coming in the morning! We are having our house appraised because we are going to be making some changes in the future.

Now, you have to realize that our house has not been the same really, since Phil died. My interest in its upkeep has slipped dramatically as it has simply become four walls that house our bodies. The contents do not mean what they used to; they are simply possessions that we cannot take with us when we go. My energy level and interest in cleaning these possessions and the house that holds them is not the same. I have other ways that I feel called to spend my time now. But the APPRAISER WAS COMING! My first reaction to this news was not great, and Jim let me know that the appraiser had said he could either come in the morning or in three weeks. I voted for the morning. I knew that if I had three weeks to prepare I would make myself crazy. The morning it would be!

The next morning I woke up at 8 a.m. This was the night after my return from Florida where it would have been 11:00 a.m. What was I doing sleeping? I had work to do! The appraiser was supposed to be here by late morning. I got up and started talking with God about this whole thing, telling Him how much I hated having to do this, and the pressure I felt about it, and what if the appraiser sees this house a mess and doesn't give us the value of the house that we need! (All those thoughts that wander around in our heads.) God gently reminded me that if He does not build the house, the men labor in vain. (Psalm 127:1) What He meant was that whatever we were to get out of our house would be coming from Him. It wouldn't matter how much I cleaned and scrubbed. That brought me back to reality and I gently told Him that He knew I had to clean some though. And guess what? He even helped us do that. You should have seen the white tornado that went through this house! By 10:30 when the appraiser came, this house looked better than it had in almost ten months. I even put on a pot of coffee to add an aroma to the air and the job was finished. The appraiser came, did his thing, and left. Jim and I met in the hall, smiled at each other, hugged, and thanked God for His help!

God knew. He knew I would hate this. He knew it would make me crazy. So, He gave me the choice. Would I allow the appraiser to come on my first morning back and let Him carry me through this whole thing, or would I choose to put it off for three weeks, make myself crazy with the cleaning and do it on my own strength in my own way because "I know best"? I chose God's way and He

133

carried me. Had I chosen my way, I would have been on my own. The result may have been the same as far as the appraisal, but the journey would have been so much more difficult.

God knows us. He knows all about us—what makes us crazy and what doesn't. He knows we can't change on our own. We need His help in all things and we need to ask Him for it. He has provided it. That's why He sent Jesus to die for us. That's why He sent the Holy Spirit to strengthen us. That's why we can ask Him for help when we are at our very worst—when our lives seem beyond restoration, when our hearts seem broken beyond repair, or simply when our pride is getting the best of us...even if our house needs cleaning!

Just like a best friend, God stands by our side through the toughest of days. He is a Friend who never leaves us. When I open my heart to Him, when I die to myself, He pours His love directly over the wound that bleeds and helps me want to live again, to the fullest.

I will walk with you all my days Lord, because any other way makes no sense to me.

The world may call me crazy, because I am...crazy about You!

Living in His peace,
Diane

Myself

God knew that something must die before they could enter the Promised Land, and that something was to be Moses.

We all have things in us that need to be cut away from our lives, and it's not fun. We want to keep our "stuff," the good, the bad, and the ugly. We are human. We like our stuff, or at least we like to convince ourselves that we do. But it's not all good for us. I'm not saying that in grief, what is being taken from us is a bad thing being taken away. No, these are our loved ones, and of course we want them to live. They are not what had to die. But what dies because they have left us is more what I'm talking about. It's putting our hopes, our dreams, and our life's expectations in the wrong places, instead of on Jesus, that must go. I heard, just the other day, that most of us fill up our lives with about 50 percent Jesus, 20 percent spouse, 10 percent kids, etc…until we reach our 100 percent. But what we need to be doing is filling up with 100 percent Jesus, and then anything beyond that is surplus. This made sense to me, and it makes sense in grief if we are ever to heal from it. The person who is gone from us will not be coming back to live with us here again, so if we are not filled up with 100 percent Jesus, we will always have a hole inside that cannot be filled. But when we are filled to the brim with Jesus, we can live fully again even if part of our life is now missing. Our loved ones, our health, our jobs, our hobbies…these are all surplus. These are all gifts. When one or more is taken from us, we don't have to live the rest of our days incomplete when we are complete in Jesus.

In reading John 3:32-33 (NLT) this morning, John said this about Jesus, "He tells what he has seen and heard, but how few believe what he tells them! Those who believe him discover that God is true." Until we allow Jesus to be our all in all, we won't be able to discover how He can truly be our all in all. We have to dive in before we can experience that the Living Water is all Jesus says it is. It is FAITH – Forsaking All I Trust Him. (Thanks for that acronym Steve.)

I relate to this story because part of it is very clear to me. The something that must die was my son. That may seem harsh, but only because we cannot see the whole picture yet.

Here again, it's not that Phil had to die, but for me, with Phil dying, other parts of me that shouldn't have been attached to me spiritually were dislodged and gotten rid of. I need to stop living for myself, instead of for Jesus—choosing my will over God's. Obviously, God's will is far more powerful than mine, and I could attempt to argue against it, but it does no good. Until I bow down and say as Job did in 13:15 (NKJV), "Though He slay me, yet will I trust Him," I'm going to be fighting against the wrong things in this life. Fighting against God and arguing with His decisions for our lives is useless. Until we repent, turn to God, and seek His ways, we will find ourselves living in futile frustrated chaos. It's not God's fault, it's our stubbornness that has to die to rid ourselves of wrong things, and confusion about how life works best.

Example: I was at a company picnic just two days ago. The girls I work with were having a discussion that I really wasn't a part of. I was on the fringes of their circle, but my manager, Michelle, turned to me and said, "Right Diane?" I had heard enough of their conversation to know how to answer. I said, "No, I actually like depending on a man to take care of me." That was not well received by this group of co-workers, all women, mostly very young. And not one in the group was married, if I'm remembering correctly. It's not that I don't understand what they are saying. Why? Because I've been there—I've been their age, I've wanted to be "Miss Independent." I've wanted to not "need" a man, or anyone, including Jesus. But I'm not that person anymore. That stubborn independent nature is mostly gone now. (Only to be perfected when I actually meet Jesus face to face.) If they had given me the chance, what I wanted to finish telling them is that when you are with your husband, and He is a devoted man of God, loving you as Christ loves His Body, the Church, being a submissive wife is a gift, not a prison. A godly, Christ-filled husband is a person we can trust to always have our best interest at heart, and one who will lay down his life for us. Ephesians 5:24 (NIV) says, "Now as the church submits to Christ, so also wives should submit to their husbands in everything." That type of marital relationship is a very good place to be…to be cared for, nurtured, and protected by the man God has given us. That's why God put it in His Word. Our families can work the way they were designed to if we follow God's Instruction Manual. Jim and I didn't start out this way, and that's why I understand the protests from the girls I work with. We have had some very tough years. But Jim and I have grown into this relationship with Jesus, and with each other, and it is very good. I pray they find that kind of marital relationship one day.

During Phil's illness, we were wandering around in the desert. We were lost a lot of the time and seeking God's direction like never before in our lives. We needed "water" from the rock and there were probably many times that we were beating the rock with the stick instead of just depending on God's timing for things.

How true! We want to beat the answers out of God instead of wait for His answers to come. In just reading John 6:16-21 (NLT) this morning, I found it very interesting that the disciples went down to the shore to *wait* for Jesus. (Jesus had gone higher into the hills alone.) "It says that darkness fell, and Jesus still hadn't come back." How many of us feel like darkness has fallen, and we are waiting for Jesus to show up? I know I have! But what do we do many times? We do just what the disciples did. They got into the boat and headed out...with no Jesus. And what happened? The "sea grew very rough." How many of us have been out in the middle of a very rough sea? Was Jesus in the boat with us, or were we trying to go it alone? They were terrified when Jesus did show up, walking on the water, but He called out to them, "I am here! Don't be afraid." It then says they were "eager to let him in." And when He got into the boat, "immediately the boat arrived at their destination." All this to say—we need Jesus with us to get where we need to be. I don't want to wander without Him anymore. Do you?

When it was time to leave the wilderness wanderings, something had to die. But it was not just Phil who died, although that is the obvious conclusion. What had to die were pride, stubbornness, self-sufficiency, and human wisdom.

These are hard things to set aside…**very hard**. Our Father in Heaven knows that. He had to cast Lucifer out of Heaven because his pride got the best of him. It doesn't shock God that we have these human traits, but we can be rid of them in Jesus' Name! We may want to curse the very thing that God has brought into our life to help us weed these things out our lives. We don't understand the pain, and the length of time the pain is taking to work through and out of our lives. I believe we can speed things up, just a bit, if we will cooperate with God. And if we know someone who has gone before us, and has the wisdom and guidance that comes from God, let's open up our ears, listen, and learn! Let's be a fish with our mouth open, waiting to gobble up the Truth and be healed!

What had to be born were humbleness, a willing heart, dependency on God, and godly wisdom.

I believe I talked about this "head banging" experience in my previous book. I wanted to bang my head against a brick wall and have it come tumbling down, and have Phil standing behind it. That was fighting against what is. But through the years, with a willing heart and a dependency on God, we can glean some godly wisdom and stop fighting what is, and live with what isn't. Paul said he had learned to be content in whatever state he was in, Philippians 4:11 (NKJV) Can we say that? My friend, Lynn, loved her mother-in-law. Being a mother-in-law myself, I wanted to know her secret. Why did Lynn love her so much? So I asked Lynn. After some thought, she said that her mother-in-law was *content* and *flexible*. I have always remembered that, and Lynn and I remind each other of that often. We want our daughters-in-law to love us, and to want to be around us. With Jesus at the heart of all we do, we can be as Paul was, content in whatever state we are in. With grief, or any kind of sorrow or pain, we can learn to be content. I'm not saying it's easy. I'm just saying it's possible with Jesus.

God is the only One who can heal my heart and He is doing so. He will nurture my soul and offer me His peace and love if I will accept it from Him. Sometimes our Father in Heaven uses another person to let His love shine into our lives...

Many have shined God's love into my life through the years, starting with my parents who provided a home that I could feel safe and loved in. I know some don't have that kind of childhood, but even in the horrible state of some homes, we can still see God's provision. One of my friends told me of being very young, still young enough to be in a crib, and her home life was horrific. She remembers looking up and seeing Jesus reaching down to her. That was her first encounter with the living God. In later years she remembers a couple weeks each summer where she could escape the treachery of home, and spend time with an aunt and uncle who nurtured her. She even remembers being in her teens, having run away from home, and some strangers took her in and treated her kindly. Do these things fix everything that happened along the way? No, there are terrible scars from what the enemy inflicted early on in her life. But we can see God, all along the way, if we are looking up for Him through the pain and darkness.

Unfortunately, for surrender to happen, usually something must die. Did it take the death of our son to surrender? I don't know if it did. But I have. I do, every day—I surrender.

In our walk with God, when we come to a moment of surrender, it will change our walk with Jesus for the rest of our days. This moment will look different for everyone. There is no recipe to follow. I would give it to you if there were. For my oldest son, his moment came after a week of fasting between 5 p.m. and 5 a.m. each day as he prayed for his marriage. His surrender moment came with great emotion. Mine didn't. I was simply in the hallway of the children's oncology clinic. Phil was being treated in one of the rooms, and I had walked into the hallway, and started to pick up pamphlets on the wall. I picked up the one that talked about what happens when a child relapses with cancer. It was not good news, at all. I put the pamphlet back, went into Phil's room, sat down in a chair, and surrendered the control I *thought* I had in his healing process. I have never forgotten that moment, as Jimm will never forget his. I would like to know what your moment is, if we ever get the chance to talk about it. I'm not sure how much later it was that I was baptized, but Phil was sitting in the church that day, and I stepped into the tank just as the worship team decided to do a song. I stood there with my pastor as they played, "I Surrender All." And each day, I continue to surrender all, over and over again, finding God's peace in what is.

Will I now go back to the wilderness and rejoin that craziness? Or will I stay here in what the world calls "craziness," and live in peace? I choose to stay in the promised land of peace.

The girls I work with probably think I'm a bit crazy, if not a lot crazy. This old woman wants to depend on her husband? But what if he should leave? Good question. What if he should? It would not be good. It would be very hard. It would be very emotional. I'm human, and I would feel all the things that anyone else would feel. But what are we called to do with those feelings? We are called to rise above the troubles by resting in Jesus, and trusting in all He died to give us. Will Jesus pay the bills? Will He take care of the kids? Will He find us a job? Will He take care of all the practical things we think we need to worry about? But, but, but…Well, do we trust in the Word of God where it says, "But the very hairs of your head are all numbered. Do not fear therefore; you are of more value than many sparrows."? Luke 12:7 (NKJV) We are called to do that. It takes practice. It takes fixing our thoughts on what is true, honorable and right, etc… (Philippians 4:8) None of this is easy. Life isn't easy. But the best way through life is the way that God designed it when He says, "And this same God who takes care of me will supply all your needs from his glorious riches, which have been given to us in Christ Jesus." Philippians 4:19 (NLT) We can follow Jesus' narrow path and find the peaceful pathway Home, or not. It is our choice each and every day.

But He also provided a way that we could grow up. Some don't want to. Some just want to do it themselves, and they will fuss and fume and turn their back on God, refusing His helping hand.

We will never be perfect at this, but we can always continue to move toward that perfection which is in Christ Jesus. If you want, stop in this moment and think of those around you. Picture the ones you know who seem to be following a godly path. Think of who they are, and how you feel when you are around them. What is it about them that you desire or don't desire? Rest there for a moment...

Now picture the people you know who are not choosing the things of God, who have little or no interest in His plan for their life. How do you feel when you are around them? What it is about their life that you desire or don't desire? Stay there for a moment…

We have living examples around us everywhere. If we can't find clarity at the moment in God's Word, if it's not making sense to us, then let's just take a look around and see what works and what doesn't. It's pretty clear isn't it? I'm not talking about worldly wealth and possessions. I'm not talking about who's going to Europe or on their next two-week cruise. I'm talking about people, who they are, what they are about, and what we see in them when everything else is stripped away. What are they depending on to get them through each day? Are their relationships healthy with friends and family? If Jesus were to come back in the next few moments, would they, would we, be ready to meet our Savior with the choices we are making? All of life is simply a preparation for meeting Jesus one day, and standing before Him. John 3:18 (NLT) says, "There is no judgment awaiting those who trust him." When we trust Jesus, it changes the way we live for the better. Are we willing to allow Him to work in and through our lives?

Jesus said when He left us that He would be sending us a Comforter. Are you going to refuse that on a cold, chilly night of pain?

I don't like the cold! I will take heat over cold any time. I know many don't agree. I don't want humid heat. I like the dry heat of Fresno where I grew up. And I love my heated seats in the car. Wow! What a great invention! I used to love it when I was a kid and we were leaving some place late at night, and my dad would go out and warm up the car. Then he would come in and carry us out to it. The car was so comfy compared to the chill of the night. Isn't our Father God much the same? He not only sent His Son to save us for all of eternity through His death on the Cross and resurrection from the grave, conquering death for all time, He sent us a Comforter until Jesus returns. Have you ever been carried in your Heavenly Father's arms into the warmth of His Holy Spirit's comfort? It is a safe and wonderful place to be. The Holy Spirit fills us with strength when we have none. He comforts us when there is no worldly comfort around us. He gives us courage when ours is depleted. Sometimes we have to search The Holy Spirit out, going to the Word, getting quiet in prayer, "But if from there you seek the Lord your God, you will find him if you seek him with all your heart and with all your soul." Deuteronomy 4:29 (NIV) He will be worth the search.

My mom used to keep her purse in the same spot on the counter, when I was a teenager in Fresno. It was behind a wall, and when I would come in from school, or wherever, and the house was quiet, I would go directly to that place. I would see if her purse was there. If it was, I knew she was home. It was a comforting feeling for me, even though I hadn't actually seen her yet—I knew she was around. If you are having trouble seeing Jesus in your sorrow, finding the peace He left us with, or if the Holy Spirit who comforts us seems elusive...go to the place where you know God is, His Word, instead of going to the worldly comforts which will leave all of us feeling empty and cold.

Do we trust God enough to rest in His time frame for our lives? Do we trust Him enough to put it into His hands and not take it back because we think we know better?

Looking back, we see God's timing so much better. Looking forward, it seems like He is always running late. Planes usually run on time, trains do not. Trains stop for all sorts of things. But trains are calming, and there is so much to see along the way. Jim and I like to take the train. A few years ago we took it from Martinez, CA to Chicago, IL. What a treat that was. With three days and two nights of traveling, we got a sleeper car. One morning I woke up to see Idaho out the window. I texted our boys, asking them, "Is this Heaven?" (From the movie, *Field of Dreams*.) Of course the correct response is, "No, this is Idaho." There were corn fields stretching out for many acres outside our window. When we ride the train, we have to put the time frame into the conductor's/engineer's hands. We have no control, but must simply choose to ride along and watch the changing scenery as we go. That's okay if we're not in a hurry, but if we want to get somewhere quickly, the plane is a better choice. Next week, we leave on the plane for Tennessee. We don't want to spend half of our vacation traveling. We want to get there to see my brother, Howard, and his family. In life, we get to choose which mode of travel we prefer, but in life, we don't get to choose God's mode of travel for the journey we are on. In Psalm 32:8 (NIV) we are told, "I will instruct you and teach you in the way you should go; I will counsel you with my loving eye on you." We can fight it, or we can rest in it. Either way, God will get His way, and we might as well trust Him on the journey.

When I open my heart to Him, when I die to myself, He pours His love directly over the wound that bleeds and helps me want to live again, to the full.

"To Live Again," is a book by Catherine Marshall. Her husband, Peter Marshall was the Chaplain for the U.S. Senate in the 1950's. I was given this book by a friend, Jill, in my early stages of grief. She found it at a yard sale, and I know God prompted her to get it. Torn cover and all, it was truly a treasure to me. It reminded me of my grandma, and how she talked about Catherine Marshall. I'm sure my grandma related to her story as Catherine's husband died, leaving her with their young son of about ten, just as with my grandma. The story she writes tells of her grief journey, and I related to so many of her emotions. But, she learned to live again as her faith grew and emerged out of the darkness. That is why I write today. What Catherine Marshall learned, I have learned…we all can, with Jesus as our Light!

<u>Gift #8</u> – Learning to rest in what is, instead of fighting for what isn't.

A surrender point—have you experienced one that transformed your walk with Jesus?

What is the "something" in your life that must die before you can enter into your "Promised Land"?

Record today's date and other notes you'd like to make:

The Great

<u>I AM</u>

"I know the Lord is always with me.
I will not be shaken, for he is right beside me!
No wonder my heart is filled with joy,
and my mouth shouts his praises!
My body rests in hope."
Acts 2:25-26 (NLT)

CHAPTER NINE

"Test me in this," says the Lord Almighty, "and see if I will not throw open the floodgates of heaven and pour out so much blessing that you will not have room enough for it."
Malachi 3:10 (NIV)

<u>Me</u>

Let It Rain

Sunday, 15 Sep 2002

God is so good! Life truly does go on, in ways we cannot even imagine it will, when we're in the midst of what hurts most. I have seen such great evidence of God's healing power in others just this week. It amazes me once again!

How do I begin? Let me tell you about another experience I had while I was in Florida.

It was the day before Tropical Storm Edouard was to hit the coast of Florida. I figured I had one good day of sunshine left and I should use it wisely, so I canceled lunch with my friend and spent the day on the beach instead. I was sitting there in a beach chair, pulled up close enough to the waves so that they could roll under my chair from time to time without drenching me. I had my CD player with me and I was listening to Michael W. Smith's Worship CD. It is fantastic! On that CD there is a song that he sings that says "Let it rain...open the floodgates of heaven...let it rain."

Most times, when it starts to rain, I run for cover, but not on this day. There were only small patches of storm clouds in the sky, I was in my bathing suit, and it was warm, so why run from a little water even if it turned into more than just a sprinkle? These storm clouds would pass across the sky, sometimes off to the right of me, sometimes off to the left, and sometimes right over the top of me. When I ended up in the center of them, the rain would just flood down from Heaven and drench me to the point that I could have been swimming in the ocean and not have gotten much wetter! What an experience—to sit there and look up into the rain, and enjoy it. To let it pass over me, and then feel the warmth of the sun as it came out to dry me off and restore me once again. That is what it felt like—a restoration.

As I watched the storm clouds blowing around me, I thought that it was like life. Sometimes we are on the fringes of those clouds and we just feel a sprinkle. Sometimes they pass us completely by, to the right or to the left, and we feel nothing from them at all. Other times we are directly underneath them. It gets dark and cold. We wonder how long it will rain, and if we should go running. But if we sit there, they will eventually pass on by. The sun will come out again and there is no need to go running. God will move them by us, but we don't need to move if we are prepared—if we are in our "bathing suit," clothed with God's grace, we realize the darkness will not consume us, and know the sun will shine again when God is ready. We can sit through the coolness of the storm for just a while, waiting for God's warmth that will surely come when it is over.

To listen to that song, "Let it rain...open the floodgates of Heaven...let it rain..." and be sitting there watching God at work, doing that very thing, is an experience that will stay with me a long time.

When I sat in the midst of those cloud bursts, it seemed like there was no sun shining anywhere, that the whole earth must be getting rained on as I was. I could not see very far because of the haze it brought with it, and surrounded me with. But when I sat and watched those storm clouds from a distance, as they made their way out to sea, I could see that they were only a small patch of darkness that moved across the sky, sometimes blocking the sun and sometimes drenching the earth, but continually moving.

Just like storm clouds in our own lives, we wonder how the rest of the world can go on sometimes, when we are in the middle of a storm. Doesn't the whole world understand what we are going through? Don't they see the pain in our eyes? Don't they know how wet and cold and dreary it seems to us? But I think they can only really see it if they pull their chairs up to the "water's edge" and sit and watch for a while.

The world keeps spinning and our lives keep moving, and unless that cloud passes over us and drops some rain on our lives, we can be oblivious to what another might feel. Sometimes, we might see it, but we don't understand it enough to even comprehend what is happening. We see the rain from a distance, but it is not our rain, and it will move on, and we might not realize the devastation that was caused by those sitting underneath it.

Once you have felt the devastation that can be caused by a "storm cloud," I think it makes you pull up your chair to the "water's edge" more often and take notice. You recognize others' storms because you have had a similar one in your own life. You see the same pain in their eyes that you have felt, and for the first time, you can honestly say, "I know."

It's like when I went to the show the other day and saw the movie "Signs." There is a scene in that movie where Mel Gibson is standing beside the truck window as the man inside the truck tells him how very sorry he is to have fallen asleep at the wheel that night. I won't give away the movie. But when the camera pans back to Mel Gibson, he gets this pained expression on his face that shows the emotions that can surface when you have lost someone. I just sat there watching that scene thinking to myself, "I know..." Ten months ago I couldn't have said that. I had never sat under the storm clouds to the extent that I have now, and I didn't understand how deep and how painful those emotions are.

Which brings me back to the beginning of this chapter...such great evidence of God's healing power in those around me who have lost loved ones. Four women in one week—you would think I do nothing but spend time with people who are grieving. All four of these women have been drenched by a very dark cloud. It has rained all over them and they are drying out now. I can see it. I can hear it in their voices. I marvel at the smiles they wear, which are not the strained smiles that just come at the appropriate times, but smiles that come from a heart that is healing. Their hearts are feeling the joy of living again. All four women are in awe of the transformation that God has made in their lives. They are changed women, who, now, more fully trust in the God they serve.

Maybe I am able to see this and absorb this because I, too, am drying out from a good drenching. Maybe a year ago I would have not even stopped to notice the change, or maybe I could not have seen it, because I didn't understand. Maybe I would have watched Mel Gibson at the truck window and not paid so much attention to the emotions that surfaced during that discussion, because it would not have meant so much to me. But now it does. And I marvel at God's great healing power like never before.

I feel it in myself, but I can't see it. My sister and I were together recently, and later she told me that I looked younger to her—that my eyes sparkled again. Others have told me that I seem lighter. The heaviness is not so evident. These are things that I can't see. I only know what I feel inside—a new joy. But with these other women, I am able to observe from the outside what God is doing on the inside, and it is a beautiful thing to witness.

I have listened to some of these women's struggles over the whys, as I have wrestled with my own. I have sat with them and discussed what hurts most and some of the guilt and regrets that all grieving people must deal with. And now I sit with them and I see the aftermath of those storm clouds. I see the storm cloud moving on as the last of the sprinkles fall. This is not to say that it will not re-emerge in a moment and drench us to the bone, but the clouds become less frequent. We understand them better, and are able to realize that they will not last. They will pass on by, and the drenching will eventually stop. I think we realize some of the reason for the drenching, and, in a strange way, only those who have experienced them can understand how we are grateful for the storms. They have brought us to a place that makes us appreciate the Son/sun just that much more. We have been taught things that are difficult to learn, but so valuable. They have chilled us to the bone, but we know that God goes even deeper than to the bone; He heals to the marrow with His Word.

For the word of God is living and active. Sharper than any double-edged sword, it penetrates even to dividing soul and spirit, joints and marrow; it judges the thoughts and attitudes of the heart.
Hebrews 4:12 (NIV)

I know a little about bone marrow because Leukemia hides itself deep in the marrow. There is a bone marrow test that can accurately identify if the patient has Leukemia. Phil had plenty of those tests as I looked on. He had no fear of them because he was given a medication that blocked them from his memory, as well as a pain medication that kept him comfortable. How thankful I was for that. He would ask, as he was coming off of the medication, if it was over, that's how little he remembered.

Isn't it good to know that God knows us to the marrow? Isn't it good to know that God can heal us this deeply? I talked with these women and I saw it with my own eyes. I saw most of them when it hurt the most, and I see them now, and they are transformed. They smile and they laugh, and there are visible signs that God's promises are true. I know there are still tears, because I still have so many of my own. But it does get better. It really does.

There is a verse in Malachi 3:10 (NIV) that says, "Test me in this," says the Lord Almighty, "and see if I will not throw open the floodgates of heaven and pour out so much blessing that you will not have room enough for it."

This verse talks about tithing. But tithing is an offering to God, and I think in the same way as offering our money to God, we offer Him our heart. I know He wants us to, and when we do open up to Him, He will open the floodgates of Heaven and pour out blessings on us. It's not always rain that falls from Heaven.

It is hard to explain how losing someone you dearly love, and the pain that follows, can bring about a joy in the Lord that is deeper than you have ever known before. But it is true. You don't have to like what has happened. But you come to a point where the fight in you is gone and the acceptance of what is, becomes real. And I think you either hate God for it, or you love God more than you ever have before, because you have come to a place of total trust and acceptance that He only wants what is best for you.

*It took me about six months before all reserves of my own strength were gone. **Six months**, before I handed it completely over to God and said, "It's Yours now." And as Pastor Dave said in his sermon last Wednesday night, September 11th, it is when our own strength is completely gone that God's strength has only just begun. (Please forgive my loose quote there Dave.) It is when we give it over to God, that we truly begin to see God working in our lives.*

> *I have discarded everything else, counting it all as garbage,*
> *so that I may have Christ and become one with him.*
> *Philippians 3:8b (NLT)*

When I had tried everything else, and discarded it as garbage, it was then that I truly found out what God's strength in me was all about.

Verse 3:9
I no longer count on my own goodness or my ability to obey God's
law, but I trust Christ to save me. For God's way of making us
right with himself depends on faith.

My ability is worth zero, compared to God's ability. Christ alone
saves me. When I start sinking and I start thinking of all the things
that will destroy me, God reminds me to focus on Him and Him
alone.

Let your eyes look straight ahead,
fix your gaze directly before you.
Proverbs 4:25 (NIV)

As a result, I can really know Christ and experience the mighty
power that raised him from the dead. I can learn what it means to
suffer with him, sharing in his death, so that, somehow, I can
experience the resurrection from the dead!
Philippians 3:10 (NIV)

It's the "Somehow" that can puzzle me. I'm not sure how it works.
I only know that it does. I only know that when I believe in what
God's Word says, and I follow it, it works. I experience the same
power that raised Jesus from the dead when I experience that same
mighty power raising my broken heart back to life again when my
heart would rather die. I used to think this is it, I'm going down
this time and I will never come back up again—this hurts way too
much. But now, I have gotten to know Christ enough to know that
He will bring me back once again to live. We don't have to die to
be dead emotionally. We can live the rest of our lives dead inside if
we so choose. To the world, it will seem as if we are fine, but we
will know we aren't. And I think others who have been there will
know, because they will still see the pain that they once felt. It will
be visible to those that have sat under that cloud. But to those that
God has healed, it will also be evident, as it is in these women I
have mentioned.

"But now we have been given a brief moment of grace, for the Lord our God has allowed a few of us to survive as a remnant. He has given us security in this holy place. Our God has brightened our eyes and granted us some relief from our slavery. For we were slaves, but in his unfailing love our God did not abandon us in our slavery."
Ezra 9:8 (NLT)

I don't want anyone to get caught in the slavery of grief. I don't want there to be just a small remnant of people who heal from loss. That frustrates me, because the devil wins then. He is allowed to keep us captive on this earth until we go Home to Heaven. He is happy, and we are not, and God is not.

That is why I write, besides the fact that I love to do it. I write because if there is a shred of truth in what I write, if there is anything in what I write that can open an umbrella for someone who is sitting under that dark cloud getting drenched, it will be worth it. We are not called to live unhappy defeated lives. We are called to be full of joy, and rejoice!

If I can, if these women can, if others can, then we all can, if we will only look to the One who is greater than our greatest loss or struggle.

We sing a song at church that talks about God being our Rebuilder, Restorer, Redeemer, Rewarder.....and so many other things. I don't just sing those words, I KNOW those words. They are my life, every one of them! Jesus is doing it for me. He is doing it for these women I have talked about here. To see it, helps me to believe it, and it encourages me so very much!

Whatever your storm cloud in this life is, don't sit under there alone. There's no need to.
Let God brighten your eyes and grant you relief from your slavery!

Living in His peace,
Diane

153

<u>Myself</u>

How do I begin? Let me tell you...

We did a CD with my brother, Rick, about ten years ago. It was about the journey through brokenness and beyond with God's power. We called the CD, "How Do I Begin To Tell You?" When I wrote the words to the songs included on the CD, some of those experiences I was living through at the moment, some of those experiences I had passed through (but not many), and some I hoped for somewhere down the road ahead of me. I couldn't really go back now and write those same songs, just as I can't go back and write about the emotions I am sharing with you in the "Me" sections of this book. God moves us through different seasons, different phases, of our life, and that is a very good thing. Our Father does not want us to get stuck. We are to continually learn and grow. I'm thankful for the words to the songs God had me pen those years ago. I'm thankful that Rick put them to music, so I can still listen to them. And I'm grateful that I'm not there anymore. God has helped me experience the words that I hoped for back then. There has been healing through the help of His Word, and now I can live in that healing. Our Lord can, and will, do the same for you.

Most times, when it starts to rain, I run for cover.

We don't like the storms unless we are under some sort of protection. The storms of life are the same. We don't like the loss, the pain, and the length of it all. But we must always remember that Jesus is our Savior, and He is our Protector, and He is our cover. What does that mean? What does that look like? How does that feel? It's like this…the storm comes into our life. If it's a big one, it knocks us off our feet. We reel emotionally for a time. Our spirits dip. Our strength wavers. Our hope seems dimmed. Where do we run in those moments? Do we run to the bottle? To the store? To our friends? Or do we run to Jesus? The storms hit hard, and often, early on in my grief. It was the dead of "winter" in my heart. I ran to my private place with God a lot. I dropped to my knees, I opened the Word, I prayed and I cried out to God in my distress. And He met me there. Would a big glass of wine have been quicker or been easier? Most times, probably. But what would the end result have been? Wine brings some instant pain relief—granted. But when the glass is empty, and we have slept it off, where does it leave us? Does alcohol grow us in our relationship with Jesus? Do we find that He is our source of healing? Or have we blocked His healing powers by drenching our heart with what cannot heal, and will eventually harm us? On the opposite side of that, if we run to Jesus when the storm hits, and soak up the Word that is filled with the promises of God, it may take more time and effort, but what does it leave us with? A closer walk with our Creator, who knows the workings of our heart like no one else—not even the greatest heart doctor on earth. These times with our Father build our confidence in the power of the Holy Spirit who lives inside of us. It shows us when the cupboard of our soul is empty, we need not run to the store for another bottle of alcohol, because what lives inside of us, and what is found in God's Word, is all the drink we need. These times show us that by turning to what is good, and right, and true (instead of what diminishes the Holy Spirit inside of us), we come out of those storms strengthened and more ready for the next storm (instead of weakened and even less prepared for what the enemy's next attack will bring our way). Our enemy, Satan, will come again and again! That we know. But do we know that we can learn and grow in each storm, instead of being defeated by them? We can!

What an experience—to sit there and look up into the rain, and enjoy it. To let it pass over me, and then feel the warmth of the sun as it came out to dry me off and restore me once again. That is what it felt like—a restoration.

I remember this time on the beach. What a treat it was. What an awesome time in "school" with God! What an amazing classroom, as I sat there and watched it play out all around me! It was a perfect example of life...seeing those clouds far off in the distance. Those weren't my "storms," they were falling elsewhere, on someone other than me. It showed me I could pray for what was happening far, far way, but it wasn't drenching me. And then the wind would blow the clouds my way, and it would grow so dark, and it seemed as if the whole world was feeling what I was feeling in that moment, but it wasn't true. The rest of the world was back out in the sunshine, and they were looking far off in my direction, perhaps praying for me. When we are in the storm, we have a hard time seeing the sun, but it is still there, and we will eventually feel its warmth. It reminds me of the verse, "Be still, and know that I am God; I will be exalted among the nations, I will be exalted in the earth." Psalm 46:10 (NIV)

But if we sit there, they will eventually pass on by, and the sun will come out again and there is no need to go running. God will move them by us, we don't need to move at all if we are prepared.

We can't go running from our storms. They follow us. They follow us into the bottle. They follow us into the store. They follow us to our friend's house. But if we sit it out with God, seek His help, He will move the storms on by us, sometimes physically, sometimes by healing our heart in the midst of the storm so that we aren't drowning in it every moment of every day.

To listen to that song, "Let it rain...open the floodgates of Heaven...let it rain,." and be sitting there watching God at work doing that very thing is an experience that will stay with me a long time.

If you have heard this song, you can imagine how powerful this experience was. Sometimes what rains down on us is dark and hard, but sometimes what rains down on us is full of blessings. I was in a dark place that day on the beach in Florida, but what God was raining down on me were His blessings of healing. He was showing me things, teaching me things. I was listening to Him speak to the hurt in my heart, and it was helping. In reading John 6 this morning, Jesus is attempting to teach the crowd many things. It says they "began to murmur in disagreement." Jesus replied in John 6:43 (NLT), "Don't complain about what I said..." Don't we all do that? We want to argue with God about what He is telling us. We want to do what we want to do, when we want to do it. What are we thinking? Jesus said, "As it is written in the Scriptures, 'They will all be taught by God.' Everyone who hears and learns from the Father comes to me." John 6:46 (NLT) We are supposed to hear and learn, every day, all the time. And when God gives us a classroom on the beach, it can be powerful! I've sat in many classrooms, some I remember, some I don't, but this one I will never forget.

We wonder how the rest of the world can go on sometimes, when we are in the middle of our own storms.

I remember going into groceries stores when Phil was very sick in the hospital. I did the simple, regular tasks that were required of me during the not so simple, difficult tasks that surrounded me. Now I go into the grocery store, healed and full of joy, knowing that those around me may be in their very own dark place. It's how life is, and we all do it together. We all take our turn in the dark and in the light, but what we must all encourage each other to do is to walk in the Light of Jesus all of the time.

We want to rid ourselves of the pain, we wonder, "Why me?" But I've heard it said that if we could take our backpack off and throw it into a pile with everyone else's, whose backpack would we rather pick up? Are we willing to take on their unknown burdens instead of our own? I'm not. When I would drive home from the hospital in my blue convertible mustang, wind blowing in my hair, sun shining on a warm California day, someone may have wanted my "backpack" from what they could see on the outside. But they would have had no idea that what it included on the inside was their child, lying in a hospital bed, battling Leukemia. What a shock that would have been to them! I remember many years ago going to a seminar, and meeting a new friend there. I didn't talk much about my "problems," and on one of the days she questioned me about it. She wanted me to be "vulnerable" with her. I said, "So you want me to share with you that my son has Leukemia, and how difficult that is?" She looked at me, and said, "That's not really true." I said, "Yes, it is." She was shocked...as shocked as she would have been had she exchanged backpacks with me, thinking I had the perfect life and she didn't at the time because she was struggling in her marriage.

Once you have felt the devastation that can be caused by a "storm cloud," I think it makes you pull up your chair to the "water's edge" more often and take notice.

2 Corinthians 1:4 says that, "He comforts us in all troubles so that we can comfort others." Sometimes those "others," are very, very close to us. Our son, Jimm, is going through a very difficult time right now. It's his turn in the "rain" so to speak. He is 36, married, and has three children—each of which brings its own challenges. He and I have been talking a lot, of late. This is kind of new for us. Our boys are very independent. I guess we raised them to be that way. It's how I was raised, so I passed it on to them. But right now, he is calling "home" often. Not that this is his home any more, but as his parents, he is in need of our moral and spiritual support. We are happy to give it to him.

I read a simple, but probably true, quote this morning. It said, "To be old and wise, you must first be young and stupid." We all start out young, obviously, and some of us have been more stupid than others. We all grow old, of course, but growing wise is the harder part. It has to include a relationship with God to be truly wise. Now, some may want to argue with me on that point, but I'm not talking about smart, I'm talking about wisdom. There are some very smart people, but James 3:17 (NLT) says, "But the wisdom that comes from heaven is first of all pure. It is also peace loving, gentle at all times and willing to yield to others." It goes on to include, mercy, good deeds, etc… What God offers us, His wisdom, is very different than the world's wisdom—just as what I am offering Jimm right now is from the Word, not from the world. God does most things backwards from the ways of this world. Strange, isn't it, how far this world has drifted from godly things? Anyway, all this to say Jimm is young, but not stupid. I am old, and the wisdom he is calling on me for right now is from God, and it is the result of the "storm clouds" I have experienced. Through time, with God in the storm, I can now spend time with our son in his own storm, and have comfort to offer him. Sometimes he doesn't like what I am offering, but he says he goes to the Word and he sees it backed up in Scripture, so he trusts me. He also has his good friend Tim that he trusts, for the very same reason. Tim is actually a bit younger than Jimm, but it just goes to show that when it's God's wisdom, age doesn't matter because the Source of Wisdom is ageless.

I like that my storm, and the comfort and wisdom God has imparted through the years, can now be used to make me more aware of when to "pull up to the water's edge," and help not only Jimm, but others through their own storms. And Jimm makes me proud to be his mom. He *hears* and *learns*, just as Jesus talks about in John 6. It doesn't make all his problems instantly disappear, but he is growing by leaps and bounds because of his cooperation with our Mighty Lord! What more could a mom want?

But when the camera pans back to Mel Gibson, he gets this pained expression on his face that shows the emotions that can surface when you have lost someone.

This was such a powerful scene in the movie for me. This is not normally my kind of movie, one that includes aliens, but this scene, and other things talked about really drew my attention to it. You will see in the movie that a Cross has been removed from the wall—faith was wavering because hearts were broken. And any of us who have been there, can relate, and will relate to Mel's expression…we know…we have felt that pain…it is hard.

All four women are in awe of the transformation that God has made in their lives. They are changed women, who, now, more fully trust in the God they serve.

I honestly don't remember who all these women were. But I'm glad I noted them in my writings all those years ago. It helps to still build confidence in what God can do, and will do, when hearts are yielded to Him. Praise Jesus!

My sister and I were together recently, and later she told me that I looked younger to her—that my eyes sparkled again.

My mom told me that she had not heard me so happy in years as I was when I went to beauty school at the age of 50. I guess she, too, was watching and waiting for the sparkle to come back to my life. I hope you see it in me, even if we have never met. I hope you see it in what you are reading, and I hope it gives you Hope for your life, too. Those around you are watching and waiting, they want to see what Jesus can do with a broken heart. You may be the important witness they need to show them the power of our Risen Lord, Jesus Christ. Your pain, may truly be their gain. As son Jimm texted the other day, "Thinking about what Tim told me yesterday. If he and Becca can have a strong marriage that results in them raising their daughter with God's love in her heart and a love for God in all of them, and it is a result of my suffering and walk of faith, what right do I have to complain? If I could hold the two, in each hand, which weighs more?" (Their marriage has been strengthened through Jimm's difficulties by turning their relationship with each other over to God.) I texted him back with this, "Eternity and a closer walk with Jesus outweighs everything. When we can get that perspective, it changes how we do life."

It is hard to explain how losing someone you dearly love, and the pain that follows, can bring about a joy in the Lord that is deeper than you have ever known before.

This can't be explained. It can only be understood once it's lived through. I can tell you about it in the pages of this book, and I do, but that is all. It's like reading God's Word, or looking up at the screen in church as we sing worship songs, or hearing a sermon—until it speaks directly to something in our own lives, it doesn't penetrate as deep. When we own it, because we must, we grab hold of it and never want to let go!

The day of the book launch party, we attended church in the morning. Remember how I said earlier we were waiting for delivery of "It Started in the Dark," and I had to trust in God's timing for that? Well, the books came in plenty of time for the party! Praise Jesus! And the party was a total blessing. Many came and supported book number one. Maybe you were there, and now you're reading book number two, "It Ended in the Light." Thank you! You help me continue on with your encouragement! Now, back to church...that morning they sang a song called "Oceans," by Hillsong United. It spoke to me about stepping out in faith, into the unknown. It seemed God was speaking to me about the book launch. It resonated with me. It meant something because God was calling me to go where I hadn't before, in my walk with Him. My nephew, Vinny, and his girlfriend, Kerri, blessed us with their music at the party. They chose the songs to play. When they started singing this song, "Oceans", I not only connected with my friend, Joan, because it has a special meaning to her and her sister Annie, I felt a confirmation from God in where He was calling me on that day. These are rich times, deep times, in our walk with God. These things can't be fully explained or understood by others, as you know in your own experiences with God, but it is good to share them.

Six months, *before I handed it completely over to God and said, "It's Yours now."*

Grief progresses differently in everyone, as does our handing the trials in our lives over to God. Six months in was a difficult time for me. Phil being gone was becoming all too real. God uses these dark times to strengthen our faith, and when we cooperate with Him in that, it propels us forward. It's hard for me to watch others in deep pain, but what's harder for me to watch is when they choose to remain there. The struggle is not the problem. God has a remedy for that. What God won't do is force us to hand it over to Him so He can heal us. When we cling tightly to what is hurting us most, instead of handing it over to Jesus and clinging tightly to Him, that's where forward motion stops, and even causes more harm. Jimm is hurting right now. His roller coaster ride takes deep dips into times of devastation, and all I can do is pray for him, and encourage him to hang on. The coaster will come up again; and it does because each day He listens as God instructs him how to move forward—and Jimm is paying attention. This has to please

God very much, when He sees and knows our pain, but we choose to ride it out with Him and trust Him through it. The blessings that Jimm is seeing overwhelm him at times, even though the situation he is dealing with remains the same. I can't reveal more than this right now, but maybe there isn't a need to. You have your own situation that remains the same. You have your own roller coaster ride that is making you sick. Hang on to Jesus, He will bring you back to level ground again. Will there be future dips? Yes. But one day, the ride may resemble a train more than a roller coaster. Trains go through hills and valleys, but not to the degree that coasters do.

If I can, if these women can, if others can, then we all can, if we will only look to the One who is greater than our greatest loss or struggle.

You may be reading this book and you may be saying, "This Jesus thing works for everyone else, maybe, but not me." Can I be blunt with you here? You're wrong. Jesus doesn't love others more than He loves you. He didn't come to die for others, offering others eternal life and Hope, and not offer it to you. You are a beautiful, wonderful creation of a Mighty God. He has great plans for your life, and the enemy is trying to ruin them. The question that remains is, will you let Satan destroy you? If your problems seem worse than others, maybe that's just because Satan knows something about your future that you don't, that God's plans for you are super amazing! When I was a young mother of three boys, just living my life, I had no idea I would be sitting here today writing these words. And I don't know what plans God has for this book, or any other part of my future, but whatever those plans are, I don't want to miss them. We get one life, one shot at living on this earth and walking this out with Jesus. Let's let it be all that it is supposed to be. Let's hang on to Jesus, He will see us through whatever it is we are dealing with.

Gift #9 – There's a reason, there's a way, and Jesus will show us!

Are you under a storm cloud right now? What is it?

If not, are you presently watching others in their own rainstorms? How could you encourage them?

Record today's date and other notes you'd like to make:

The Great

<u>I AM</u>

As a result, I can really know Christ and experience the mighty power that raised him from the dead. I can learn what it means to suffer with him, sharing in his death, so that, somehow, I can experience the resurrection from the dead!
Philippians 3:10 (NIV)

CHAPTER TEN

Happy are those who are strong in the Lord,
who set their minds on a pilgrimage to Jerusalem.
When they walk through the Valley of Weeping
it will become a place of refreshing springs
where pools of blessing collect after the rains!
Psalm 84:5-6 (NLT)

Me

After The Rains!

Sunday, 22 Sep 2002

Can you picture a small girl skipping along the street, coming upon puddles of water left from the drenching rain? Can you picture her stomping in those pools of water with her rubber boots on, enjoying the splash she creates, and laughing in merriment? I see her yellow rain slicker, and her yellow hat, maybe an umbrella in hand—not a care in the world as she moves along down the street toward home.

Is that me? Is that the woman that was laughing today with her friend outside of her friend, Emily's, new home?—laughing about things that might not seem funny to the rest of the world, but laughing anyway just because God had put a song back in her heart? Maybe, at this moment, the cares of this world seemed far away, and what was visible to this world was not as important as what was hidden in her heart.

I came home laughing in my car and I wasn't really sure why. I came into the house laughing and tried to explain it to Jim. I don't know if he understood my laughter. I didn't. But I think I do now. Let me try to explain, if you will.

Today was a hectic day at the church office, but a great day. Some things went right, some things went very wrong. But were they wrong, really? God has a plan for all things. I love to watch it unfold. The van that had been rented for the youth became a problem. There was no record of the rental, so there was no van to haul the youth to their weekend retreat. A friend of mine, Emily, loaned her van to carry a portion of the kids, which left her at the church with no car. I was asked if I would take Emily home, and that was not a problem. So off we went at the end of the day, chatting all the way as we drove out to her new house. When we pulled up in front of Emily's house, she offered to show me around. They are in the middle of remodeling the entire place. So in we went!

Now, this is no ordinary house. Jim and I live in an ordinary house—you know, a few bedrooms, a couple of bathrooms, with a two-car garage. Cozy you might say! This house was more like a mansion! Emily and I laughed our way through the rooms. I lost count of bathrooms, and got turned around, and practically lost following Emily from room to room. The kitchen was spectacular! I knew it was way beyond what I might need since take-out is my favorite recipe.

I found "Jim's" room, but of course I thought more of it as a great Raider football entertainment room since I am the football fan in our house. Jim would have been comfortably seated in there watching Sci-fi, I imagine, and loving it.

We ventured out back to their LARGE second garage where they are living until the remodeling is done, and I got to check out their cozy living arrangement for the time-being. I laughed once again, because Jim and I are in the process of down sizing to about 400 sq. ft of living space. We want to buy an RV and live in it. More on that later... This garage living arrangement is small for Emily's family, as the larger house is prepared for their eventual move into it, but I joked with her that I would stop staying up nights crying over their living arrangements. They are not suffering in the "garage"!

And so, the tour ended and we found ourselves back out front again. I told Emily I would be sure to wash my car before my next visit, to keep up with the standards of the neighborhood! We laughed again.

So why do I share this story with you? Because of who we are—my friend and I. We are two women who are married to great guys, we both have three wonderful sons, we live a good life, and both serve the same God. We have a deep desire to find God's will for our lives and follow the path He has for us. But our journeys are very different. Mine has been filled with heartache as of late. Emily's has not. Mine is simpler and "cozier," hers grander and more spectacular. I would rather talk with one person at a time. She would rather be on a stage in front of 500. But we laugh together, and we talk together, and we question God together. Why does God provide so much for some, and so seemingly little for others? But is it little, or does it just appear that way? Who can judge something like that?

As I dove into God's Word tonight seeking answers to these questions, I saw myself once again out in front of that beautiful home, and God gave me a picture of my heart. He showed me a heart big enough to hold all the blessings He has given to me. It was like God was saying my heart is His home, He lives in there *and it is **His** mansion. It contains all the things the world can't see, but the things that I can feel—His love, goodness, kindness, gentleness, and faithfulness. It is a vast "home" filled with all the things He wishes for me in this life.*

*I wondered how I could stand outside of Emily's home and laugh about the fact that we could be living in a "trailer" soon, and considering the fact that my son had died, I still laughed. What was I laughing about anyway? Surely not the fact that my son died, don't get me wrong. That was not it at all. I think I was laughing because I felt blessed beyond measure. How do I explain that to the world? Could Emily understand my joy? I think she could, because she is so overwhelmed with God's blessings in her own life. Some may say, of course she is; Emily has it all. She has the perfect life. What more could she want? And yet, would it be the perfect life without God? I think not. I know not! That vast space in my heart that fills with the good things of God is the very same space in Emily's heart that needs God's filling, no matter what the wealth. It doesn't matter what the living arrangements are, we all have the same need of God. That space is not filled because Emily "has it all," it is filled because she has it all **with** God. She knows God personally, and she knows where all good things come from.*

What would that house be worth, what would those possessions be worth, if Emily should find herself in my shoes emotionally? You might as well burn the house to the ground with everything in it for all that it would be worth. You might as well pitch a tent in the yard and sleep in that for all that Emily would care if she suddenly had a son in Heaven. The specially chosen tiles, the beautifully painted walls, and even the large screen TV would become a blur compared to the loss that was felt. And then what would you have...God living in your heart. God occupying that vast space in your heart—or maybe not? Your heart could be empty. Maybe the Holy Spirit would not be living in there at all because you have said "No" to Jesus over the years. He may not have found a home in your heart as yet, and you would then be left with nothing to fill that empty space. Everything that matters, suddenly wouldn't, and you would be left empty. And would you be laughing? No way! No how!

You may wonder how I can even be laughing at this point. I wonder that myself. I am astonished at the healing that has gone on in ten months. I am shocked that I can feel the way I feel after only ten months of my son being gone—truly shocked, and I don't mind telling you that. When this all started, I told you that I would tell you if God's promises were true. I would tell you if He really could heal a completely broken heart. Well, I'm here to tell you that there is healing beyond measure already, and I know He has only just begun.

*Psalm 84:1 (NLT) says, "How lovely is your dwelling place, O Lord Almighty." That is how I live, in His dwelling place. And the Lord's dwelling place is in me. It occupies a mansion-sized space right in my heart, and each day I live, Jesus keeps filling it with more and more blessings. They are not blessings that the world may notice. They are not huge homes, expensive cars, or the latest outfits. But they are blessings that nourish my soul. And they are blessings that keep me laughing when there is **nothing** to laugh about! They are blessings that make me look forward to getting out of bed in the morning because of what Jesus has in store for my day.*

I was so foolish and ignorant -
I must have seemed like a senseless animal to you.
Yet I still belong to you; you are holding my right hand.
You will keep on guiding me with your counsel,
leading me to a glorious destiny.
Whom have I in heaven but you?
I desire you more than anything on earth.
My health may fail, and my spirit may grow weak,
but God remains the strength of my heart;
he is mine forever.
Psalm 73:22-26 (NLT)

What do I desire on this earth? Nothing compared to the desire of having God in my heart. "But as for me, how good it is to be near God! I have made the Sovereign Lord my shelter, and I will tell everyone about the wonderful things you do." Psalm 73:28 (NLT)

*It doesn't matter what kind of "shelter" we have on this earth when what is most precious is gone. What matters then, is to know **where** they have gone, and **how** we are going to get there. I know both, and I can live satisfied all my days until I see Phil again. Satisfied and laughing with Emily in front of her beautiful home. Satisfied and laughing because these earthly possessions don't matter one bit—they are only the things in life that God has given us to enjoy for a short while. If Emily lived the rest of her days with her family in that temporary garage space, it really wouldn't matter because she would be on God's path for her life. She knows that.*

Psalm 84:4 (NLT) says, "How happy are those who can live in your house, always singing your praises." Emily "sings" God's praises every day. She feels blessed beyond measure and wonders, why her? So do I. I feel blessed beyond measure, and the world may wonder how I can? The world may not see it the way I do. Some would see that she has everything, and I have lost everything. Some may think my life should not go on with joy while Emily's has no blemish. The "world" has no idea! Only God can know the heart and bless accordingly. And only those being blessed can truly know what those blessings are because they don't always match up with what the world would need to "see" to call a person blessed.

Psalm 86:4 (NLT) says, "Give me happiness, O Lord, for my life depends on you." All our lives depend on the Lord, whether we know it or not. Take God out of the picture and what do we have? No sun, no moon, no stars, no flowers, no mountains, no people, no world whatsoever! The Lord is the Creator of all things! Without Jesus, what we'll have is that place down under, and I'm not talking about Australia!

Is there a bit of Heaven on earth? I believe there is. A little bit of Heaven is when you can laugh and feel joy, when you thought there would be no possible way. A little bit of Heaven is standing with a friend in front of her mansion while talking about moving into a trailer, and it makes no difference at all. A little bit of

Heaven is peace and contentment in whatever our circumstances are because the One we trust in knows all, sees all, and controls all. And there is not a thing in the world to worry about beyond that. "O Lord, Almighty, happy are those who trust in you." Psalm 84:12 (NLT)

For now, a little bit of Heaven is happiness in this crazy world we live in. Stomping in the rain puddles with our big rubber boots on because the cares of this world seem as they did when we were a small child and our parents handled all our worries. They provided our home, our food, our clothing, and all the comfort and love we could ever want or need. And we didn't even have to think about it. We didn't even have to be thankful for it. Most times, we didn't even know we should be. It was a given.

But now that we are grown, and now that we may have our own children, our own home, or our own set of responsibilities, we may long for that simpler time when someone else took care of all our needs. Guess what? We have a Father who will, who wants to, who longs to. He will give us a little bit of Heaven on earth by coming into our heart and building a mansion there that becomes His storehouse of goodness. Jesus will bring the laughter back. And it will feel so good. It won't matter where we live, because Christ will be living in us!

I have been crucified with Christ.
I myself no longer live, but Christ lives in me.
So I live my life in this earthly body by trusting
in the Son of God, who loved me and gave himself for me.
Galatians 2:20 (NIV)

When all is stripped away, what is left is the beginning of all that is good. Only then can we truly enjoy that mansion or that cozy house to its full extent. Before then, it might be the very thing that puffs us up and makes us proud and arrogant, or takes us down and gives us shame. But when all is stripped away, it might be the very thing that keeps us humble, or makes our hearts burst with gratitude to the One who provided everything we have need of.

God gave us everything we need when He gave us His Son, Jesus Christ. When we start there, all the rest will make more sense than it ever has before. Then God's earthly gifts to us will give the enjoyment they were meant to—like the enjoyment we experienced as a child, who was content to splash in the puddles after the rains with not a care in the world, because we were loved, and we knew it...so we laughed!

Living in His peace,
Diane

<u>Myself</u>

Can you picture a small girl skipping along the street, coming upon puddles of water left from the drenching rain?... Is that me? Is that the woman that was laughing today with her friend outside of her friend, Emily's, new home?

I love how these writings take me back to a certain day, a certain time, a certain place. I remember that day so well, standing out in front of Emily's new house. For some reason, it made me so joyful. That had to be a gift from God. There was such a contrast in our lives at that moment. It struck my joyful bone, if you know what I mean. God was truly showing me it's not what we have in this world, it's what we have in His Son, Jesus, that makes all the difference. My heart was not only full of friendship with Emily on that day, it was full of friendship with Jesus, and I was grateful.

So why do I share this story with you? Because of who we are—my friend and I.

Emily and I still live very different lives, but very similar lives. She has three sons, and so do I. I still have one in Heaven and two on earth, and she still has three on this earth. Our boys are now men, and they have gone on to marry. I have grandchildren, but Emily is still waiting for hers. We get together from time to time. We share the ups and downs of life. We both have them, in different ways. We are both still learning and growing in our relationship with our Lord, and it is good. Emily is much more the comedian when she shares Jesus from a stage, I am much more serious. God designed us differently to accomplish the various tasks He asks of us.

Why does God provide so much for some, and so seemingly little for others?

It seemed, on this day, that Emily had everything, and I had very little. We both knew that wasn't true from God's viewpoint, only from the world's. What God provides cannot be measured by the world's standards. Who can measure the peace in a person's heart? Who can measure the joy? Who can measure the heartbreak? The more we open our heart to what Jesus offered us when He walked this earth, died for our sins, and ascended back into Heaven after His resurrection, the more we will know that we have everything we need in Him. All the rest just adds to our experience here—it doesn't make it or break it.

As I dove into God's Word tonight seeking answers to these questions, I saw myself once again out in front of that beautiful home, and God gave me a picture of my heart.

Diving head first into God's Word at any time is the right thing to do. But especially when we have questions that need answers. Many of our questions are probably heart questions, which is fine because God usually goes right to the heart of an issue in His Word. While reading John 8 this morning, I was once again seeing the total honesty of Jesus as He talked with those He was with. Jesus said, "You say, 'He is our God,' but you do not even know him. I know him. If I said otherwise, I would be as great a liar as you!" (vs. 54-54 NLT) Jesus pulls no punches. He is not afraid to offend. He is also not afraid to love. Jesus is the perfect example of living this life as our Father would want us to. Jesus said in John 8:26 (NLT), "I have much to say about you and much to condemn, but I won't. For I say only what I have heard from the one who sent me, and he is true." Like we should, Jesus seems to be biting His tongue here when there is so much the human side of Him would want to say. We can see the heart of Jesus in these verses. I hope the world can see the heart of Jesus in those of us who know Him.

*It was like God was saying my heart is His home, He lives in there and it is **His** mansion. It contains all the things the world can't see, but the things that I can feel...*

"Even in laughter the heart may ache..." Proverbs 14:13 (NIV) Right in this very hour, my good friend, Ann, is hurting deeply. Her long time companion, Bear, is being put to sleep in her home by a visiting vet. Bear has gotten old, and has gone blind, along with many other physical ailments. Ann is being kind to her beloved dog, even though it causes her great pain to do what must be done. Ann's heart will ache the rest of this day, and many days to come, although when I see Ann again, soon we may share some laughter. God has given us a wonderful mixture of emotions, and even though we can't explain them all, and why they ebb and flow as they do, we can trust, that with God in control of all things, on all days, it can be well with our soul.

I wondered how I could stand outside of Emily's home and laugh about the fact that we could be living in a "trailer" soon...

The "trailer" does need some explanation here! I don't want anyone pulling out their violins for us having to move into a trailer. (Unless it's my nieces Haley, Delaney, and Libbey who I love to hear play.) The trailer was a 39' fifth wheel attached to a Medium-duty Freightliner. We purchased this new "home" of ours to travel full time while Jim worked in different cities around the United States. It was a wonderful, fun way of life, and also provided a "mountain cabin" of sorts for me to do a lot of writing in. The simplified life style was very healing for both of us. We didn't crawl into a bunk at night. We had a king-sized bed, a dishwasher, recliners, and eventually even a flat screen TV when they became available. It was a small space, but a very comfortable way of life that we willingly chose. In fact, Phil knew this was our plan when he was old enough to move out, and voiced that he hoped we would at least wait until he graduated from High School. I assured him we would.

What was I laughing about anyway? Surely not the fact that my son died, don't get me wrong. That was not it at all.

I was laughing at the contrast. It just struck me funny that day. As Emily and Gregg remodeled their mansion, we were planning on down-sizing to a trailer. And we were all very happy with our decisions to do so. Just as people enjoyed visiting our trailer, we also enjoy visiting mansions. It keeps life interesting and exciting, to see how different people live.

I think I was laughing because I felt blessed beyond measure. How do I explain that to the world?

I was happy to be so satisfied in our "lack" compared to Emily and Gregg's "abundance." I loved that God was able to make that so real in a person's heart because of His satisfying grace and love in our lives. Often when I see very large, very well-to-do homes, I wonder about the lives of the people living there. Do they know Jesus? Are they at peace? Recently we visited my brother in Tennessee. He and his family live on a beautiful, three acre piece of land, right on the Tennessee River. There is so much peace there. But as I stood outside of his home on his sprawling green grass, looking at the water, I knew that peace only reigns in a person's heart when Jesus lives in their heart. I had all of Jesus in my heart on that day. The Holy Spirit was filling me with contentment and joy as we visited their home. I didn't go to Tennessee searching for peace. Peace traveled there with me because the gift of the Holy Spirit lives within all who believe in Jesus Christ.

*That space is not filled because Emily "has it all," it is filled because she has it all **with** God. She knows God personally, and she knows where all good things come from.*

Emily would not want me to paint her life as perfect here. No one has a perfect life on this earth, no matter how big the mansion may be. The sad news of Robin Williams' recent death tells us all that. I can't even imagine the wealth he lived in, and perhaps no one knew the sadness he also lived in. To take his own life, when surrounded by such opulence, surely must be a lesson to us all that it is not what we own, but who owns us. With Jesus as our Savior, our inheritance in Him outweighs anything this world's money could ever provide for us. Sometimes even when Jesus is our Lord and Savior, we still make decisions that take us from this world. It's hard to understand, but we know the One who does understand our greatest struggles, and we can trust our God in that. Some say that suicide is the one unforgivable sin. I beg to differ. God's Word says, "And so I tell you, every kind of sin and slander can be forgiven, but blasphemy against the Spirit will not be forgiven." Matthew 12:31 (NIV)

What would that house be worth, what would those possessions be worth, if Emily should find herself in my shoes emotionally?

I know that Emily has thought about our loss. She was up close and personal with it. She took pictures at Phil's Celebration of Life Service. She brought flowers to our doorstep shortly after Phil's Homegoing—what a sweet gift they were when I discovered them. She and I have had many godly conversations, and I know she cherishes her grown sons each day, knowing that we don't have all three of our sons on this earth. She has said good-bye to loved ones, and knows the heartache of grief. There are very few who have not, as we get later on in life. Gregg and Emily have seen the ebb and flow of life, and they both serve God whether they are rich or poor.

I am shocked that I can feel the way I feel after only ten months of my son being gone. Truly shocked, and I don't mind telling you that.

I didn't realize that this story happened only ten months after Phil went Home, but it makes sense now. We moved into our RV about a year and a half after Phil was gone. I would not have thought on day one that in ten months, there would have been a day of chuckles. It is good to laugh, whenever it comes. There were still many months and years of pain to endure.

*They are not blessings that the world may notice. They are not huge homes, expensive cars, or the latest outfits. But they are blessings that nourish my soul. And they are blessings that keep me laughing when there is **nothing** to laugh about!*

Some would say there was nothing to laugh about on that day. But there was because "…the joy of the Lord is your strength." Nehemiah 8:10 (NIV) I love the pictures I see of Jesus where He is not so serious. Some have been painted where He is in full blown laughter. I look forward to meeting that Jesus one day. I'm not a crack up, but I do enjoy fun and laughter. I'm sort of like my dad in that I don't have real high highs, but I don't have real low lows. For the most part, my emotions, when not grieving, are not mountaintops and valleys, but mostly just a wavy line of ups and downs. I don't need to be the center of attention, and sometimes I just enjoy stepping into the shadows and watching the going's on from a distance.

We recently attended our nephew, Erik's, wedding. As he and his bride, Allison, enjoyed their festivities, I took a couple of chairs and set them away a bit. It was an outdoor wedding, and it made it possible to move back and observe. Jim sat there with me. I almost get as much enjoyment out of that as I do being in the thick of it and visiting with everyone. I love watching their fun. It's a peaceful place to retreat to. It also gave me some perspective on the evening—Erik was a huge support to Phil when he was battling the early stages of cancer. Phil was just a year younger than Erik, and they were great buddies. When we lived in Fresno for Phil's initial chemotherapy treatments, Erik provided the friendship that Phil had left behind. We had returned to the states, from our home in Germany, for Phil to be treated at Fresno Children's Hospital. (Jim was a private contractor on a military base, and we spent eight years overseas.)

I know in my heart that God's plan for Phil's life never included growing into adulthood, and marriage. But it was interesting for me to observe Erik. He is a tall man, now, 30 years of age, a full beard, and deep voice. He and Phil were just teenagers together, and Phil will always remain a teenager in my memory. But with Erik, I can see what his future might have held. I am happy for Erik and Allison as they start their life together. It was a good time to sit back, take it in, and reflect on all that God has done and continues to do in this life.

*What matters then, is to know **where** they have gone, and **how** we are going to get there.*

If we don't know this, we don't know what we need to know. Where Phil went is vital to me, as it should be to you with your loved ones. And how he got there is also vital, because it's the same way you and I are going to get there. My sister-in-law, Marlene, has been helping with the care of her 91 year old mother, Neva. Neva left this earth for Heaven just last Friday. We know where she went, because we know how she got there. Neva loved Jesus. She believed that Jesus is God's only Son, sent to this earth to die on a Cross for our sins. Neva's sins were cleansed with the blood of Jesus, and she was on the narrow road that led her Home—the road to Heaven. Her family is sad today—as they should be. They miss the wonderful woman that God blessed them with as a mom and a grandma. But they don't grieve as those who have no Hope. (1 Thess. 4:13) They can rejoice that her suffering is over, and grand reunions are taking place even as I write this. They believe that. I believe that. Do you believe that? Do you live in that Hope of eternity? If not, you can, even as soon as right now by believing that Jesus is who He said He is—by believing why He came to this earth, to cleanse you of your sins—by believing that His death and resurrection conquered sin and death, and that Hell is no longer your destination, but Heaven is. This is as close to Hell as believers in Jesus will ever get. And this is as close to Heaven as unbelievers will ever get. Which group are you in? Be at peace today, and say yes to Jesus. Then you will know **where,** and **how**, and you can rest in God's promise of an eternal life with Him.

Is there a bit of Heaven on earth? I believe there is. A little bit of Heaven is when you can laugh and feel joy, when you thought there would be no possible way.

I'm no different than you. I grieve deeply and miss terribly. The only difference for any of us is if we do grieve as those who have Hope. I do. And because of that, I was able to go back to Nashville a few weeks ago. If you read my first book, "It Started in the Dark," there is a chapter in their called "How-deee." I made a trip to Nashville just 13 weeks into my grief walk. It was a terribly hard trip. I had to keep going back to quiet times with God for strength to even have a good time 12 years ago. But this time, upon returning to Nashville, I wanted to put God's healing to the test. I wanted to go back to the exact spots that I had been in at the Grand Ole Opry Hotel, and see what it would feel like—sort of like returning to the scene of the "crime." Last time I was there with my best friend, Deb. This time I returned with my husband, Jim, and my dad, Vince. We were pushing dad in his wheelchair, and he was giving us quite the workout. There are many levels, and many ramps to go up and down. It was a very different visit in many ways. The greatest of which was that there was no pain in my heart. I looked for it. It wasn't there. I searched for it around every turn, but it didn't appear. Last time, I remember fountains that went off playing songs that Phil played on the piano. I remember boys with their moms. I remember Deb pointing out blue roses in one of the shop windows. (We put blue roses on Phil's coffin.) I didn't spot a blue rose in the place. We even went over to the mall next to the hotel to eat afterwards. That's where I saw Hilo Hatties 12 years ago, and had to escape back to our hotel room to refuel. Too many painful memories bombarded my every step. Twelve years ago my tank was on empty, and I NEEDED to be filled up with God's strength to keep going. But this time…there was no pain…only the memories of how hard it was last time, and the blessing of how God can heal. I told our son, Jimm, I was entering into these places to face my demons. I found that the demons had fled, and they have been replaced by the healing power of Jesus. My heart is so grateful!

When all is stripped away, what is left is the beginning of all that is good.

Hard times separate the wheat from the chaff in our lives, just as Jesus will do upon His return. "His winnowing fork is in his hand, and he will clear his threshing floor, gathering his wheat into the barn and burning up the chaff with unquenchable fire." Matthew 3:12 (NIV) When our Father strips away things that are not Heaven-bound, all that will be left in Heaven is all that is good. We can get a taste of that in our own lives here on earth. The hard times are not meant to harm us. They are meant to heal us. As we grow from childhood into adulthood, many things in this life start to cling to us: bad memories, hurts, fears, bitterness, unforgiveness, pain. The list is endless. We sometimes will wear those things like a big heavy coat. But Jesus says His yoke is easy and His burden is light. (Matt. 11:30) Jesus doesn't want us carrying around a lot of unneeded baggage. He wants to set us free so we can live and serve Him fully. We can either add grief to our heavy coat, stuffing all the pain into our pockets along with everything else that's already there, or we can allow God to empty out our pockets of pain, lift off the heavy coat of darkness, and allow Jesus to walk us into the light of all that He has waiting for us. "The light shines in the darkness, and the darkness has not overcome it." John 1:5 (NIV) No matter how dark it seems, the light of Jesus Christ can dispel it when we give our heart to Him to be healed.

God gave us everything we need when He gave us His Son, Jesus Christ.

It may seem too easy, too simple, but all we need is Jesus and the Holy Spirit that the Father sent us. If we needed anything or anyone else, our Father God would have sent it to us. But He sent us His One and only Son to be our Savior. People flocked to Jesus when He walked this earth. They asked Him questions He shouldn't have been able to answer. Wasn't He just a carpenter's son from Nazareth? He spoke in the Temple like He knew what He was talking about. He opened the scroll and read about Himself in Isaiah—a book that had been written before He ever walked this earth. And now I just read today that they are discovering more scrolls in Rome that, once interpreted, point to the Truth of Jesus' miraculous healing powers while He was here. Is there anything on this earth that disproves Jesus other than the heart of a person that tries to because he/she doesn't want/choose to know Him? God will not force us to love His Son. But when we do...when we choose to believe the gift of eternal life Jesus is offering to us, we will find that He is all we will ever need. A heart that is fully surrendered to the Lord, Jesus Christ, is a heart that is filled with the power of the Holy Spirit. And God can, and will, do amazing things through that heart. And as my sister-in-law, Sandra, said just this last week in Tennessee, "It really can't be understood until it is experienced." So true Sandy. But once experienced, we will never be the same.

Gift #10 – Finding that we have absolutely everything we need in Jesus.

Do you feel spiritually rich even when your money and/or possession might not be so plentiful?

Are you finding a surrendered heart brings greater healing than a resistant heart?

Record today's date and other notes you'd like to make:

The Great

<u>I AM</u>

Whom have I in heaven but you?
I desire you more than anything on earth.
My health may fail, and my spirit may grow weak,
but God remains the strength of my heart;
he is mine forever.
Psalm 73:25-26 (NLT)

CHAPTER ELEVEN

"They will be my people," says the Lord Almighty. "On the day when I act, they will be my own special treasure. I will spare them as a father spares an obedient and dutiful child. Then you will again see the difference between the righteous and the wicked, between those who serve God and those who do not."
Malachi 3:17-18 (NLT)

<u>Me</u>

'gator Infested Waters

Saturday, 28 Sep 2002

Did you know that people in Florida actually rent canoes to paddle around in alligator infested waters? They do! I was just talking with my friend, Deb, last night and they are camping this weekend. They rented a canoe, which they have done many times in the past, and were out paddling around with the 'gators. In fact, as they paddled, Deb's oar hit a 'gator under that dark murky water and made the 'gator a little mad. So it swung its tail into the side of the canoe, hitting it with a thud. I think that would increase anyone's heart rate immediately! Deb said if the canoe had tipped over, which they easily do, she would have probably been like Peter...walking on water! Oh, the crazy things we do for enjoyment. It seems sort of strange to people like me out here in California, but then again our freeways could be feared, and we think nothing of driving on them all the time!

Do you know that we actually live in 'gator infested water all the time? You were wondering how this was going to tie in, weren't you? I was too! And who saves us from that "dangerous" water? God does, of course!

> *As for me, I look to the Lord for his help. I wait confidently for God to save me, and my God will certainly hear me. Do not gloat over me, my enemies! For though I fall, I will rise again.*
> Micah 7:7-8a (NLT)

In the ordinary things in life, we are able to glide pretty easily over those dark waters, knowing that should our "canoe" tip over, it wouldn't be much of a problem. There are only small 'gators down there and they won't hurt much. A small nip or two in the leg, a loss of a little toe perhaps, maybe a finger, but nothing life threatening. We think we need not worry about the boat tipping over or needing to walk on water until the "water" gets deep and the 'gators are huge—until it gets so dark there is no light under there and we wouldn't know which way to turn if not for God's help.

I experience two types of challenges in my life right now—the ordinary kind of decisions about our future, about the car, the house, the job, whatever it may be—and then there's the big "Gator," the one that will eat me alive if I'm not walking on the water, so to speak. You probably know what that big 'gator is; it's the loss of Phil. It waits to devour me any chance it can get. I wouldn't dare bump it with my oar or it would probably do more than swing its mighty tail at me; it would chomp the canoe in half, taking me with it. It lurks, and it prowls, and it waits for me to lose my focus so it can take me down into the deep, dark water of life.

185

BUT, I can stand strong if I keep my focus on Jesus as I paddle with care through the murky waters of this world. I have been going through the school of "professional canoeing," and it has taught me so much—hard lessons, for sure—but important ones.

Lesson Number One:
Allow God to steer.
God knows where we are going and He will guide us there.

Lesson Number Two:
I may not see the final destination, but there surely is one.
1 Peter 1:5b (NLT) "...which is ready to be revealed on the last day for all to see."

Lesson Number Three:
The 'gators are there only to test our faith in the One who saves. They can't harm us.
1 Peter 1:9 (NLT) "The reward for trusting him will be the salvation of your souls."

I'm sure there are many more lessons along the way, but these are getting me started.

We have to keep away from those "gators" that seek to kill and destroy us! We are not meant to be swimming around with them. In their water, we are unprotected! If not for God's strength and protection, we would be eaten up by the evil in this world.

> *And God, in his mighty power, will protect you until you receive this salvation, because you are trusting him.*
> *1 Peter 1:5 (NLT)*

Do you know that when we get into the "canoe" of faith with God, we are only small babies? When we take that step and say "yes" to Jesus in our lives, we're just youngin's. We start out this journey with God knowing nothing about Him, really, except that we are drawn to know more about Him. We get into that canoe/relationship with Him by stepping in of our own free will,

186

and then the rest of our lives we are on an entirely new journey. The rest of the world, who may have no belief in God, feel that this world is their home. Those of us in a relationship with Jesus know it is not. We feel like foreigners here—a fish out of water, so to speak, because we are. "Dear brothers and sisters, you are foreigners and aliens here. So I warn you to keep away from evil desires because they fight against your very souls."
1 Peter 2:11 (NLT)

When we step into the canoe as babies, what happens then? We are reborn!
Your new birth announcement might look like this. (You can fill in your name.)

A New Life:

All honor to the
God and Father of our Lord Jesus Christ,
for it is by his boundless mercy that God has given

(Your Name)_____

the privilege of being born again. 1 Peter 1:3a (NLT)

> *Now we live with a wonderful expectation because Jesus Christ rose again from the dead.*
> *For God has reserved a priceless inheritance for his children.*
> *1 Peter 1: 3b-4 (NLT)*

God has delivered (You)_____

The Lord will bring (You)_____ out of the darkness into the light...
Micah 7:9b (NLT)

> *Obey God because you are his children. 1 Peter 1:14 (NLT)*

For you have been born again. Your new life did not come from your earthly parents because the life they gave you will end in death. But this new life will last forever because it comes from the eternal, living word of God.
1 Peter 1:22 (NLT)

Congratulations!

Wow! We are born right into this new life! God welcomes us into His family and loves us like no other person has ever loved us before. Does that get rid of the "gators"? No! They are still lurking. Why? Because we were born again into God's family, but we still must live on this earth with the enemy. Satan has always wanted to destroy us, and he won't quit trying until we are Home with Jesus. Can the enemy destroy us? He will surely try, but one way to find protection from him is to "grow into the fullness of your salvation." 1 Peter 2:2 (NLT)

"You must crave pure spiritual milk so that you can grow into the fullness of your salvation. Cry out for this nourishment as a baby cries for milk, now that you have had a taste of the Lord's kindness." 1 Peter 2:2-3 (NLT)

Do you crave God? I do, now. I can't say that I did before I experienced the things of late...this sorrow. But now that I have seen the 'gators up close and personal, I am addicted to God. I need Him every day! I need His spiritual milk, which eventually becomes a soft food, and then becomes the meat of my existence.

*We are God's children, and we were born into this world, but this world is not our home. When Phil was born, we as his parents gave birth to him, but it ended in death just as that verse in 1 Peter 1:22 above said it will. **God** gave Phil life when he died, because of Jesus' very own death on the Cross. After Phil's earthly death, he began a new life, in Heaven, which will last forever!*

1 Peter 1:24 (NLT) says "People are like grass that dies away; their beauty fades as quickly as the beauty of wildflowers."

And that is the "gator" that will eat me up. Death! The death of my son. It seeks to destroy me. But I seek God more! I place my confidence in the promises of an eternal life with God. It's like a "Twilight Zone" TV show that Jim and I watched the other night. In this episode a young doctor dies, and from his sitting position on a bench he slumps to the side...gone. Then his spirit gets up and looks back at his body lying there. The doctor is now changed. He no longer looks tired...his brow is no longer furled from the aneurysm that was giving him headaches. He is no longer sweating and rumpled. He is calm and refreshed. I loved it! That is what Phil must have felt! He must have looked back at his body lying on the bed, swollen, bruised, and pale, and he must have felt so refreshed. It is what I believe, but do not see. That is what believers will do—we will leave this tired body behind, and feel so calm and refreshed in God's presence.

It also says in 1 Peter 1:20 (NLT) that God chose Christ "for this purpose long before the world began, and He was sent to earth for all to see." And God did this for us.

I was watching some ants a few weeks ago, remembering something I had read before, as they were crawling along the seam in the sidewalk. There they were, the whole bunch of them scurrying about, to who knows where, bumping into each other, going around clumps of dirt in their way that must have seemed like mountains, all the while thinking this is all there is to the world. It's all they know. They had no idea that I was standing there watching them. They had no idea I even existed. And yet, I had such power over them. I could have picked them up and carried them away, or put my finger down in their path and changed their direction, or maybe blown on them and scattered them to different places—whatever I chose. They wouldn't have even known where the wind came from—they would have just gone on as best they could, doing whatever it was they were doing. Ants have no idea that the world they live in is HUGE, because all they knew was that little piece of the cement for now. They are oblivious that the universe even exists. Oblivious to all of us! They don't care, they don't know, and they never will.

*That's why Christ came—to make us aware—to pull us out of our oblivion. Jesus wants us to **know** that there is so much more than what we see. The Bible says, "He is the image of the invisible God, the firstborn over all creation." Colossians 1:15 (NIV)*

Christ became visible so we could see God. He is God's image. Jesus became an "Ant," so to speak, so we "ants" could see and know God. Human ants "stumble because they do not listen to God's word or obey it, and so they meet the fate that has been planned for them." 1 Peter 2:8b (NLT) "But you are not like that, for you are a chosen people. You are a kingdom of priests, God's holy nation, his very own possession. This is so you can show others the goodness of God, for he called you out of the darkness into his wonderful light." 1 Peter 2:9 (NLT)

We may be foreigners here, now that we have been born into God's family, but at least we know the way Home. We were brought out into the light and we look forward to the special blessings that will come at the return of Jesus Christ. We can know more about who and what the "gators" are and how to avoid falling into their jaws—they are anything that take our focus off of God and place it on this world, especially during those fiery trials that we must endure for the time being.

These trials are only to test our faith, to show that it is strong and pure. "It is being tested as fire tests and purifies gold - and your faith is far more precious to God that mere gold." 1 Peter 1:7 (NLT)

The Bible says, no matter what, keep your faith intact. Should life take a turn, we don't want to be sucked under it all and eaten alive! We have to keep our focus on Jesus, and then one day, the whole world will see Jesus Christ! The Bible says that even the angels are eagerly watching these things happen. (1 Peter 1:12) There is a world that we can't see, just like there is a world that the ants can't see, but that doesn't mean it isn't there. That is what faith is all about. We are God's children. We have been adopted into His family when we stepped into the "canoe" and believed.

> *So you must live in reverent fear of him during your time as foreigners here on earth. For you know that God paid a ransom to save you from the empty life you inherited from your ancestors. And the ransom he paid was not mere gold or silver. He paid for you with the precious lifeblood of Christ, the sinless, spotless Lamb of God.*
> *1 Peter 1:17-19 (NLT)*

I don't like the idea that Phil inherited an empty life from Jim and me. But it is true. We gave birth to him in this world, but it was temporary. When He accepted Christ and was born into God's family, he inherited a full life, a life that will last forever. That I do like! Phil lived as a foreigner here for a very short time, but now he is not a foreigner where he lives for all of eternity. He is Home with the family of God.

Phil trusted, when he could not see, that God was standing above him watching over everything. He trusted when it hurt and dirt clods got in his way. He trusted when strong winds blew and it didn't make sense. He trusted when the rain fell as the cancer came back over and over. He trusted. The reward for that trust was the salvation of his soul. Phil might have left this earth pretty much still drinking "spiritual milk," although in his last days I believe he quickly moved from that to soft food and onto thick steak. He was doing serious business with God toward the end, and it required serious nourishment. He "cried out for this nourishment." He needed all God had to give.

> *And now God is building you, as living stones, into his spiritual temple.*
> *1 Peter 2:5 (NLT)*

Hopefully we are growing from babies, to living stones—
something very soft into something Rock solid. That is not to say
our hearts are getting hard, it is to say that what is in this foreign
land cannot penetrate into a heart filled with God's love. It cannot
harm us. Yes, it can hurt, and it does. Losing Phil hurts. But that is
different than it harming me to the point of destroying me. This
pain will seek to devour me, but it has no power to do so when I
focus on the Hope of my Savior. With faith, we can be in that
canoe, and it can be overturned by those very 'gators, and we can
walk on water right over the top of them as one of God's
children—safe and secure in Jesus.

"They will be my people," says the Lord Almighty. "On the day
when I act, they will be my own special treasure. I will spare them
as a father spares an obedient and dutiful child. Then you will
again see the difference between the righteous and the wicked,
between those who serve God and those who do not."
Malachi 3:17-18 (NLT)

Are we God's people?

Are we even in the "canoe" yet?

Are we wise to the ways of the 'gators?

Living in His peace,
Diane

Myself

You probably know what that big 'gator is, it's the loss of Phil. It
waits to devour me any chance it can get.

I wonder what your 'gator in life is as you read this? Everyone
either has one, did have one, or will have one. No one escapes life
without trials—some trials we contribute to by making harmful
choices—some trials are thrust upon us simply because we live in
a fallen world. Either way, it doesn't make them easy. But getting

out of them, or through them, is done the same way—with Jesus. I've been thinking lately, what if God had abandoned us after His children went against His commands in the Garden of Eden? What if our Father had just turned His back on this world, and His created beings, and never had a plan of Salvation through Jesus? What would the world look like with no God in it? Those who have Jesus living in their hearts are not perfect, far from it, but at least with the Holy Spirit being given half an opportunity to work in this world, it's a better place. So many may not want God. But He still wants us—all of us—and He continues to work on our behalf. And sometimes that work comes in the form of 'gators that show us our need for Jesus, and His saving grace.

It lurks, and it prowls, and it waits for me to lose my focus so it can take me down into the deep, dark water of life.

Those dips, those pits, they come so quickly, don't they? We try to avoid them, in so many ways. We keep busy, we go shopping, we eat that piece of chocolate cake…any number of things to keep from feeling bad. So what is the answer? How do we keep our focus and not let the 'gators in our life eat us up? We get pumped up each morning! We become intentional about our thoughts, and our habits. We don't just roll out of bed and do the same old thing expecting different results. What do they call that?—a form of insanity? It is! I can't feel good by stuffing myself full of chocolate cake each day, although I would like to. The other day I just wanted chocolate cake for breakfast, so I helped myself to a piece. I regretted it afterwards—too much sugar too early in the day. This morning I was tempted again to start my day with the same "hearty" breakfast. I resisted. I remembered how I felt last time I did that, and I didn't do it again. I waited until at least after lunch before partaking. And that was fine. I wasn't going to do the same thing again, and expect a different result. I knew the result, I remembered it, and chose a different plan for my morning. That is how we grow, and learn, and progress through life. We have to stay focused on a good plan each day, and learn from it. How does it make us feel when we actually take time to be in the Word, to pray, to ask for and receive forgiveness each day? I know if I took a poll, it would be unanimous...one hundred percent of believers would say that was a good choice, a good focus to have. It benefits all believers to start our day with God in His Word, because the world will be distracting. The world will pull hard on our emotions. We need to know where our Hope lies.

Lesson Number One:
Allow God to steer.

They say if God is your co-pilot, He is in the wrong seat. We want to steer our own lives. We all do. But when we give up that control to our Father, it is a much better ride. Thinking I was in charge, once again, the other day, I began to visualize a picture my son, Jimm, sent me. It was all the planets and the sun, with their size in relation to each other. The earth is very, very small. And when I think about that, and how I am just a small speck on a very small planet, I am able to put myself back into the place where I belong...as a child of a mighty and powerful God who knows and sees all, and doesn't need my help to run the universe.

Lesson Number Two:
I may not see the final destination, but there surely is one.

As we get older, we have seen a few final destinations. We have seen things that have worked out how we would like, and those that haven't. And we have learned that most things can't be rushed, if we are getting the picture at all. When Phil was first sick, probably his second day in the hospital after his diagnosis became sure, I remember walking out of the hospital and saying to my mom, "It's not over until the fat nurse sings." I had hope on that day that Phil would live—that he would survive a very survivable cancer. He had ALL, Acute Lymphocytic Leukemia. He was only 10 ½, and initial tests showed that it had not progressed too far. He was a good candidate for a cure. I could not see the final destination on that day, but there surely was one. It was not the one I was hoping for, but it was the one God could already see. I didn't like God's answer. I didn't like God's "cure" for Phil five and a half years later. But on this day, almost 13 years after the fact, I understand it so much better. Sometimes God gets the glory by healing in miraculous ways, and sometimes God gets the glory by healing shattered hearts so those hearts can share with others that life will go on. If this life were perfect, we would already be in Heaven. Obviously, we are not. So those that will walk out their pain, and continue to give God the glory, can help another make it through until Jesus comes back. It's not a fun job, but it is a fruitful one. In reading John 15 this morning, I see that branches that are cut off are in big trouble because apart from Jesus, we can do nothing. But branches that are pruned, that stay attached to the Vine, Jesus, produce even more fruit. There is great satisfaction in bearing fruit for Jesus, even though the pruning can be very painful.

Lesson Number Three:
The 'gators are there only to test our faith in the One who saves.
They can't harm us.

Satan has no power over us, none that is not in God's will. In John 14:30, Jesus says about the enemy, "He has no power over me, but I will do what the Father requires of me…" This can give us all great confidence. It's not that 'gators aren't everywhere, and aren't attacking us a lot, because they are…it's that they are not God, nor will they ever be God. We have only one true God, and He is all powerful. Jesus did what He did on purpose, He did not die by accident, or by man's power, but because it was all in God's plan. He even told Judas to "Hurry. Do it now." (John 13:27 NLT) When Jesus was asked at the last supper who would betray Him, He said it was the one "whom I give the bread dipped in the sauce." (NLT) He gave it to Judas. Jesus was not caught by surprise. Judas was probably surprised Jesus knew it was him. The rest of the disciples probably were surprised—but not Jesus. We can take great comfort in that. What we are going through may have caught us by surprise, but not God. He is well aware of our circumstances, and well in control of them. That may make us angry at God for allowing them, but that, again, is a choice that we will make. Jesus said, "Father, bring glory to your name." Can we do the same? Some may say, "Well, I'm not Jesus." That is true, but Jesus also said, "The truth is, anyone who believes in me will do the same works I have done, and even greater works, because I am going to be with the Father." John 14:12 (NLT) There is power in the name of Jesus Christ. Are we living in it?

We have to keep away from those "gators" that seek to kill and destroy us!

I don't run into the enemy's camp if I don't have to. I don't look for trouble. I try to avoid it. Sometimes it catches up with me, and seemingly over takes me, but I don't choose to invite dangerous 'gators into my life. I am not overly cautious, but I'm not a daredevil either. That's an interesting word there, "daredevil." Why would we ever want to dare the devil to do anything in our lives, when he already feels invited to mess with us? I love C.S. Lewis' book, "The Screwtape Letters." What a perfect example of the behind the scene workings of darkness—it's going on constantly. That's why God's Word says in Ephesians 6 that we are to "stand firm against all strategies and tricks of the Devil." Satan's full of ways to cause havoc in our lives!! As my friend Aimee says, "The enemy comes in with our favorite flavor of ice cream." In talking with someone right now, who is going through a very hard time, I can see the "favorite flavors" clearly. Each day it seems to be a new one, especially if the one the day before didn't work out as the Devil would have liked. The person going through it can't see it quite so clearly. Why? Because it seems so very real to them! The lies seem real, and they have to be reminded of the Truth. That's why we need each other, especially as we go through difficult times. We need people we can trust who can call plays in from the sidelines, seeing how the opposing team is lining up. And we need those people to be grounded in the Word of God, so that the plays they are calling in to help protect us will be God's plays, and not human ways. "For we are not fighting against people made of flesh and blood, but against the evil rulers and authorities of an unseen world," on the field of life. (Eph. 6:12) If we call on the worldly to help us with the things of Satan, it simply won't work because the world and Satan are on the same team. It will be the wrong play, at the wrong time, and our opponent the Devil will get the upper hand. We need the Word of God to be our playbook to beat our opponent Satan.

We feel like foreigners here—a fish out of water, so to speak, because we are.

Do you believe in aliens? Most of us would say no, of course, so as not to be thought crazy. But this last Sunday our pastor, Rick, preached a great sermon about being foreigners here on this earth, with our real Home being in Heaven. He said we are the aliens on earth, we the children of God, and we are only passing through, as God's Word tells us. That's why the closer we get to knowing the ways of Jesus, the more we feel uncomfortable in the world around us. If we're comfortable here, we're resting our feet on the wrong "ottoman." Psalm 119 (NLT) says, "I lie in the dust, completely discouraged; revive me by your word." Our feet should be resting on the firm foundation of Jesus Christ and the Word of God. Jesus is our only Hope. Jesus died to give us eternal life. The world doesn't recognize our Savior, and most times the world thinks we are missing out on all the fun because we want to be more like Jesus. But that's okay. "It is better to trust the Lord than to put confidence in people." Psalm 118:8 (NLT)

But now that I have seen the 'gators up close and personal, I am addicted to God

We all have addictions. I have mine. You have yours. No one is exempt. But I think my son, Jimm, paid me a compliment last night when he said that I have the 1000 yard stare. I didn't know what he was talking about. He had been watching a war movie, and he was talking in military terms. He explained, "Soldiers get this stare when they have been in battle too long. It is a look that makes them look like they're seeing beyond—a look of disassociation caused by seeing great trauma. It can't be faked. It only comes from gross humanity." (Jimm just texted me that explanation. Thanks Jimm!) Because of the battles that I have seen, he has noticed that I can look beyond, and disassociate myself from the worldview, and seek God's view on most things. It is because I have watched my son die. It is because I have lived almost 13 years without him. I have seen a great war for Phil's life, that Satan seemingly won, but didn't. Jesus won the war! Satan only won the

cancer battle. Jimm now sees my "addiction" to Jesus that gives
me that "stare." He hears it in my voice. Jimm knows when he asks
me something about life, I'm not going to give him my opinion,
I'm going to give him Jesus' opinion out of the Word, even if it's
not what he wants to hear. (Even if it's not what I want to tell him.)
Why do I do this? Because it's what works. It's what brought me
this far, to this day, writing what I am writing. And if it has worked
for me, why would I tell Jimm, or anyone, anything different? And
I know that even if we don't see immediate results, and even if it
seems it's not helping, and sometimes even hurting more, that it's
still right because it is of God. God didn't heal my heart in a day,
or a week, or a year, but He healed it. I'm not a perfect counselor;
only the Holy Spirit is. But I can help others with what I have
learned. And when I am wrong, it's not God who is wrong, it's me
who is making a mistake. And for that, I will apologize. But I will
never apologize for God's ways—even when life doesn't turn out
like we want it to. Psalm 118:13 (NLT) says, "You did your best to
kill me, O my enemy, but the Lord helped me." That is all I know.
That is all I share.

*God gave Phil life when he died, because of Jesus' very own death
on the Cross. After Phil's earthly death, he began a new life, in
Heaven, which will last forever!*

My best friend, Deb, called me last night. She had something she
wanted to run by me. She is singing in her Christmas musical this
year, and although it is only October, they are already in
rehearsals. She had a question about the second to last song they
are going to sing. I had never heard it before, but she read the
words to me. It is about a loved one who has gone Home to
Heaven, and how they are missed, but how the person still on earth
is happy for them, that they will be celebrating this Christmas in
Heaven, in God's Throne Room, with the angels all around
worshiping God together. Not that Deb has any choice in the songs
they sing, but she just wanted confirmation from me so that she
could be at peace with it. After I heard the words, I told her how
much I liked it, and agreed with it being in the program. She
thought it was so sad, that it was going to make everyone cry. It
will. But that's okay. Christmas is a hard time for those who have

great sorrow and missing in their hearts. They have a hard time
going to Christmas programs and listening to merry tunes. They
want their pain to be addressed, and with this song, it will be. And
the end is good, so they don't have to be too emotional the whole
time. Deb said that their pastor will speak after the song, and then
they will finish with a joyful tune. I think that is perfect. My
husband, Jim, said, after telling him about this, that the song leads
right into the Gospel message—and without the message of the
Good News of Jesus, Christmas is worthless. If we avoid the pain,
there will be no gain. What if someone is there just hoping to get
happy, and they get saved instead because they hear the Truth
about Christmas, and not just the Santa Claus version? We can't
shrink away from what's most important, especially in the times
we are living in, and especially at Christmas. Hurting hearts are
already sad, and acknowledging their pain is being compassionate.
Like our pastor, John, preached about having an empty chair at our
Christmas table on the first Christmas Phil was not with us. He
talked about Jesus filling that chair. It helped us get through that
very hard time because he was speaking to our need, and where
our Hope is...just as this song will do. Deb hung up the phone
satisfied. She thought I might be offended if I had been there, and
this song was performed, as one who has grieved deeply on past
Christmases. Instead, I told her I would be encouraged. Deb will
sing that song with a new song in her heart now. I was glad she
called!

*Ants have no idea that the world they lived in is HUGE, because
all they knew was that little piece of the cement for now.*

For some reason I'm intrigued by the world of ants. This last
summer we were out at the pool here by the condos we live in. I
had the grandkids out there, and our grandson, Jackson, loves
science, and such. He was out of the pool, and we spotted a lone
ant crawling along a crack in the ground. We watched it together,
and then we decided to put some food down by the crack. It didn't
take long at all and there was a whole army of ants there, working
hard to carry away the food. We were having a blast watching all
the ants join in on the party. I wonder if Jesus does that...He sees a
person alone, and He drops some nourishment in the vicinity, and

it attracts others to the lone person, and they start to work together? We can't know what God is doing from His vantage point as we scurry along on this earth.

Jesus became an "Ant," so to speak, so we "ants" could see and know God.

This is a very simplified view of Jesus' visit to this earth, but it's one that makes some sense to me. Ants are so oblivious to us, and so many of us are so oblivious to Jesus. God is so big, and we are so little, we can't even look at our Father with our eyes or we would die, that's how powerful He is. But Jesus came to this earth, became very small, one of us in many ways, and still very much God, and He walked among us and taught us. He displayed God's attributes, and His character. He showed us how to treat one another, and how to forgive one another. Through miracles, Jesus showed us how powerful God really is. What is impossible for man, God can just speak into being. The other day we prayed for a friend whose knees were very painful. I had just read about Jesus smearing the mud on the man's eyes, having him wash, and then he could see. We prayed for healing, I prayed about the mud...my friend's knees still hurt, but that's okay. God's answers are not always yes. Sometimes they are no. Sometimes His answers are wait. My friend will have knee replacement surgery in the next few weeks, so her "wait" will become a "yes" as she heals through that. God provides in different ways, but He always asks us to pray. So we should, believing, and allowing God to be God as He answers.

There is a world that we can't see, just like there is a world that the ants can't see, but that doesn't mean it isn't there. That is what faith is all about.

Faith is powerful. It is life-changing. We all want to have faith, but we can't drum it up. We can't pretend and have it work. We have to learn to rest in who God is, as we learn to trust Him, and then we can watch faith work itself into our lives because of our Hope in Jesus Christ. It all comes back to Jesus and the Gospel message. Always. The Gospel is our foundation. When the cement dries, after the Holy Spirit has been poured into us upon first believing, we can be transformed into believers who say, "The LORD is my rock, my fortress, and my savior; my God is my rock, in whom I find protection. He is my shield, the power that saves me, and my place of safety." Psalm 18:2 (NLT)

Phil trusted when he could not see that God was standing above him watching over everything.

The moment Phil died, I looked up above his bed and said good-bye. I don't know how long it takes for a person's spirit to leave the room, but I wanted him to know that I knew where he was, and that I was okay with where he was going. One day, maybe he and I can discuss that moment in time—maybe not. But it won't matter by then. I do know that Jesus was watching over everything that was happening in Phil's room on that night. Much of that I have already written about in, "It Started in the Dark." God was with us even in the midst of such horrific emotional pain. Many have asked if Phil was in physical pain, because they have told me that Leukemia is a very painful death. Phil's was not. He had a sore throat from a sinus infection, but other than that, he had no pain whatsoever. I'm still coming to an understanding of what a miracle that was. I do know that he should have been bleeding out, and he wasn't. As the petechiae (small bruises) spread up his neck and onto his face, we knew that his platelets were practically gone. He had had a blood transfusion on the previous Friday, and was due for another one on Monday, but when we put him in his wheelchair, and rolled him to the front door, he looked pale and very ill. We stood by the door and we prayed if we should go. We didn't. We rolled Phil back to his room and put him back in his bed. We worked with Hospice to try and get some platelets brought to the house. They were okayed for the following Friday. Phil was gone by Wednesday night. I remember our neighbor, Annet, coming over to see how things were going. She was a nurse at one time who worked with dying children. She knew how badly Phil needed platelets. She was frustrated. I remember calmly telling her it will be okay. I didn't even know how or why I could be saying that. There again, I think it was the Holy Spirit in me who knew something I didn't know. And I believe it was God who heard our prayers by the front door, and spared Phil a non-stop nosebleed, as well as other things, during his final hours on this earth. There is so much that we don't see that God is doing. That same God that Phil trusted, that I continue to trust, is still watching over everything.

That is not to say our hearts are hard, it is to say that what is in this foreign land cannot penetrate into a heart filled with God's love.

When our hearts are filled with God's love, it can keep so many of the 'gators in life at bay. It pushes them away with Truth, and we all need that. If our hearts aren't filled with God's Word each day, it leaves too much room for doubt, fear, anger, bitterness, and all the rest. When the things of this world try to move in, let's not give them any space. Let's jump ahead of them, and fill up any emptiness with heavenly goodness.

Gift #11 – Recognizing the 'gators and winning the battle against them.

When and how do the attacks come in your own life?

Are you finding that by filling up with God's Word and time with Him, it gets you through those tough times?

Record today's date and other notes you'd like to make:

The Great

I AM

*Through Christ you have come to trust in God.
And because God raised Christ from the dead and
gave him great glory, your faith and hope can be
placed confidently in God.*
1 Peter 1:21 (NLT)

CHAPTER TWELVE

*Before you Gentiles knew God, you were slaves to so-called gods
that do not even exist. And now that you have found God (or
should I say, now that God has found you), why do you want to go
back again and become slaves once more to the weak and useless
spiritual powers of this world?*
Galatians 4:8-9 (NLT)

<u>Me</u>

'tis The Season

Monday, 07 Oct 2002

*Is it? The season that is...probably not for you. Not yet. There's
many more shopping days left until Christmas. The season I speak
of is my season—the season that starts when the leaves begin to
change their colors. It's the season that starts when September
slips into October. This season is the most difficult because Phil
would be 17 this month, and then as October slips into November,
we will remember his going Home, and his first Thanksgiving in
Heaven. Then we will remember his service on December first, and
buying a Christmas tree shortly after that. We will remember doing*

practically all of our Christmas shopping in one day, in one store, and thinking that was just fine, because it just didn't seem to matter much.

We will remember. And we will pray. We will pray harder than we probably ever have, that this season will not take us back to that very difficult place we were in last year.

Before you Gentiles knew God, you were slaves to so-called gods that do not even exist. And now that you have found God (or should I say, now that God has found you), why do you want to go back again and become slaves once more to the weak and useless spiritual powers of this world?
Galatians 4:8-9 (NLT)

I don't want to go back. We don't want to. We have come so far, we have learned so much, and we have begun to heal...and yet, what we must face now can seem larger than life. It can seem larger than death—even larger than God, if we let it.
Will we?
I pray we won't!

There seems to be an unwritten law in the world, one that says this season must take us down. It must seek to destroy us, and we must submit to it. I struggle with that because I know that God is greater than this unwritten law. Maybe I have gone too far. Maybe I am hoping for too much. I don't know. What I do know is—God is greater than any power the devil has, and He can rescue us from anything. I guess the question is, will He?

It was the same with Phil and his leukemia. I know that God has the power to heal anyone from anything. We prayed that for Phil. The question was, would He? I believe He did, right before he died, but God still took Phil Home. So to the world, the answer seems to have been "No."

Perhaps this season will be the same. Perhaps God will say, "No, there are things that you will learn that are necessary for your future, and it may hurt as I am refining you, but there is good reason for it. This will be an extra tough season in your life."

Perhaps... But I can still pray. Just as I prayed for Phil's healing and trusted God even when He took him Home. I can still pray that God will spare me from this hurting season.

I will trust God, no matter what.

As September slipped into October the battle began to rage. It seemed the evil one stepped up with extra forces and arrows to sling into my heart, trying to reopen wounds that have recently just healed. The enemy is trying to force his way into areas that would take me back months and months if allowed to penetrate. Strangely, I think they should. And yet, I wonder. Is this the law of the world, and if I am no longer under that law, but under the law of God's love, do I have to comply?

I am a stubborn sort. I have told you that, and God knows that. Sometimes I just don't want to go with the flow. Tell me I can't, and I'll show you I can! If the devil tells me I must crash and burn during this season, I'll show you where God says I don't have to!

He died for our sins, just as God our Father planned, in order to rescue us from this evil world in which we live. Galatians 1:4 (NLT)

So Christ has really set us free. Now make sure that you stay free, and don't get tied up again in slavery to the law. Galatians 5:1 (NLT)

"Make sure that you stay free." That's easier said than done if we don't remember Who fights these battles for us.

"The old sinful nature loves to do evil, which is just opposite from what the Holy Spirit wants. And the Spirit gives us desires that are opposite from what the sinful nature desires. These two forces are constantly fighting each other, and your choices are never free

from this conflict. But when you are directed by the Holy Spirit, you are no longer subject to the law." Galatians 5:17-18 (NLT)

I am not subject even to the "law" of grief. I can be free from it if I will stay focused on the One who sets me free from it. But the "forces" are battling hard right now.

The devil wants to remind me that my son has died.

God wants to remind me that Phil lives for all eternity.

The devil wants to remind me how he suffered.

God wants to remind me that Phil suffers no more.

The devil wants to remind me that if I truly loved Phil, I should not smile, and laugh, and enjoy my life.

God reminds me that I will love Phil all my days and because Christ's Spirit is greater in me than the spirit who lives in the world. (1 John 4:4) I can smile, and laugh, and enjoy my life because I will see Phil again.

The "forces," back and forth, forth and back, every day, every night, the battle rages and yet:

> *So don't get tired of doing what is good.*
> *Don't get discouraged and give up for we will reap*
> *a harvest of blessing at the appropriate time.*
> *Galatians 6:9 (NLT)*

A harvest of blessing awaits. That reminds me of Thanksgiving, and it reminds me how thankful I am to God for all He has done. So many say, "Anything God. Anything but my child. Please don't take my child." Believe me, I was one of those. Aren't all parents? But God has taken my child Home, and now I am on the other side of that experience, and because God is God, and His promises are true, it is possible to go on. Sure, there was a time when I really didn't want to, and I have to tell you, I still don't mind the thought of death. I even dream about it! Let me tell you about a dream I had last week.

Jim and I were driving along the road in our RV, and we came around a corner and fell into a huge pothole. HUGE! The whole rig was falling down, down, down into this pit. I remember the sides of the pit being green, and I remember putting my arms up into the air and saying "Here I come God!" I knew this was it. I was going to die and see God. And then, I hit the bottom. My back hit, then my head, and it went dark...and then I woke up in the hospital. Alive. Others had died in my dream, but not my friend, Linette, who has also lost her son. I walked into her hospital room and we laughed together because we had wanted to die, but God had spared us. He had work for us to do.

Two strange things about this dream... One is, it was in color, and two is, I actually hit bottom. My friend told me that people don't hit the bottom in their dreams. But I did! I think I was just a little too anxious to go "Home." But, I am a mother with a son who is waiting for me there!

So yes, I get tired sometimes, and I get discouraged, but God knows that. That's why He tells us not to give up because there is a harvest of blessings awaiting us. Those blessings happen every day, even in our grief.

> *Don't be misled. Remember that you can't ignore God and get away with it. You will always reap what you sow!*
> *Galatians 6:7 (NIV)*

If I ignore God during this most difficult time, I will reap what I sow. I will end up fighting my own battles and I will be defeated. I will crash and burn into a pit of despair, and I will have only myself to blame. I will have chosen the darkness over the light, because I want to. And, I may just want to. The human fleshly side of me may say, "I want to go there. I want to wallow in my misery during this season. I deserve it. I lost my son. I am miserable."

That's what I may do.

Or...

I will choose not to, and I will focus on the One who saves. This is not to say I won't shed tears, I won't feel pain, and I won't miss my son with everything I have inside of me, but I won't stay there for the whole month of October, November, and December, coming up for air in January wounded from the fight. I will feel the battle going on, and I will call for help. I will be taken down with moments of great despair and missing, but I will call out "Medic!" and God will come right over and bandage my wounds. I will hear the arrows whizzing past my head, and I will put on all of God's armor for protection against them, (Eph. 6:11) and I will call for back-ups, and reinforcements, by asking all of you to pray for us. We are not in this alone.

Dear brothers and sisters, if another Christian is overcome by some sin, you who are godly should gently and humbly help that person back onto the right path. And be careful not to fall into the same temptation yourself. Share each other's troubles and problems, and in this way obey the law of Christ.
Galatians 6:1-2 (NLT)

I think we have no idea what prayer does in this world. I think we have only been given small glimpses of the power it yields. I have a feeling when we get to Heaven that we will see how much others have helped us along the way because they stopped to pray for our needs. I am still in the process of learning about prayer. But one thing I don't want to have happen is to get to Heaven and see that if I had only whispered a small prayer for someone, I could have helped them greatly. I don't want to have missed out on that opportunity because I neglected to do it.

We are all in a battle in this world. Sometimes it doesn't rage quite so much, but other times it does, and we all need each other more than we could ever know.

> *Whenever we have the opportunity, we should do good to everyone, especially to our Christian brothers and sisters. Galatians 6:10 (NLT)*

> *For you have been called to live in freedom - not freedom to satisfy your sinful nature, but freedom to serve one another in love. Galatians 5:13 (NLT)*

So, will you please pray for us during this intense season of battle? It is not something I have experienced before. I don't know how it will be. I only know that if it is anything like the calendar simply slipping over from September to October, it will be a rough road if I don't have my complete focus on God. I'm not sure why. I can't even explain it except to say that it's those "forces" that seek to destroy us.

Satan may be saying, "Oh, here's an opportunity boys! Let's get them!"

But God is greater!

> *From now on, don't let anyone trouble me with these things. For I bear on my body the scars that show I belong to Jesus. Galatians 6:17 (NLT)*

I bear those scars on my heart. They are scars that will always be there, but they are scars from battles that have already been fought and won. They are reminders of God's goodness and healing power in my life. They were not the first scars in my life, and they will not be the last, but I hope each and every one of them brings me closer in my relationship with God the Father and His Son Jesus Christ.

> *Because of that cross, my interest in this world died long ago, and the world's interest in me is also long dead.--What counts is whether we really have been changed into new and different people. Galatians 6:14-15b (NLT)*

Jim and I are new and different people. And that is good! We are happy to be where we are, and happy to watch where God may be taking us. We will be driving up to Tahoe for a couple of days to spend what would have been Phil's 17th birthday among the beauty of the trees and the lake. I can smell it already! We don't want to sit home and think about it. We can think about it there, and hopefully draw closer to God by enjoying the wonderful places He has created for us to go when our hearts have been broken.

We see God's hand upon our lives as He gently guides us into the future. Even when we are in a fog of despair, we hear Him calling us to follow Him out into the light. We see His perfect timing in all things, and are comforted to know that we don't have to know all things, because God does. We miss Phil every single day. But every single day brings new Hope, and new ways of coping with not having him here with us. We hear of others who are suffering with leukemia and we pray for them and are reminded of all that Phil endured while he was here. Phil fought such a good fight and was so very patient through it all.

> *The strength of a horse does not impress him;*
> *how puny in his sight is the strength of a man.*
> *Rather, the Lord's delight is in those who honor him,*
> *those who put their hope in his unfailing love.*
> *Psalm 147:10-11 (NLT)*

Our Hope is in Christ's unfailing love, just as Phil's was.
What else can we hope for in this world?
What else is there that never fails us?
Nothing!
Our strength is pitiful compared to God's!

The arrows will fly, the battles will rage, and the only one true "Medic" we have is God. We will call on Jesus during this season of battle knowing that the victory has already been won.

Living in His peace,
Diane

Myself

This season is the most difficult because Phil would be 17 this month, and then as October slips into November, we will remember his going Home, and his first Thanksgiving in Heaven.

I find it very interesting that I am writing this chapter this week. It is Tuesday, and on Thursday Phil would have been 29. God's timing is always perfect. I believe God wants to remind me of His great healing power over the last 12 years. Jesus is talking about His departure in John 14, and he says to His disciples, "I have told you these things before they happen so that you will believe when they do happen." It reminds me of reading Scripture in the early days of grief—about God's great healing power, and how Jesus came to bind up the brokenhearted. He told me those things **before** they happened, so that **when** they happened, I would believe. I **believe**!

We will remember doing practically all of our Christmas shopping in one day, in one store, and thinking that was just fine, because it just didn't seem to matter much.

I can't remember what I had for dinner last night, most days, but I do remember this day. Jim and I did that first Christmas shopping together, which is not the norm for us, and we got everything we needed in one store. I have been prayerfully shopping with God since, and He really does help us find what we need. I have to believe that God's holy angels were guiding us through the aisles that first Christmas, pointing out what was needed, and giving us the strength to even care enough to do it. "They will hold you with their hands to keep you from striking your foot on a stone." Psalm 91:12 (NLT) The greatest gift that Christmas, and every Christmas since then, is the peace Jesus left us with 2,000 years ago.

I don't want to go back. We don't want to. We have come so far, we have learned so much, and we have begun to heal...

The firsts were SO painful, and the seconds weren't much better. I know that I was hoping they would be, but grief takes a long time, and the holidays are the most difficult time. There's many things we can rush in this world—we can rush through crowds, speed down freeways, hurry through the grocery stores... But healing comes in its own time. Just the other day my friend, Michella, had surgery. When I saw her scar just the next day, I was shocked. It looked a week old. She said she heals quickly. She must! The hard part is, she still has a lot of pain inside her neck and back to heal through. Grief could look more healed on the outside than it is, while on the inside, the pain still runs very deep. We have to give it time, even when we don't want to.

Maybe I am hoping for too much. I don't know. What I do know is that God is greater than any power the devil has, and He can rescue us from anything. I guess the question is, will He?

Will He? I really asked this question of our mighty God? Wow! I was still struggling with many things at this point. I wanted God's healing, but I wasn't sure after almost a year that it was truly possible. It still hurt so badly. I think it's the world view on grief...the world operates differently than what God's Word says. Jesus said, "The world would love you if you belonged to it, but you don't." (John 15:19 NLT) I think we must view grief, many times, in a very worldly way. I did too. I wasn't totally confident in the promises I read in God's Word. Just the other day I heard it said once again, "You never really heal from the loss of a child." And I had to disagree. A heart can heal because God is just that powerful! Missing is quite a different matter. We will always miss those we love who have gone Home. But we don't have to always hurt from it. As the leaves turn golden this Fall, my heart does not hurt. I remember, and I remember well, but I am not in pain. I am just in missing. I am enjoying the memories, even if tears may well in my eyes when I see pumpkins in front of the grocery stores. Life has continued on fully and joyfully. What more can I ask for? I don't want to forget Phil and not miss him. I want to remember the things we shared and praise God that we had that time together.

Perhaps God will say, "No, there are things that you will learn that are necessary for your future, and it may hurt as I am refining you, but there is good reason for it.
I can still pray that God will spare me from this hurting season.

We wanted to be spared from the pain. I did. We all do. We want it to be over, and done with...quickly. But there is much to be learned during those painful times. We will learn that God is our pain relief, as nothing and no one else can be. When we need to return to Jesus again and again, reading God's Word, praying, taking all our grievances right into the Throne Room and laying them at the Father's feet, we will learn. If God spared us this process in healing what hurts most, would we ever really get to know Him as we should? Would we find that the peace Jesus left us with is real? If Jesus had not left this world after His resurrection so that He could send us the Holy Spirit, who actually now lives inside of us, we would be missing out on so much. Jesus said, "But it is actually best for you that I go away, because if I don't, the Counselor won't come. If I do go away, he will come because I will send him to you." John 16:7 (NLT) Sometimes, it seems so wrong, but it is so right! We have to change our thinking and get in agreement with what God is doing, because what He is doing, works for our best interest.

"Make sure that you stay free." That's easier said than done if we don't remember Who fights these battles for us.

We can't do this on our own. We can't even do it with the help of only our friends and family, because they are in similar battles. They need us as much as we need them, so we all ultimately need Jesus! Others will fall short, and then we will get angry. Jesus never falls short, and if we get angry at Him, He understands and helps us through it. Satan wants to pull us under, to veil our eyes, to confuse us as he lies to us about EVERYTHING. He is the father of lies. He is full of deceit. Jesus is full of Truth and Life. He's not only full of those things, He **is** those things! He said, "I am the way, the truth, and the life." John 14:6 (NLT) God cannot lie, and Jesus is God, so He cannot lie. The Holy Spirit cannot lie as He guides us from within. We get confused because we don't know who we are hearing sometimes, who is guiding us. The other day I was told by someone two things they were struggling with. Just upon hearing them, it was clear which one was Biblical and which one was not. I asked this person to take a look at that, and they did, and then it became very clear to them which answer was from God, and which was not. When we hold things up to the light of Scripture, we will find our answer. Sometimes it is not so clear cut, but most times it is. Satan doesn't want us to know that it can be that simple. He wants us to be wound up tight as a top and as entangled as a large ball of twine. That is his world, and he tempts us to live in it, but we don't have to. We can stay free of all of that by focusing on Truth, Truth, Truth!

The enemy is trying to force his way into areas that would take me back months and months if allowed to penetrate. Strangely, I think they should. And yet, I wonder. Is this the law of the world, and if I am no longer under that law, but under the law of God's love, do I have to comply?

The answer is, "No." We don't have to comply with any of Satan's tactics. We will be tempted to, for as long as we live on this earth; it is a constant battle. But we can learn, grow, and do better by knowing the Holy Spirit better. Satan still wants to draw me back into hurt and sadness. And it's tempting to do so, even 12 years later. But I've been there, and I don't want to be there anymore. It is a choice that I make, daily. When we do what God tells us in Philippians 4:8-9, and fix our thoughts on things that are true, honorable, right, pure, lovely, admirable, excellent, and worthy of praise, "the God of peace will be with you." What are we looking at each day? Are we watching TV shows that lift us up or bring us down? Are we reading books that depress us, or books that encourage us? Are we spending time with people who are negative and full of criticism? Are **we** full of negativity and criticism? I have heard that wherever the mind goes, the man follows. If I dwell on pumpkins in front of grocery stores, I will be heading into a pit, even today. But if I glance at them, take note of them, remember sweet times with Phil and his excitement during his birthday season and all that it entailed, and then move on, I find that the peace of God will be with me. It is a choice for all of us. One road makes us miserable; the other leads us up to the heights with God.

The devil wants to remind me that my son has died.

And the devil does, still to this day. And I remind the devil that Phil is the most blessed of all of us. He doesn't have a care in the world, because he is not in this world anymore. Phil lives in a place that Jesus prepared for him, and it is wonderful. Sorry, Satan, you were thrown out of Heaven, and you are stuck on this earth, and much worse...the blazing furnace awaits you when all is said and done.

God wants to remind me that Phil lives for all eternity.

Thank You, Lord Jesus! Who is our friend here? Satan or God? That's obvious! Who is wanting us stuck in our pain, and who is wanting to free us from the hopelessness of this world? Our Father in Heaven has a plan, and it is a good one! Jesus came so that we could all have Hope, no matter how dire our circumstances are. We have a friend, Sharon, who loves Jesus and now lives with Him in Heaven. She was paralyzed, from the neck down, 15 years ago in a car accident. She and Don had two young children at the time. Just a month or so ago, Sharon was in another car accident. This one took her life after about two weeks in the hospital ICU. Don was by her bed every day, sending out messages of Sharon's condition, and ending each message with GOD IS REAL. When Sharon went Home to Heaven, Don had an empty wheelchair added to his already tattooed back. Don's focus is right and true; he knows where Sharon is and that she doesn't need wheelchairs in Heaven. His heart is broken, as are the hearts of their two now nearly-grown children, but their faith in Jesus will carry them through this time until they see Sharon again.

The "forces," back and forth, forth and back, every day, every night, the battle rages...

We are never to feel alone in our struggles, because we all have them. If I don't today, you probably do, and mine will be returning tomorrow. That's why we all need our Hope to be in Jesus, our God who never wavers, who is the same yesterday, today, and forever. I don't have a personal storm right now, no huge winds blowing through my life, but I know some very close to me who do. My calm seas right now allow me time and energy to help them. Not that I can calm their seas, but I can continually point them to the One who can. I don't have all the answers, but I know where they can be found, so I turn there often. A person I know, who is having a difficult time, has another person helping them along the way. The interesting thing is, we both give the same "advice." And we haven't even talked to each other. We are only talking to God and the person who is struggling. That is confirming and encouraging when we are looking for answers. The Holy Spirit, who lives in each one of us, can keep us connected and on the same page when that page is God's written Word. I love seeing God work in that way. It is faith building to the helpers, as well as to the person who needs help.

...it is possible to go on. Sure, there was a time when I really didn't want to, and I have to tell you, I still don't mind the thought of death.

Life has gone on, and it continues to. Jim and I enjoy this time in life, just the two of us, with a simple routine, and a togetherness that we've worked hard to sustain. Marriage is not easy, and there were times when we really could have thrown in the towel. I am so thankful now that neither of us did. We also agree on the subject of death. I'm not trying to be morbid here, I'm just being real. In the beginning of deep sorrow, death seems welcomed. But now that we are not at that place any more, one would think death does not seem quite so welcomed. But it is, for both of us. It's not because our lives are miserable—our lives are good, and we enjoy good health, for the most part—but it's because our view on eternity is wide, and long, and Hope-filled. Leaving what is not our home for our heavenly Home is something we look forward to. And above that, what we really look forward to each and every day is Jesus' return for all those who believe in Him. The Bible tells us, "Two men will be in the field; one will be taken and the other left." Matthew 24:40 (NLT) The movie, "Left Behind," was just released. Jim and I saw it the other day. The series of books written are not totally Biblical, but what is correct is that many will be left behind. The mayhem that will cause in this world will be catastrophic. We have to believe this will happen if we believe the Bible. "The word 'rapture' comes from the Latin word rapturo, which is a translation of the Greek verb 'caught up' that's found in 1 Thessalonians 4:17. (Taken from the site *Rapture Ready*) The site went on to say that "Those that think the rapture is not spoken about in the Bible need to understand that even the word Bible is not in the Bible. There are no English words in the original text because it was in Hebrew and Greek." The Truth is there in print. It's important that it's also in our heart, and that we share it with others so as few as possible get left behind when Jesus returns. Jesus said in John 14:3, "When everything is ready, I will come and get you..." We don't know when everything will be ready, only the Father knows the time of Jesus' return, but we **can** know if we are ready!

Let me tell you about a dream I had last week.

I am going to go cautiously here...or maybe not. Most of what I write is bold, so why not the subject of dreams? This last year I was introduced to how God can and will speak to us through dreams. It's one of those things I'd never really paid much attention to. It's sort of like when you get a new car. Suddenly all you see is that make and model of car on the road and you never noticed them before. When I learned a bit about dreams, my eyes were opened to how much God spoke through dreams to people in the Bible. Just look at Mary and Joseph alone. One example in Matthew 1:20, "But after he had considered this, an angel of the Lord appeared to him in a dream and said, 'Joseph son of David, do not be afraid to take Mary home as your wife...'" And in Genesis 31:11, and 31:24 God spoke to Jacob in his dreams. The list is many, but I never spotted them, until they were shown to me. Not only was I not paying any real attention to my dreams, I never realized the symbolism they held, and how God can use dreams to warn us, encourage us, teach us, etc...

Jim and I were driving along the road in our RV, and we came around a corner and fell into a huge pothole... I remember putting my arms up into the air and saying "Here I come God!" I knew this was it. I was going to die and see God. And then, I hit the bottom. My back hit, then my head, and it went dark...

When I got to this writing, and I was recalling this dream, I was intrigued. I had never really tried to interpret it. I didn't know anything about how to do that. But looking at it today, it doesn't need much interpretation. It's pretty straightforward. It seems to be saying that Jim and I are on a journey, and we will go into a very deep dark pit, thinking we will die from it. We will be willing, and it will hurt. When we hit the bottom it will be dark.

...and then I woke up in the hospital. Alive. Others had died in my dream, but not my friend, Linette, who has also lost her son. I walked into her hospital room and we laughed together because we had wanted to die, but God had spared us. He had work for us to do.

I remember when reading this how it felt to hit the bottom of the pit in the dream. I hit with a hard thud. My head snapped back into the ground. I can look back now and know that dark pit was grief, and it was a long way down, and it hurt, and I was ready to die. But it didn't kill me. And it didn't kill Linette after the death of her son. We are both still here, fighting the good fight in the varying forms of ministry God has for us to do.

Two strange things about this dream... One is, it was in color, and two is, I actually hit bottom.

God usually gives something in the dream that ties into real life in a way so we realize we are on target with what it seems He is trying to convey. I know, now, why the sides of the pit were green. Green was Phil's favorite color. I lived through hitting the bottom in the dream, and I lived through it in real life, too...not just on Phil's first birthday in Heaven, but every one after that. I never would have thought that dreams would be part of my relationship with God—but they can be, and are, in very interesting ways.

If I ignore God during this most difficult time, I will reap what I sow. I will end up fighting my own battles and I will be defeated.

It's a temptation to ignore God and do things our own way, because we want to. I read recently that it's not that the temptations are too big, it's that our God is too small—the way we perceive Him. When we really understand all that Jesus died to give us, how He suffered on our behalf, and how undeserving we are of His Grace, we will be much more willing to say no to what drags us away from Him, and yes to what brings us toward Him.

That's what I may do.

Sounds like I was still deciding 12 years ago, which way I would go. I'm so thankful, on this day, that I kept on the path of healing. It does pay off. I could have chosen some very destructive ways of getting through such a tremendous loss, but thankfully, by the grace of God, I didn't. When I see others on a similar path now, I keep encouraging them to keep doing what they are doing with Jesus. Jesus has the answers to all of life's challenges.

Or... I will choose not to, and I will focus on the One who saves.

Jesus saves. That's why I am writing here today. If He didn't, I wouldn't be here doing this. I'd be involved in some other activity on this day.

I think we have no idea what prayer does in this world. I think we have only been given small glimpses of the power it yields.

How much should we pray? How should we pray? With whom should we pray? All good questions, but the best answer is, just pray! We can pray when we wake up in the morning, just thanking God for the day and His love. We can pray when we are making breakfast, thanking God for His provisions. We can pray when we are sending the kids out the door for their safety. We can pray when our husband calls from work and is having a hard day. We can pray when we aren't feeling well. We can pray about anything, at any time. If we make prayer into a huge chore with a big long list, chances are we won't do it. But if we pray like we are just talking to our Friend, it can be enjoyable. I'm heading off to a women's retreat this weekend. I don't know one woman who is going, since we haven't been at our church for a long time. There would have been a time when I wouldn't have gone alone. But I know I'm not alone anymore. Ever. As always, I will have my Friend with me each step of the way. I look forward to what Jesus has planned, who I will meet, or not meet, and what He will show me that I've never seen before. I expect to have a good time with my Friend. I will pray this weekend, and enjoy each minute with God! One added note, if we are asked to pray for someone, do it right then and there with them. Let's not wait until we get home. It's such a good way to connect with others and with our God. And if we get a message that someone needs prayer, let's pray immediately, just a whisper up to God will be better than the guilt we will feel later because we unintentionally forgot. We don't have to wait for a specific time to pray, God is available 24-7.

Jim and I are new and different people. And that is good... We will be driving up to Tahoe for a couple of days to spend what would have been Phil's 17th birthday among the beauty of the trees and the lake.

We had a very difficult, very blessed time on that trip to Tahoe. We did things we had never done, and made new memories. We just tried to get through Phil's birthday as best we could. It was extremely painful. That's to be expected. But this Thursday will be different. I will be working, Jim will be working, and God will continue to work in our hearts showing us the tremendous blessing it is to follow Jesus.

We miss Phil every single day. But every single day brings new Hope, and new ways of coping with not having him here with us.

I love thinking about Phil, but sometimes there are hard memories. Today on Facebook someone posted a picture of a boy. It was sort of a joke, matching the boy's face up with a cartoon character. No harm was meant, really, I guess, but it made me sad. The young boy had features much like Phil did when he was taking steroids. It makes the face very round, the cheeks prominent, with a slight hump in the upper back by the neck. At least, that's the way Phil looked. I wanted to comment on that picture. I wanted to say how it hurts when others are teased, and how one never knows what might be going on in a person's life. I haven't commented on it, as yet. I may still. But I took note of it, and I want to be more understanding and kinder when someone might look a little different. We can't know their struggles, but we can be loving. Twelve years ago that "joke" would have had me in a puddle of tears. Today it only stings a bit. There are a lot of things that come into a grieving person's life that hurt deeply, and we do learn to cope. What Satan means for harm, God can surely use for good when we focus on our Hope instead of our despair.

We will call on Jesus during this season of battle knowing that the victory has already been won.

And we continue to enjoy Jesus' victory every single day. What we have learned, not only helps us, it helps those around us, and those who come after us. The ripple effect that goes out when a life is dedicated to Jesus started with the disciples, and trickles down to us still today. Who are we passing it on to? Let's never give up the fight, when we know the One who goes before us.

Gift #12 – Learning, living, and sharing with others.

What past days are coming back around again for you?

Have you learned a new way of walking through them with Jesus that you can share with others?

Record today's date and other notes you'd like to make:

The Great

I AM

Because of that cross, my interest in this world died long ago, and the world's interest in me is also long dead. -- What counts is whether we really have been changed into new and different people.
Galatians 6:14-15b

CHAPTER THIRTEEN

If you really love me, you will be very happy for me,
because now I can go to the Father, who is greater than I am.
John 14:28 (NLT)

<u>Me</u>

...Circle 'round The Moon

Wednesday, 16 Oct 2002

As I woke this morning in our darkened room in Tahoe (I think
they put black-out shades on those windows for late night
gamblers), I opened my eyes...and realized that this was it. It was
the 16th and just as in my dream, I woke up knowing I'd fallen to
the bottom of the "pit." And I was alive. I looked around and sort
of took an inventory—no pain, and still breathing. I got up and I
lifted the shade and let the sun into the room. It was a beautiful
day! Phil's first birthday in Heaven. I wondered what it would
hold. I grabbed my notebook and wrote a poem:

Birthdays in Heaven

Your first birthday in Heaven, will they make a birthday cake?
Are there mothers there to do it? I bet Mary knows how to bake.
Will they serve your favorite foods? Are you allowed to pick?
Breakfast, lunch and dinner...Will there be a measuring stick
To see how you have grown, especially since you're well?
Will you be at your full height? It's hard for me to tell.
Will you get to make a list, of all the things you'd like?
Are there toy stores up in Heaven? Have you ordered a new bike?
Will Jesus come a calling, to sing these words to you,
Happy Birthday Philip...we've so many things to do!
There are no limitations, as you have always known
We'll fly through all the galaxies, count the stars as we go
We'll visit with our Father, and sit upon His lap
He'll give you a birthday hug, and oh how we will laugh
We'll run along the clouds, and circle 'round the moon
Spending this day in Heaven hasn't really come too soon
It's just the way we planned it, long before your birth
Sixteen years with your family, then you'd leave the earth
And join us all in Heaven, we're so happy that you're here
We know how much they miss you, but it won't be too many years
Until you're all together, and then they all will see
Birthdays spent in Heaven, are the best there could ever be!

"If you really love me, you will be very happy for me,
because now I can go to the Father, who is greater than I am."
John 14:28 (NLT)

This is what Jesus said before He left this earth. I smile when I read it because I know I should be happy for Phil. He is with the Father. And you know what? I am happy for Phil, because I love him that much! I thought of what he would be doing if he were still here for his 17th birthday, and if it meant that he was barely able to do the things he enjoys, if at all, then please Lord, let him be with You! I want him to fly through all the galaxies and circle 'round the moon!

A new bike? Who needs a new bike when there are no limitations any more?
Not Phil. Not now!

We were in Tahoe, as Phil spent his first birthday in Heaven. It is a beautiful mountainous area with a lake so large it could supply the United States with water for five and a half years, including showers, before it would run dry. If it did run dry, it would take over 700 years to refill it! That's one big bathtub!

How did I find out this information? Because we took a ride on that beautiful lake today in a steamboat. We left from South Shore and cruised over to Zephyr Cove and back. The day could not have been more beautiful. We could have seen North Shore if not for the curvature of the earth. I told you it was a big lake! Tahoe means "big water" in Indian—just some of the facts.

This was not a planned adventure. Nothing, today, was planned except to rise and make it through the day, anyway we could. It turned out better than we could have expected. Why? Because God is so good, and because we were covered with all your prayers. We felt them. When it seemed as if we should be so miserable, we wondered why we were not. We weren't fighting it either. It was just a peace that settled over our day—a joy, or as I've heard it put before, a calm delight. We weren't jumping up and down, laughing our heads off in glee. We were putting one foot in front of the other, as God led us through the day in the way He would have us go.

We arrived at the boat a half hour before it was due to leave the dock, so we bought our tickets and boarded. We ordered lunch and as it arrived, we set out...with just a slight delay. You've heard about the narrow path in the Bible? Well, there is a narrow path in Lake Tahoe, too—the one this boat takes away from the dock and into the deep blue water. The wind was blowing and the boat kept getting stuck in the sand to the left of this narrow path, and it took an extra hour to free it, along with the help of all the passengers moving to the right side of the ship to take the weight off the left side. I told Jim it was turning into a "three hour cruise," and we all know what that could mean. Skipper?

> *You have died with Christ, and he has set you free from the evil*
> *powers of this world.*
> *Colossians 2:20 (NLT)*

Do you know that this is what happened today? The evil powers of this world wanted us to be miserable and Christ set us free—just like that boat! We listened to God, and we moved where He told us to move, and we prayed as He told us to pray, and we waited on Him...and we were set free.

Here's how it all went...

The days leading up to Phil's birthday, the ones that God has not provided for because He has told us all not to worry about tomorrow for it has enough trouble of its own, were spent worrying. Okay, that's a little harsh. But let's just say the fear wanted to overtake the peace that God was providing, big time. I could feel it rising up inside of me, and I thought it might devour me like lions do! But God kept reminding me of this:

> *Don't be afraid, for I am with you.*
> *Do not be dismayed, for I am your God.*
> *I will strengthen you. I will help you.*
> *I will uphold you with my victorious right hand.*
> *Isaiah 41:10 (NLT)*

That fear wanted its way. But, God is true to His Word! He is with us. He was with me. He kept the fear away and allowed me to get to the 16th without going crazy just thinking about it. That is the hardest part. I could feel it, and it felt so overwhelming. Why is the thinking about it harder than the actual doing of it? It's crazy how it works. But when I thought about it, I thought of that verse above, I thought about my dream when I said, "Here I come God," and I thought about putting my arms up in the air and letting go and falling into Him, and Jesus always caught me, especially today.

*I thought about the battle being the Lord's. I would work at
pushing the fear away, and giving it up to God, then thanking Him
for fighting this battle for me—and it worked. But it was work,
because I was fearing what was not yet time to be feared, if at all.
When the day actually arrived, I didn't work. I was carried,
completely—by your prayers, to the Father, through His Son, and I
was given comfort by the Holy Spirit in me.*

*I looked up at that blue sky today, from that boat on the lake, and I
thought about Phil and where he is. I thought about why it is so
hard to really believe that he is out there somewhere, because my
mind cannot fathom what it must be like in Heaven. I know that is
what faith is all about, and I have faith, but I still think about it.
Who wouldn't? And then it came to me... Why is it so hard to
imagine that Phil is with God at this very moment, when I KNOW
that God is with me—that He lives inside of me? I don't question
that. I know it to be true, if by no other way, than by the way He
carried me through this day without a struggle. That is a miracle
to me! Why did I not crash and burn today in a pile of tears? Only
with the grace and mercy of God! Yes, there were moments when I
could have "gone there," but very few—unlike the last week or so
of a constant bombardment of painful thoughts. Not today. Today
was a day of calm delight...of being glad that Phil was spending
his birthday in Heaven and knowing that he is well at last! Crazy
you may say, but I'm only sharing with you what happened, piece
by piece.*

God blesses the people who patiently endure testing.
James 1:12 (NLT)

*I don't know how patient I have been. But God surely blessed us
today above all days!*

*After we left the boat, we started our drive home. Jim took
Highway 88. I have never seen such fall colors in the state of
California! There were a gorgeous mixture of gold, orange, some
reds, and other colors mixed in. We had to stop the car more than*

once so I could get out and take pictures just because they were so beautiful. Others, along the way, were doing the same thing.

We were high in elevation and there were so many spectacular scenes that would take our breath away. It made me think about our drive around the lake, the day before, when we stopped at different places to look out over the beauty, as so many people did. I thought about all that God has created for us to enjoy, and especially when our hearts can be so broken. He has provided a way to endure it all, and grow, just as the Bible says.

> *Dear brothers and sisters, whenever trouble comes your way, let it be an opportunity for joy. For when your faith is tested, your endurance has a chance to grow.*
> *James 1:2-3 (NLT)*

I believe it! We have had some troubles, as you know, and getting through each piece of the puzzle, while searching for the picture that God is creating, sometimes gets to be a bit much. As much as we want God's will for our lives, it is so hard to give up our son in the process. We don't understand it all. But we know we may never understand it all. In the meantime, there will be joy, as there was today. And each time we feel the joy of the Lord, during the difficult trials, our faith in God expands in new ways. We know that if we just hold on, just hold on and keep the faith, we will grow through the experience and we'll be that much better for it.

> *But if you keep looking steadily into God's perfect law - the law that sets you free - and if you do what it says and don't forget what you heard, then God will bless you for doing it.*
> *James 1:25 (NLT)*

It really works! Today I was holding God to His promises, and He passed with flying colors. I wanted all that He had offered me.

This was written about Abraham:

You see, he was trusting God so much that he was willing
to do whatever God told him to do. His faith was
made complete by what he did - by his actions.
James 2:22 (NIV)

I will do what You ask God. I will surrender this day to You. I will
put my arms up into the air and fall into You, and rest, and see if I
find perfect peace there, on a less than perfect day.

So humble yourselves before God. Resist the Devil,
and he will flee from you. Draw close to God and
God will draw close to you.
James 4:7-8 (NIV)

I willingly admitted that I couldn't do this. My strength is gone,
long gone, and this day is too big of an assignment for me. I
couldn't pass this test without God to help me. It's not that it would
kill me, but I wanted more. I wanted peace and joy on this day.
That's what is offered. That's what I wanted!

I'm here to tell you that if you resist the devil, if you resist the
world and what it tells you, that God is bigger than all of it. He
can give you perfect peace in the middle of a terrible storm. I'm
here to tell you that when you crawl under the shadow of His
wings and let the storm pass, it's not dark under there! The sun
shines, the birds sing, and the water laps against the rocks on the
shoreline. The breeze blows through the trees, and there is peace
that transcends understanding.

When you bow down before the Lord and admit your
dependence on him, he will lift you up and give you honor.
James 4:10 (NLT)

Why do we get so prideful and stubborn and think we can do it on
our own when we don't have to? Why do we even want to? I know.
I was there. And yes, sometimes I still go there and think I can do it
on my own. But I'm also here to tell you how much easier it is
when we let God do it for us. He doesn't mind, really. He wants to!

He has allowed something so tragic in our lives that words cannot even describe it, although I try as I write this. It is a loss that I never thought I would experience, and it is a path that I never would have chosen. But it is what it is. (This is about Job)

From his experience we see how the Lord's plan finally ended in good, for he is full of tenderness and mercy.
James 5:11b (NLT)

I want this to end in good. I already see so much good out of it, and it has really only just begun. The first year of grief has been an amazing process of finding God when it seems I can't find my shoes. I have been blinded by the pain at times, and yet God shines through. God is taking me step by step until His healing is complete in me. And He is asking me to share this process with you, I believe, because He doesn't want those in situations similar to mine, to suffer more than is absolutely necessary. I'm not saying it doesn't hurt, and it won't hurt for a long while, but there is also peace and joy in the process—even in the first year—even on the first birthday missed. It may be spent in tears from morning until night, and that may be what is healing for someone else. But it doesn't have to be that way just because the world tells us that proves the person was loved sufficiently. How many of us don't love our children? Even when they make us absolutely crazy at times, we still love them, always. How many of us think we can ever live without them? Not many. I'm with you. I want all three of my boys right here on earth with me—I go first, then my children. But life doesn't always work out the way we want it to, and God provides for that. For whatever the situation, God provides!

I command you to love each other in the same way that I love you. And here is how to measure it - the greatest love is shown when people lay down their lives for their friends.
John 15:12-13 (NLT)

That is why I do this. I want to lay down my life in writing for you because I don't want the devil to gain any ground in what he's

*already lost. Our peace and joy belong to Jesus. I don't want to
freely hand anything back to Satan, and I don't want you to either.
It's not his. Everything comes from God!*

> *"I am leaving you with a gift - peace of mind and heart.
> And the peace I give isn't like the peace the world gives.
> So don't be troubled or afraid.
> Remember what I told you: I am going away, but
> I will come back to you again."*
> *John 14:27 (NLT)*

*The world will tell us how things should be. But it is probably a lie.
The world will tell us that on the first birthday of your loved one in
Heaven, you should be miserable. I'm here to tell you that if you
surrender the day to our Father in Heaven, He has the power to
make it a day of calm delight. God will make the lake water
glisten, and the golden leaves of autumn sparkle in the breeze. God
will take our broken heart and hold it in the palm of His hand on
the worst day of our life and help it to keep beating. He will listen
to the prayers offered up by so many and answer them ten-fold!*

> *Are any among you suffering? They should keep on praying
> about it. And those who have reason to be thankful should
> continually sing praises to the Lord.*
> *James 5:13 (NLT)*

> *The earnest prayer of a righteous person has great
> power and wonderful results.*
> *James 5:16b (NLT)*

*Those prayer results were felt today. That righteous person is you!
We have been made righteous by our Lord. He hears our prayers.
We are thankful. We praise our God!*

*As we were driving home tonight, my cell phone rang. I had not
planned on talking with anyone today, wanting to spend the day as
quietly as possible. I went ahead and answered it for some reason,
even though the number was blocked. It was my friend, Linette—*

the one in the dream who "survived" the fall into the pit also—the one who I went to see when I woke up and walked into her room, where we laughed together knowing that God had spared us because He had work for us to do. Of course she would call—she completed the day. God was working through each and every detail of this process. We talked for just a short while, as she assured me that we were in her prayers. And we laughed a bit, too.

On a last note, the tears that were shed today were not shed because of devastation. They were shed because of the kindness, of people like this friend who cared enough to call, or left a message, or sent a note, or a card, or said a prayer on this day. Because of your love for us, we were lifted up, and we won! The devil was shown to be the weak fraud that he is, and God's refreshing Living Water nourished us all day long. It's more unlimited than all the water in Lake Tahoe. With Jesus, we need never thirst again!

Living in His peace,
Diane

__Myself__

It was the 16th and just as in my dream, I woke up knowing I'd fallen to the bottom of the "pit." And I was alive.

I woke up today, and it is the 16th of October, **2014**, 12 years since I wrote this sentence above. I **am** alive, fully alive! Life is not perfect, Phil is still gone, but God has grown in me. It's not that God changes, or grows, it's that He has grown in my heart because I have made efforts to make room for Him. I have invited Him to push the pain out, and bring the healing in. It's not always easy; in fact, it's very challenging most times, especially in the beginning. I want my own way, I want to say the things I want to say, and do the things I want to do, and most those things are not very godly. But over the last 12 years I have not had the luxury of doing things my way if I want to be fully alive each day. That is one of the benefits of grief. That is one of the blessings for those who mourn. We either allow God to change our way of thinking, or we give

Satan permission to do so and lead us down a very dark path. As I
heard today, "You can't ride two horses at the same time."
(Allister Begg) One leads to joy, the other to misery. Today, I'm
not in a pit. Instead, I feel the firm foundation of a Hope in Christ
beneath my feet.

Spending this day in Heaven hasn't really come too soon
It's just the way we planned it, long before your birth
Sixteen years with your family, then you'd leave the earth

That doesn't sound like a very good or fair plan does it? But
Psalm 139:16 (NLT) says, "You saw me before I was born. Every
day of my life was recorded in your book. Every moment was laid
out before a single day had passed." That means God knew in late
May of 1996 that Phil was going to be diagnosed with Leukemia.
It means that God knew on November 14, 2001, Phil would take
his last breath on this earth. And God knew, and knows the reason
why. We don't. I don't. But there comes a time when we have to
stop asking why and start living in the what, trusting that *what* God
does is work everything together for good to those who **love Him**.
(Romans 8:28) We may get tired of hearing that verse, but we
should never get tired of the Truth of God's Word. We have to
believe that God's plan is to get as many people safely Home
before He closes the door. "When the master of the house has
locked the door, it will be too late. You will stand outside knocking
and pleading, 'Lord, open the door for us!' But he will reply, 'I
don't know you or where you come from.'" Luke 13:25 (NLT)
That will be a very wonderful, very terrible day. If we are inside,
because our faith in Jesus Christ has provided the way in, we will
be safely Home. If we are outside, because we have chosen to
follow someone, anything, other than Jesus, there will be no worst
day in our life. Our Father loves all of His creations, and He sent
Jesus to this earth so that all who believe in Him, and are therefore
saved by grace, can be called His children. But not all will do so.
Some are still just creations, and some have become God's
children. There is a difference. And God has to take strong
measures to get His Word out before that final day. Whatever that
takes, He will do. And He asks that we who do believe, trust Him
with what must be done. I don't like that Phil had to suffer and die,

but our Father God didn't exactly enjoy watching His Son suffer and die either. But it is for our good. Always! Because God is a good and loving Father.

I am happy for Phil, because I love him that much!

The more I see of this world, the happier I am for Phil. It's not because I don't love him more than words can say, but it's because I do. When we truly believe in the goodness that awaits us in Heaven, we can't help but feel some relief for those that have gone ahead, having escaped the things that happen here on this day. And for all I know, Phil would be enjoying a pretty good life. I mean, we are. But even a good life here doesn't compare to what's going on there! "A single day in your courts is better than a thousand anywhere else! I would rather be a gatekeeper in the house of my God than live the good life in the homes of the wicked." Psalm 84:10 (NLT)

Nothing, today, was planned except to rise and make it through the day, anyway we could.

This weekend I will head off to a women's retreat with our church. Being that we haven't attended this church for long, I don't think I know anyone who is going. Years ago, I wouldn't attend a Bible study without my sister, Karen, at my side, practically holding my hand. And she's my "much younger" sister! But times have changed, and I look forward to going into this weekend not knowing how it will be, who I will meet, and most importantly, how God will meet me there and teach me many new things. Years ago I attended a retreat, and my roommate was a woman I had never met before. When she arrived, she needed help in assembling her wheelchair. She came, knowing no one, needing assistance, and God put us together. He showed me what true courage looked like on that day, and I have always remembered our weekend together. I was once a very planned person, but it has been good to experience God breaking me out of that mold as I become a new creation in Christ—to be able to go where and how God leads. His plans are so much better than mine.

When it seemed as if we should be so miserable, we wondered why we were not.

God can do this for all of us. He can take, what should be a miserable day and make it a pretty decent one, if not a good one. We worry so much about how things will be, and the worrying will cause headaches, and all sorts of ailments. But if we will simply trust that God will get us through, we will see that He will. It is something that I've had to practice a lot through the years. Not worrying is hard for most of us, but as we see God's faithfulness, it can get a bit easier. That's why the book of Deuteronomy is one of my favorites. Moses reminds God's people over and over to not forget all that He had done for them. "Oh, that their hearts would be inclined to fear me and keep all my commands always, so that it might go well with them and their children forever!" Deuteronomy 5:29 (NIV)

The evil powers of this world wanted us to be miserable and Christ set us free! Just like that boat!

The boat on the lake was quite a memorable experience that day. Not only was it peaceful and beautiful, but it had its share of problems. To be on a semi-large boat, and to have been asked to all stand to one side so as to dislodge the boat from the sandy bottom of the lake, was an adventure. It was not a scary thing, just interesting. If we will go where God tells us, stand where He directs, we can be set free in Christ.

The days leading up to the birthday...

I love when I am writing along, and then I read a line and it makes me take in a deep breath. I know that I have just hit on something that was extremely difficult on the journey through grief. I just took that breath when I read about the "days leading up to the birthday." I know, know, know how difficult those days can be. They are heart-wrenching! It seems we might surely die. How will we ever make it through such a day? And yet, we do. The question becomes, do we grow and learn through it, or does it just destroy us that much more? I was just reading in John about Jesus preparing His disciples for His departure—the days leading up to it. In a way, the days leading up to Phil's departure were probably similar to what the disciples went through. I couldn't really see it clearly, couldn't fully grasp it, as they couldn't. As plainly as Jesus was explaining it to them, they had a hard time grasping it. But we, as believers in Jesus, looking back upon it, see clearly what He was telling them, now.

Yesterday, one of our sons had a difficult day, or I should say, the days leading up to it were difficult. I could not deny him that, I understood. But I hoped when the actual day came, it would be different than what he expected. He was praying. I was praying. I had asked others to pray. Sure enough, when the actual day came, he said it was one of the best days he had had in a while. I could not explain it to him clearly enough, before, for him to grasp how that can work, but now he can look back on it and understand how God's "manna" is sufficient for the day we are on. God told the Israelites not to collect more than a day's supply of manna, except for the day before the Sabbath—that way they wouldn't be working on the Sabbath. It is such a great lesson on God's provision for each day. But grasping it, is something that we have to walk through, and out of, to begin to understand how it works. God provides for the day we are on.

When the day actually arrived, I didn't work. I was carried, completely—by your prayers, to the Father, through His Son, and I was given comfort by the Holy Spirit in me.

Our son found that the prayers, and his faith, actually carried him through the day. Not to say there wouldn't be difficult days still ahead— but it's one day at a time, sweet Jesus.

I looked up at that blue sky today, from that boat on the lake, and I thought about Phil and where he is.

How many of us have done that...looked up and wondered...or looked out the window of an airplane and wondered how far we were from Heaven? It seems we are closer to Heaven at 30,000 feet. I'm not sure how true that is, but I did this a lot in the beginning, and I still do it from time to time. On our recent trip to Tennessee, my dad sat by the window both ways. On the way there, he slept some. On the way back, he stayed awake the entire trip. I don't know what he was thinking, but I do know what I was thinking...it could very well have been his last trip on an airplane and perhaps he didn't want to miss a minute of it. He watched the terrain below skim past, and he commented on how many planes are in the air at one time. When we got close to home, he pointed out the cities below us. He was born in the Bay Area, and has lived a lot of his life here. He has worked in most of those areas, that he saw from the plane, as a salesman. He was taking it all in...perhaps for the last time. We don't know how much longer we will have dad with us, but we do know where he is going when he leaves here. And when I take another flight some day, I will look out the window at that blue sky and I will wonder how far away my dad is when he is in Heaven. But one thing I know today, and will know then, is that we are all only one heartbeat away from finding out where Heaven or Hell really are.

And then it came to me... Why is it so hard to imagine that Phil is with God at this very moment, when I KNOW that God is with me?

The more we know that God is with us, the more we know that our loved ones are safe in His arms. In reading John this morning, I was very touched to read again how Jesus prayed for us in John 17:20 (NLT), "I am praying not only for these disciples but also for all who will ever believe in me because of their testimony." Jesus knew I would be sitting here today, Bible on my lap, reading His love letter to me—to all of us who will believe. Isn't that an amazing thought? How many other love letters have we gotten in our lives like that? And Jesus was telling His Father, that He wants those the Father has given Him, to be with Him, so they can see His glory. He has gone to prepare a place for us, and He wants to show it to us. We should be excited to see it, and Him, the Lover of our souls!

Jim took Highway 88. I have never seen such fall colors in the state of California!

We missed the fall colors in Tennessee. They were just coming out as we left. But we also missed the rain. We had gorgeous weather, but it was supposed to start raining the day after we left, and I heard that it did, for many days thereafter. What a blessing from God to have enjoyed such wonderful weather on our trip. We don't see fall colors in California like some other states do, but on our trip home from Tahoe in 2001, we did. In the midst of such sadness and missing, God's was showing us His glory.

As much as we want God's will for our lives, it is so hard to give up our son in the process.

Isn't this one of the age-old questions...is it worth it? If we could choose our path of pain, which one would we choose for the end result to be God's glory? None of them, probably. We would never choose a path of pain on purpose, and yet sometimes our decisions do lead us there, and sometimes God's plans do, too. It's hard to explain the peace I have about all that has happened in a way that doesn't make me sound like some crazed lunatic—or at least makes me feel that way because I don't know what you might think about it. Once again in reading John this morning, Jesus said, "Truly, you will weep and mourn over what is going to happen to me, but the world will rejoice. You will grieve, but your grief will suddenly turn to wonderful joy when you see me again."
(John 16:20 NLT) As I read that, I saw that the "world" would be rejoicing, but the followers of Jesus would be grieving. The world put Jesus to death, and when Jesus rose from the grave, the world was in BIG trouble! It was either time to get in line with the Savior, or they were going down with the ship. One day, this world will be finished, and God will create a new Heaven and a new Earth. (Revelation 21:1) These things are going to happen. They must! It's God's good plan for us. We have to trust Him with that. And what the loss of our son has taught me is that God cannot only get us through anything, we can also trust Him with **everything.** And our perspective can change so much when we start to grab

hold of who God is and what He is doing. His plan is to bring us all into His Heavenly Home, and whatever that takes, He will do it. Somehow it works out as a gain in God's Kingdom work here on earth.

When I hear it said, "We lost our son," I just let it go. But in my mind I am thinking, we didn't lose him, we know where he is. And we know we will see him again. And that is the ONLY reason why I can confidently know and feel the peace that Jesus left us with. Because it is a peace, not as the world gives, but as only our Savior can. "Peace I leave with you; my peace I give you. I do not give to you as the world gives. Do not let your hearts be troubled and do not be afraid." John 14:27 (NIV) I don't know how to explain it to you in written words here in this book. I only know that I believe it and experience it. I write about it so that in some way, perhaps, you can know it is possible to be okay with even a child dying, even when it seems to be, and probably is, one of the most horrible things in all the world.

Sometimes, lately, God wakes me up with a thought, and I jot it down. The other night it was this, "The angle we are viewing things from changes how we see it, but not how it really is." I drew a circle and an oval next to what I wrote. They were both still a circle, but I was looking at them from a different angle, giving me a different perspective. Phil died an earthly death, that's how it really is. But I need to always view it from the angle I find in the Hope of Jesus so that I can see it as Phil living a heavenly eternal life. That is the Hope-filled perspective our Father God wants us to have.

There is no worldly explanation that can really capture what only comes to us in the supernatural way of our Savior. It's like the blind man that Jesus healed. (John 9) They kept questioning the man about who Jesus was. The man couldn't really explain what had happened, or how it had happened, or even who Jesus was, as yet, but he knew he was once blind and now he could see. When Jesus finally got back to him and asked him if he believed in the Son of Man, he said, "Who is he, sir, because I would like to know?" The once blind man was willing to believe, because he had experienced what was beyond this world, and what comes only from our Father in Heaven. God changes hearts. He renews minds. And He designs it so that when we love Him with all our heart, all our soul, and all our strength, we will want His will for our life, no matter the cost. I hope this helps you in some way to understand how we can live in peace each day without our precious loved ones.

I willingly admitted that I couldn't do this. My strength is gone, long gone, and this day is too big of an assignment for me.

I am back from the retreat now. I didn't finish this chapter before I left for the mountains. I think that is a good thing. I learned some things on the mountain. God had an assignment for me there, many, actually. I went, not knowing anyone. I came home knowing many, and their stories. I asked my sister a few days ago how many people she meets who are grieving? She had to admit, not many. It seems on the mountain everyone I met was...and I believe it was that way because those who were grieving were God's assignments for me over the weekend.

I arrived, checked in, went to my cabin, made up my bed, and didn't return until late that night when all my roommates were already asleep. I hadn't even met them yet. I had been at the fire talking with a woman whose husband went Home about 13 months ago. He was a pastor. She loves him deeply and misses him so much. God brought us together to talk, to share, and to encourage one another. And so the weekend went...meeting person after person as I asked God where He would have me be. The next night I went out to one of the fire pits and asked God if this is where He wanted me. Someone was playing a guitar, and I love that, but it seemed not—it didn't feel right. So, I went on to the next fire pit...but it didn't seem I was to be there either. I went on to a third one...it seemed I was in the right place at last—but that's all I knew. Two women were talking, but it didn't seem I should be joining in with them, although they were friendly and pleasant. There were about six woman gathered on the other side of the fire pit. I asked if they were all from the same church. They were. I got to talking with the woman who stood next to me. She began to tell me about her dear nephew who went Home seven months ago. We talked at length. We bonded in our Hope in Jesus. It was inspiring, heart-warming, and amazing. I also met many women from my church, and they were sweet and welcoming, and I enjoyed my brief times with them. But for the most part, it didn't seem that I was to hang out with them—I could do that back home.

On the last day, a song was sung. It had been sung a few times, but this time it was different. The woman singer, with a powerful voice, stood at the back of the room that held about 250 women, and she just started singing out, "You make me brave," over and over—no instruments, no mike. She then walked through the crowd, up the aisle, and onto the stage, where she reached for a mike and the musicians joined in with her one by one. It was powerful, and it spoke to my heart. I knew that Jesus had made me brave over these last almost 13 years and more now. He has healed my heart so that I can now share with others around the fire, at the dinner table, or on the patio all that is possible with a God who loves us and wants the very best for us. He has made me brave enough to walk this out with Him, and walk beside others who grieve. It is a privilege to serve Him in this way. I am not the same me. Even as I told my best friend, Deb, about this retreat experience, last night, she said, "Who are you?" She knows me now, but she knew me then...and she knows God has been at work in my heart.

It's not that it would kill me, but I wanted more. I wanted peace and joy on this day.

I have found the "more," so much more! I see God in ways that astound me every day. I see His miracles, large and small. As I came out of the dining hall on one of the days at the retreat, I needed to head up the hill to get some of my books (*It Started in the Dark*) out of the trunk of my car. But the meeting down the hill was about to begin. There was really no time, but I figured I would just be late to the gathering—which is hard, because I don't ever like to be late. But God provided—there sat one of the golf carts, driven by a woman that I had been talking to throughout the weekend. It was like she was my personal taxi there waiting for me. I walked up and asked Velma if she would drive me up the hill? Of course, she said she would. When we got up to my car, I jumped out and grabbed some books. Then she gave me a ride to the meeting down the hill. On the way down, I gave her one of my books as a thank you. She began to tell me how her best friend's daughter had died suddenly a year ago...and she was wearing the young woman's tennis shoes. I said, "Maybe this book is for her."—another of God's assignments. There is peace and joy in working for Him, as He leads.

He has allowed something so tragic in our lives that words cannot even describe it, although I try.

As I stood with, sat with, and rode with so many women this last weekend, I didn't need a lot of words. What I needed was a heart filled with the Hope of Jesus, and two listening ears. The women wanted to share—most of us do—but it is hard to find those who will take the time to listen in this busy world. Retreats are great for that, as the busyness gets left in the valley. I was blessed to not only have this retreat to attend, but when it was finished, I joined three long-time friends in the mountains for a couple of nights, and we shared an intimate time together, talking about the things of God. It was there that my friend, Lynn, told me how she is not a big fan of retreats. She doesn't really like crowds. She used our four-women retreat as an example of what she prefers. I had to tell Lynn what I had just experienced in this crowd of 250 plus women, and how personal and intimate it was. I have been at retreats where I was connected to a large group, and it was very social and different than this retreat. But we can go into any retreat weekend seeking God, His ways, and come home with a different experience with Him each time.

The first year of grief has been an amazing process of finding God when it seems I can't find my shoes. I have been blinded by the pain at times, and yet, God shines through.

I went to bed that first night at the retreat, and the word *amazing* kept running through my mind as I thought about the woman I had just met. Karen was there, missing her husband, hurting so deeply, and yet wanting to praise God in the midst of it. She had her best friend, Sharon, with her. Karen and Sharon—I think that's so fun, that their names rhymed! Karen was grieving, and Sharon was her support. Sharon reminded me so much of my friend, Deb. She would stand by, stand back, or move in, as called for. She was loving, kind, and helpful to Karen, and I knew how blessed Karen was to have her. I had many, many friends supporting me when my heart was shattered. Each one had a part to play in the healing process, and I appreciated all they did. And then, when we have one who is closer than a sister/brother in all of our pain, it is huge. I remember Phil's service. The family was getting ready to go in. Deb mentioned where she was going to sit, and I said, "No, I want you right next to me." She didn't want to assume that's where she would be, but it's certainly where I wanted and needed her to be. God will bring us who we need, when we need them, if we will be open to all that He is doing. It would have been so much easier for Karen to not attend the retreat last weekend, to curl up into a ball, and cry. But she came, and I was amazed by her, and the strength she allowed God to fill her with. I encouraged her to write her story, because, personally, I want to read it one day!

I want to lay down my life in writing for you because I don't want the devil to gain any ground in what he's already lost.

With writing that first book, "It Started in the Dark," God has given me tools that I can carry in the trunk of my car. That's what I had to run and get—I had to get the tools out of my tool bag to be a part of God's healing team in this broken world. I also grabbed a couple of the CD's we did ten years ago, "How Do I Begin To Tell You." It is the grief journey put to music—more tools. It is easier to praise God up on the mountain, surrounded by women who love Jesus. It is a lot harder to come back to the valley and continue praising Him when the world presses in. We leave those retreats with many types of survival skills, and renewed strength. I came down with the song, "You Make Me Brave" reverberating in my head. I love it! Some came down with a new or renewed faith in

Jesus. Some came down with books, or CD's, to inspire them to keep on when life hurts most. When we fight the devil with God's tools, God always wins because He already has the Victory. Jesus is the Savior, now and forevermore. He is our greatest weapon against the enemy! He conquered death for us! What more can we ask of Him?

God will take our broken heart and hold it in the palm of His hand on the worst day of our life and help it to keep beating.

I started writing this on what would have been Phil's 29th birthday. It is now more than a week later, and I feel like so much has happened between then and now. On that day, I was able to take some of my grandkids out for ice cream to celebrate their Uncle Phil's birthday. My son, Chris, called as we were driving home. He wanted to reach out to me on his brother's birthday, and I appreciate that so much. He said they were going out as a family that night to have Cheeseburgers—one of Phil's favorite foods. They were going to talk about Phil, and remember him in that way. I think that is so important. Not to idolize Phil, or to get out of balance about who he is, but to demonstrate that because of who *Jesus is*, our hearts can keep beating. We can grieve as those who have Hope, and should continue to share that Hope. (1 Thess. 4:13) If we don't talk about those we are missing, the devil wins. If we remain sad forever, the devil wins. If we don't find Jesus is more than enough in our storms, the devil wins—or thinks he does, because Truth be told, Satan has already lost! Our loved ones are not lost, but Satan is—lost in the lies he believes, because Satan is the father of lies. (John 8:44) Whatever day we are living in, or whatever day is coming up, we can still rejoice because of who Jesus is! I have heard it's not, "What would Jesus do?" It's "What Jesus has done." It is finished!

As we were driving home tonight my cell phone rang... It was my friend, Linette. We talked for just a short while, as she assured me that we were in her prayers. And we laughed a bit, too.

It is interesting to me how God can speak to us in our dreams, so specifically. I had gone into Linette's room in my dream, and we had survived the fall into the pit. And we laughed with each other. And then Linette called me, and I decided to take the call, not knowing who it was. God knew she would call, and He knew I would answer, and we laughed together. God is truly in the details of our lives, and it is a joy to be in them with Him.

The devil was shown to be the weak fraud that he is, and God's refreshing Living Water nourished us all day long... With Jesus, we need never thirst again!

As I sat in the last worship session at the retreat, I noticed the t-shirt the lady in front of me was wearing. It said, "September is Childhood Cancer Awareness Month." I had placed a copy of my book under the seat, wondering who God would have me give it to. The retreat was just about finished, and we would all be heading home soon. When we took our seats I noticed some writing on the front of her shirt, so I asked her what it said. She explained about a run that had been done in honor of Baily, a little eight year old who had died of Leukemia. I reached under the seat and handed her the book, telling her it was for her. Maybe Baily's mom will eventually get it, maybe this woman needed to read it, maybe someone else did...all I knew is that it seemed right to give her that tool in that moment. All day long, all weekend long, this retreat was refreshing, and inspiring, and I left overwhelmed with God's all-knowing, all-loving, all-caring nature. As I came down the hill for breakfast on the last morning, I was talking with God and saying that we were probably done, there couldn't be any more that He had planned after all He had already done. I highly underestimate God much of the time—He is beyond busy working on His children's behalf. Shortly after saying that to God, I was in the dining hall and a new friend, Lori, called me over to her table. Funny thing was, she was sitting with one of my roommates, who I had barely had time to say "Hi" to. It wasn't two minutes into the conversation when I found out my roommate's mom had gone Home two weeks ago. We were able to pray for her, and love on her. God knew what I didn't. Wouldn't it have been sad to leave the weekend without even knowing the hurting of one of my roommates? But God, who is ever faithful, did not let that happen.

There was a lot of Living Water to drink on that mountaintop, and I would venture to say that everyone who was there came home refreshed!

Gift #13 – God can turn miserable into memorable.

What has God poured into you that could be refreshing for someone else in your day?

How has God made you *brave* in a way you never thought possible?

Record today's date and other notes you'd like to make:

The Great

I AM

So humble yourselves before God.
Resist the Devil, and he will flee from you.
Draw close to God and
God will draw close to you.
James 4:7-8 (NIV)

CHAPTER FOURTEEN

*"I know the Lord is always with me.
I will not be shaken, for he is right beside me."*
Acts 2:25 (NLT)

<u>Me</u>

In Tune With God

Wednesday, 23 Oct 2002

One week after Phil's first birthday in Heaven...

Phil's fingers were long and thin. He loved to play Billy Joel songs on the piano. They were complicated pieces of music that went on for pages, but he would work through them and eventually learn them to his satisfaction, and then we would hear them over and over. I loved hearing him play. It was a favorite time in my day. Frequently, I would request a song or two and he would play them for me. He already knew what they would be. One of the songs I loved to hear him play was "Misty." It flowed so beautifully from his fingers.

The piano is quiet now. Phil spent many hours at those keys, taking lessons, practicing, or simply enjoying the songs he already knew. I miss hearing him play. I miss hearing the songs that were his favorites, and mine. I miss the way he would joke with me when he played a song. He would stop right before the final note and wait...and wait...and wait...and laugh, knowing that it made me crazy to have that last note missing—and then finally he would strike the note and we would laugh together with his teasing.

God knows how I miss that music and the fun we had. How do I know? Because on Sunday, as I sat at the dining room table looking at the piano, I grew tearful thinking about Phil sitting there playing for me. I didn't pray about it. I just thought about it, and my heart cried out silently as I thought about Phil. Shortly after that, Jim put in an old video of an "Eric Clapton Unplugged" concert. We had not watched it for a very long time, and we both used to enjoy it so much. I heard the music and went in to sit and listen to it with him. There was a piano solo during one part, and I thought about the young man who was playing, and about Phil. Then later that same evening, we were watching Charles Stanley, as we normally do on Sunday night. Sometimes he will have music, or singing from the choir, or a quartet. Sometimes he will have a soloist who will sing before he preaches, but not always. On Sunday night, as we tuned in, there was a young man playing a piano. No singing, just this young man, alone. They showed the close-ups of the keyboard as his fingers moved beautifully along the keys, and I thought of Phil. It made my heart ache, but it also gave me joy, because about halfway through his song I realized the gift that had come from God. He had heard my heart cries earlier, even though I had not asked Him for anything in prayer. God had heard the missing of a mother who simply would love to hear her son play a song, so God played it for me...through this young man. My heart was filled with joy knowing that God loves us so much that He cares for our every need—that He is listening when we are not even speaking, but He is listening to our hearts and He answers our cries.

Then they all prayed for the right man to be chosen.
"O Lord," they said, "You know every heart."
Acts 1:24 (NIV)

This verse is about the disciples asking God to help them pick a new member to serve with them since Judas had betrayed Christ. But it reminds me that God does know every heart. We can hide nothing from Him, the good, the bad, the joy, or the sorrow. God knows our hearts. I like that. I like that He heard my heart cry out on Sunday and He came and gave me a wonderful gift of music. What is there not to like about a God who loves us that much? Why do we refuse the easy way that He has made for us to love Him?
Why do we refuse the gift of the Holy Spirit when He gives us such comfort?
Is it because we don't believe we are sinners...that we have never committed a sin of any sort?
Who are we fooling?

Peter's words convicted them deeply, and they said to
him and to the other apostles,
"Brothers, what should we do?"
Peter replied, "Each of you must turn from your sins and
turn to God, and be baptized in the name of Jesus Christ for
the forgiveness of your sins.
Then you will receive the gift of the Holy Spirit."
Acts 2:37-38 (NLT)

Who doesn't want to be forgiven? Isn't that a cry of our heart, even when not spoken, too? When we wrong someone, that's exactly what we want of them. Some are not willing to forgive, because we are human, but God is always willing to forgive. We may think it wasn't that bad...that we don't need to ask for forgiveness. Wrong! God is perfect. His Son, Jesus Christ, is perfect. And to get into Heaven, we must be made perfect. We must be washed clean before we can enter in. The ONLY way to do that is to accept the sacrifice of the Son of God, who was the spotless Lamb, and let His blood wash us clean. It may sound crazy but:

"There is salvation in no one else! There is no other name in all of heaven for people to call on to save them."
Acts 4:12 (NLT)

I am watching the World Series right now, even though the A's are out of it! I like sports, and this is a big event, so I'm tuned in. While watching the game I noticed there is a player named Eckstein. Now, don't ask me which team he plays for; I don't really know, but I will probably pay closer attention to that after writing this e-mail. Do you know what Eckstein means? It means Cornerstone. Having lived in Germany, and picked up some of the language, I've noticed his name. Eck is corner, stein is stone.

For Jesus is the one referred to in the Scriptures, where it says, "The stone that you builders rejected has now become the cornerstone."
Acts 4:11 (NLT)

This young man playing in the World Series carries one of the names of Christ on his back, Eckstein. Jesus, the Cornerstone of the Church. We are His church, the people, and "We who believe are carefully joined together, becoming a holy temple for the Lord." Ephesians 2:21 (NLT) In my reading this morning in Ephesians, it talked a lot about the Jews and the Gentiles being joined together as one body.

By his death he ended the whole system of Jewish law that excluded the Gentiles. His purpose was to make peace between Jews and Gentiles by creating in himself one new person from the two groups. Together, as one body, Christ reconciled both groups to God by means of his death, and our hostility toward each other was put to death.
Ephesians 2:15-16 (NLT)

We are all one body, we have the same Spirit, and we have all been called to the same glorious future. There is only one Lord, one faith, one baptism, and there is only one God and Father, who is

over us all and in us all and living through us all.
4:4-6 (NLT)

It reminds me of that simple game we played as children where we linked our fingers together saying, "Here is the church, here is the steeple, open the doors and see all the people!" In that childish game, I saw something new this morning. I saw two sides of a church full of people, joined together as finger became intertwined with finger. We are no longer two sides of a church divided by an aisle down the center. We're no longer the groom's family and the bride's family, the "Smiths" and the "Greens," but all as one, united in our love for the same God because of Jesus Christ alone, our Eckstein.

Under his direction, the whole body is fitted together perfectly. As each part does its own special work, it helps the other parts grow, so that the whole body is healthy and growing and full of love.
Ephesians 4:16 (NLT)

And it all starts with the Cornerstone, with the Eckstein. Jesus holds it all together. Otherwise, there is no firm foundation for the church to stand on. "People of Israel, listen! God publicly endorsed Jesus of Nazareth by doing wonderful miracles, wonders and signs through him, as you well know. But you followed God's prearranged plan. With the help of lawless Gentiles, you nailed him to the cross and murdered him."
Acts 2:22-23 (NLT)

God is still doing wonderful miracles today, He is still doing wonders and signs through Jesus. I know when God "played" the piano for me, He was telling me that He cares, He hears, and He is with me. I just have to listen, watch, and be aware to "see" Him. Even in a baseball game Jesus can be our focus. There are so many that are blinded to all that God does for them—to all that God has for them. He has planned each and every day of our lives, just as Jesus' death was prearranged. We may think it is a mistake, but God already knows what each day holds from the moment we are born until the day we die. And we worry? Like that will change something? And we fret? Like that will help? Please! Let's stop, and trust God! Let's watch for God and His goodness, even in the hard times. He is still there. He never leaves! If it seems God is far away, think about who turned away...it's us. And we need to turn back. Our Savior is right there waiting for all of us.

He has never left me one day of this entire journey. Not even on the night Phil died. He was there with us. At times I have been blinded by the pain, but that does not mean God is not with me. I just may lose sight of Him for a while. When I re-focus, I find Him right there, waiting to help me take the next step on the journey. Our Cornerstone, our Rock, is dependable and sure!

> *I pray that your hearts will be flooded with light so*
> *that you can understand the wonderful future he has*
> *promised to those he called.*
> *Ephesians 1:18 (NLT)*

He has called all of us! Have we answered that call or are we still thinking about it? If we have answered His call, are we enjoying all the benefits that come with it? We don't want to miss out on them because of the lies of Satan that are so deceptive.

> *The Spirit is God's guarantee that he will give us everything he*
> *promised and that he has purchased us to be his own people. This*
> *is just one more reason for us to praise our glorious God.*
> *Ephesians 1:14 (NLT)*

Do you know how much I praise God for the blessed day He gave to Jim and me on Phil's first birthday in Heaven? Do you know how I will remember that day as a day of such peace and beauty? Is that not a wonder? God has given us His guarantee, His Holy Spirit. When our hearts are broken, when our lives are broken, when we think there is no way to fix the situation we are in, we can go to God with the guarantee He has given us. We can take our guarantee to the Maker, and ask for His help. We can claim it! And we can sit there in His "office," in His presence, until His peace floods into every part of our being. It's then that the world and all its trouble fade far into the background.

There have been many times in the grief journey I have needed to do just that. When I will come home, go to my room, and stay there until God meets me there, restoring the peace that I have lost. Then I can re-emerge, an hour or so later, renewed and refreshed because God has made good on His guarantee. I was broken, and He "fixed me" during that time with Him. I still need to go often for adjustments and refilling, but that is fine. That only develops a closer, more intimate relationship with our Maker. And as time goes by, I know more and more what to expect on these "visits" with our Maker. I am always a satisfied customer!

> *I pray that from his glorious, unlimited resources he will give you mighty inner strength through his Holy Spirit. And I pray that Christ will be more and more at home in your hearts as you trust in him. May your roots go down deep into the soil of God's marvelous love.*
> *Ephesians 3:16-17 (NLT)*

My roots have had to go down deep into God's soil, so that I will not topple over when the strong winds blow. When the gale force winds set in, I hunker down in the Word and find my peace in God's guarantee. And when the days come, like Phil's first birthday in Heaven, and I begin to wonder if this one mighty blow might be the one that will do me in, I dig in deeper and wait...until God rescues me from the battle. If there are no atheists in fox holes, there should be no atheists among parents who have had to say good-bye to their children. We are as much in the midst of the battle as any soldier on the front line. Our very lives depend on where our faith lies.

> *"And may you have the power to understand, as all God's people should, how wide, how long, how high, and how deep his love really is. May you experience the love of Christ, though it is so great you will never fully understand it. Then you will be filled*

with the fullness of life and power that comes from God."
Ephesians 3:18-19 (NLT)

If I am to have the fullness of life, I need to understand death. I need to know that Jesus conquered death for us all when God raised Him from the dead. I need to know that Jesus now sits on the throne of highest honor in heaven, at God's right hand. (Acts 2:32-33)

If I don't know that, I have no Hope. I would live in this world without God and without eternal Hope. (Eph. 2:12) That is not good enough for me. I want more than that. As much as possible, I want to see the full, clear picture of what we are doing here. I want to have a purpose for being here. I need a reason to walk through each day when I would rather run away. I want the fullness of life that has been promised to me!

Now glory be to God! By his mighty power at work within us, he is able to accomplish infinitely more than we would ever dare to ask or hope.
Ephesians 3:20 (NLT)

On Phil's birthday I dared to ask for something. I dared to ask God if He would carry me through the day. I took my "guarantee" up to the counter and I asked to see the Owner. I sat down with the Owner and I discussed my written guarantee down to the fine print. I pointed out where it said peace, and joy, and healing. The Owner shook His head in agreement. It surely did say that, and if I would just "wait a moment," He would see to it. So, I waited on the Lord, and He granted me the favor. He saved me, and He will continue to save me each and every time I enter His "office," step up to His "counter," and read the "Word." His guarantee says, "May grace and peace be yours, sent to you from God our Father and Jesus Christ our Lord." Ephesians 1:2 (NLT)

There is no other name to call on that will save us. There is no other god that will touch the heart of my own husband to pop in an old video with piano music, or the heart of someone thousands of miles away to schedule a program on TV with a piano soloist on the very day it is needed by a hurting mother, and in that soften the heart of the producers to include this solo in their TV programming before the preacher speaks. There is no one else in Heaven and on earth that can know and do things like our God can and does. No one else knows each intricate detail of our lives, of our hearts, to such an extent, and cares to such a degree that they will provide exactly what we need right when we need it. "When I think of the wisdom and scope of God's plan, I fall to my knees and pray to the Father, the Creator of everything in heaven and on earth." Ephesians 3:14 (NLT)

I am so grateful for God's plan, for His wisdom, and for His scope. I am so grateful that when I would like to say, "Play Misty for me," to my son, who is no longer here, God moves in the hearts of others and plays a gentle tune through them to help mend a broken heart.

> *By God's special favor and mighty power,*
> *I have been given the wonderful privilege of*
> *serving him by spreading this Good News.*
> *Ephesians 3:7 (NLT)*

Living in His peace,
Diane

<u>Myself</u>

He loved to play Billy Joel songs on the piano.

Doesn't music just take us to certain places in our memories? It can be so wonderful, or uplifting, and sometimes quite painful. We were in Florida one Christmas after Phil went Home, and we were headed to our friends', Deb and Alan's, house for dinner. We had stopped at the beach first, because that's what you can do in Florida, walk on the beach in December. It was a peaceful walk. We called our family back in California to let them know we were on the beach in the warm weather, just to rub it in a bit, and then we got in our very large truck that pulled our fifth wheel, and drove to our friends' house. That's when the song, "Only the Good Die Young" came on the radio. It was painful, in more ways than one, but it was also a gift because it was a Billy Joel song. Phil was a good boy, he did die young, and God knew that. We embraced the song instead of rejecting it and changing the station. Those are the choices we make in life, what to embrace, what to reject, what we allow to change us, and what we allow to harden our hearts. We have so many choices to make along the way, and allowing Jesus to work in and through all those times in life is what makes life possible. We have to get down on our knees and learn to walk with Jesus. We went on to have a good Christmas day, remembering the birth of our Savior, and His eternal gift to us.

The piano is quiet now.

The piano was quiet for a time, and then came the day for it to be moved out of our home. The piano actually belongs to my dad. My parents had given it to us for Phil when they were traveling for five years in their RV. My dad still plays it, to this day, in his home in Salinas. But the day the piano was to be moved, I was out walking, as I did quite often. Walking and listening to worship music helped me keep my sanity when the pain was so great. I was talking to my friend, Deb, on this walk, and telling her that this was the day the piano was being moved. During that conversation, I remember not being able to speak for a time, the tears were too many, and the hurt was too deep. She understood; we had had many of those types of conversations previously on the phone, and there were many more to come. Deb patiently waited on the other end of the phone that day, until I could engage in conversation again. Those are the kinds of friends we need when life hurts most...the kind that will call during life's worst heartaches, and be still, and listen even when we can't speak.

He would stop right before the final note and wait...

Phil was a jokester. He loved to be funny, and make people laugh. He lost a lot of that humor during his chemotherapy treatments.

Just thinking about that now, he probably went from a happy-go-lucky guy to just a pleasant guy. I guess, maybe, if he had started out just pleasant, he would have gotten grumpy. But with Phil, that was rarely the case. Even on Steroids, which were supposed to make him grumpy, he wasn't. He was just hungry, ALL THE TIME! Steroids cause hunger, and weight gain, and face puffiness, so Phil was never slender with cancer. Even when he went Home to Heaven at age 16, he was 5'10" tall and weighed 210 pounds.

I remember one day, sitting in our living room, and in walks Phil, shirtless, with his pajama bottoms pulled chest high! He looked super silly! We laughed, and then he left the room. When he came back around the corner, he had his pajama bottoms way low on his hips and was sticking his big belly out. I said, "Phil, put that thing away!" We laughed again. The great thing about Phil's personality was that he wasn't self conscious of the way he looked. He had an inner, quiet confidence that I always admired in him. Phil dressed up as Drew Carey one Halloween—business suit, slim tie, dress shoes, and black glasses. He finished his costume off with his accordion that Phil loved to play. Did you know that Drew Carey played an accordion? He does. I took Phil to High School that day, and he got out of our van and walked onto campus playing the accordion. I never, in a million years, would have had that much courage at his age. The kids at school loved it! When the word went out that Phil was gone, those that didn't know him well, wondered who he was. But all they had to be told was that he was "Drew Carey," and everyone knew exactly who Phil was. I was so proud of Phil's courage throughout his illness, but that Halloween day, I saw it so clearly. When peer pressure could have stopped him, it didn't. I also found out later that because he was wearing his brother's dress shoes, they were too small for him and hurt his toes all day. He ended up with a blackened toenail for months and months after that. He had never said a word.

God had heard the missing of a mother who simply would love to hear her son play a song, so God played it for me...through this young man.

261

I hope if your heart is missing someone as you read this book, that what I write helps you see God's love toward you in so many different ways. God meets us in our time of need, and He hears our prayers that are sometimes never even prayed. I know the young man on TV was not Phil, and it didn't come close to having Phil actually play for me, but it was still a gift that God gave me on that day. It soothed my heart, just a bit, and helped me know that I was being watched over by a loving Savior. We can chalk these things up to coincidence if we want to, and we can dismiss God from such seemingly tiny miracles if we so choose. But why would we when they can help to heal our soul? We need all the gifts, people, music, love, etc...that God extends to us as we journey through such difficult days.

What is there not to like about a God who loves us that much?

The quick answer to this might be, "I don't like God because He took my loved one." I understand that answer, and it is tempting to go there, but there is a much bigger picture to it all than what we can see. It comes down to trusting a God that wants the best for all of us...not just you, not just me, but everyone that He created. And life doesn't always look and feel like we want it to. In fact, many times, it's far from what we would choose, and in that, we have a choice to make once again. Are we going to trust our Father in Heaven who sent His only Son to die for us, or not? It might seem like I am simplifying it, but if we don't trust God, life can get very, very, very confusing. And confusion can be a ploy of the enemy, Satan. "For God is not the author of confusion but of peace, as in all the churches of the saints." 1 Corinthians 14:33 (NKJV) There are verses that talk about God causing some confusion, as in Exodus 23:27, and others, but there again, God has good reason for what He does. You will see it if you search out some of those verses. Mainly, God wants our attention, and obedience, and His peace, which will come when we are striving for His will in our lives. In that, a relationship will develop with Him. The confusion comes in, most times, when we want our own way. When we are fighting against what might *appear* wrong, but is right from God's vantage point, it can seem very perplexing. Many will argue against God's plans—like what could possibly be right about a 16 year old dying of cancer? But, "Seek the Kingdom of God above all else, and live righteously, and he will give you everything you need." We can live *in* God's peace no matter what we are living *through.* Matthew 6:33 (NLT)

I am watching the World Series right now, even though the A's are out of it! I like sports, and this is a big event, so I'm tuned in.

I love writing this when it lines up with the very time period I am in now, 12 years later. The Giants played the fifth game of the World Series last night against the Royals. Giants now lead five games to two—a very happy day for most Bay Area fans. We were at our friends, Jon and Lilia's house for dinner, so we weren't tuned in last night. Instead, we were tuned into God in an amazing way. As our friends, Steve and Joan, joined in, we all cooked pizza in the outdoor fire oven, and then sat around the dinner table and talked for hours about the things of God. That is the BEST way to spend an evening! We talked about everything from end times, Scriptures, miraculous healings, dreams, you name it...it was on the table. It was a time of rich fellowship...so rich, that at the end I asked Jon if he would pray before we left. It just seemed to be appropriate after all we had discussed. We could have tuned into the game, and that would have been fun, too, but evenings like these don't come along very often, and we all cherished it. Everyone at that table has gone through, and may still be going through, difficult things in life. And everyone at that table loves the Lord. It makes me ask, "Is there any excuse not to love God, no matter how hard life can get, when God can heal hearts and bring us to a place of peace and harmony with kindred spirits like we experienced last night?" Acts 2:42 says, "They joined with the other believers and devoted themselves to the apostles' teaching and fellowship, sharing in the Lord's Supper and prayer." (NLT) When we do, even if the Lord's "Supper" is pizza, it's a time when we can truly say, "God is good, all the time, and all the time, God is good."

If it seems God is far away, think about who turned away...it's us. And we need to turn back. Our Savior is right there waiting for all of us.

Are we paying attention to our Savior? Are we reading the Word to strengthen our hearts? Are we calling on Him in our time of need? If not, we are probably wondering where Jesus has gone. We may leave Him—but He never leaves us. This world is so distracting, the enemy is so distracting, and our trials are so distracting, "So we fix our eyes not on what is seen, but on what is unseen, since what is seen is temporary, but what is unseen is eternal." 2 Corinthians 4:18 (NIV) That is what helps us keep putting one foot in front of the other, every single day. There is no other way to make it through this life and experience the joy of the Lord. He is our strength. We cannot do it alone, or even only with others. We need Jesus!

He has called all of us! Have we answered that call or are we still thinking about it?

Our pastor, Rick, preached a sermon this last Sunday about Jesus that would be hard to refuse. In fact, Rick does that most Sundays—he explains exactly who Jesus is, and why we need Him, and then he asks for those who would like to say yes to raise their hands. One gentleman not only raised his hand this last Sunday, he gave Rick a thumbs up. How do I know that? Because, Rick noticed it, and told us about it. We all have our heads bowed while people are making their decision for Jesus. It is a personal decision, one that needs to be taken seriously. If we hear the Truth about Jesus and we don't have any arguments against who He is, and what He came to do, then what are we waiting for?
In Acts 2:37-38 (NLT), Peter was preaching to a crowd. It is written, "Peter's words convicted them deeply, and they said to him and to the other apostles, 'Brothers, what should we do?' Peter replied, 'Each of you must turn from your sins and turn to God, and be baptized in the name of Jesus Christ for the forgiveness of your sins.'" They gave Peter a thumb's up that day after he preached. They were ready to be adopted into God's family.

We cannot wait for Jesus' return to ask Him what we should do. We must turn from our sins today, and turn to God, because when Jesus returns it will be too late for those that haven't given their hearts to Him. The Bible says, "That night two people will be asleep in one bed; one will be taken, the other left." Luke 17:34 (NLT) I don't write this to scare you, I write this so that you will know if you should wake up one morning and your spouse is gone, they have not been abducted by aliens, as the news might report, but they have been taken Home by the Savior of the world, Jesus Christ. He is returning for all those who believe in Him. We can't know the day, but we can know it is getting closer every single day.

When our hearts are broken, when our lives are broken, when we think there is no way to fix the situation we are in, we can go to God with the guarantee He has given us... There have been many times in the grief journey when I have needed to do just that. I will come home, go to my room, and stay there until God meets me there, restoring the peace that I have lost.

This morning I got a wake-up call, but not what you would expect. Jim was looking for some voice work he had done in his files on the computer, and I was helping him with it. In the list he was looking at, there was a video testimony that I had done and had been shown at our church over 12 years ago. Jim clicked on it and we both sat in silence and watched it play out before us...the grief on my face and in my voice was overwhelmingly obvious. I sat in our home, and talked about prayer. And like Jim said afterward, they showed the good parts. If they had kept the camera rolling, it would have showed the breakdowns I was having in between the shots. It was a wake-up call to me as to just how tender we are in those early months and years of grieving. It looked like you could have blown me over with a wave of a feather. It was a good reminder of how far God has brought me, and how gracious I need to be with those who have just started on the journey. I can get running too fast now, and I don't want to be over zealous and inconsiderate. I'm glad we have that video as a reference. And I'm thankful beyond words for what Jesus can do in a life submitted to Him. I don't say that boastfully, I say that because I know that if I am not submitted to Him, I will remain in that pain. Phil is still gone, just as he was on that day, and I can live in that pain if I so choose. But each day that I chose Jesus, all those years ago, brought me here today. Jesus took me by the hand and helped me with each individual step. He didn't rush me. He didn't leave me. He cared for me and understood my pain. "He was despised and rejected— a man of sorrows, acquainted with deepest grief." Isaiah 53:3 (NLT)

And when the days come, like Phil's first birthday in Heaven, and I begin to wonder if this one mighty blow might be the one that will do me in, I dig in deeper and wait.....until God rescues me from the battle.

In a Bible study that I am attending, we are learning some of the differences between soldiers and warriors for Christ. I had never really thought a lot about it, but it is an interesting contrast. It seems that warriors are more of the heart, and soldiers are more of the gut. King David was a warrior, and he wrote in Psalm 16:8, "I know the Lord is always with me. I will not be shaken, for he is right beside me." (NLT) Since my son, Jimm, is interested in military things, I was talking with him about this, and he said, "A soldier has gone to boot camp. A warrior is battle tested." I think, for the most part, we all start out as soldiers. But with an intense focus on Jesus, we finish our life as warriors. It seems to me that fresh grief is like the boot camp Jimm talked about. We are new at this, and we don't know what we have "signed up" for. Oh, we've seen it on TV, and we've heard stories from others, but we haven't actually been the one being yelled at by the sergeant (our enemy, Satan), or had to crawl in the mud (muck and mire). We haven't had to do the physical training of running many miles (when we have no strength left). You may be reading this book today and never been to the boot camp of grief. Thank you for reading it anyway. But if you have been there, you know what I'm talking about. I sat with a new friend today. Her name is Bronzie. I love that name! She is a writer, too, so we had a lot to talk about. She told me they had nine close deaths in one year. Parents, siblings, friends—she said it got to be so much that she had to deaden her emotions to those close to her for a bit. I understood. If we keep our heart open and continue to love, we keep the door open to more pain. It's a hard choice, but a right choice, to continue to love. I told her she will relate to many of the things I write about. She is reading "It Started in the Dark" right now. She is a warrior, I am a warrior, and you may be, too. We are battle tested. We have some substantial medals on our chest that tell what we've been through. We can wear them with honor when we give the entire honor to our Lord, Jesus Christ, because He is the greatest Warrior of all.

If I am to have the fullness of life, I need to understand death. I need to know that Jesus conquered death for us all when God raised Him from the dead.

We can only really understand life, when we understand death. And the way we understand death is to leave the decisions about it up to God, our Father. Because if we are going to try and figure it all out, about what is right, and what is wrong, we are not going to be able to. We have to take everyone we have ever had to say good-bye to into the Throne Room, lay them at our Father's feet, and walk away. That's not disrespectful, that is faith! Acts 2:24 says that death could not keep Jesus in its grip. Death has been turned into eternal life through Jesus Christ. Our loved ones are **living** in Heaven, and we have to rest in the FACT that they are fine, and we need to continue on doing what we are being called to do here. It is HARD! I know! But the other choice we have, is to argue with God about it, get mad, stomp our feet, and live a very sad, frustrated, angry life. Then the enemy wins for a time. But he is not THEE Winner! Jesus conquered death for all of us. Mohammad didn't. Buddha didn't. Jim Jones didn't. Those "claiming" to be Jesus didn't. Jesus *did* it! It is finished. Why? Because Jesus said so!

On Phil's birthday I dared to ask for something. I dared to ask God if He would carry me through the day.

I was a heavy load, emotionally, on that day, and many other days along the way. I was like dead weight. I always think if someone tried to kidnap me, and get me to move into a car, or whatever, I would just go limp. I think I have seen that that is a good thing to do. Why are we so much heavier when we are limp? I don't understand, but we are. And yet God, in His mighty power, picks us up when we are at our heaviest—easier than we can pick up another person, even in a swimming pool. Have you ever tried that? They are light as a feather. But the weight of the world's sin, that rested on Jesus the day He hung on the Cross and died for our sins, was beyond description. I don't know how the nails kept Him secured to that crossbeam. If we think we are carrying a heavy load with our trials and tribulations, it isn't even a tiny fraction of the load Jesus carried for us. "He personally carried our sins in his body on the cross so that we can be dead to sin and live for what is right. By his wounds you are healed." 1 Peter 2:24 (NLT) I know we feel like we have a right to complain, and that our burden is heavy, because it is. But if we keep Jesus in our sites, we can make it through. We can, because He did, and does for us each day. His wounds heal ours.

God moves in the hearts of others and plays a gentle tune through them to help mend a broken heart.

We don't have to walk this out alone. God brings others to help us. Will we open our hearts and let them in? The Father brought His Son to help us. Will we open our hearts and let Him in? A wound does not heal over night, and neither does our heart, or our relationships. But with God, and time, there is always Hope. It's not our job to repair our broken heart, it is our job to let God do it. After watching that video this morning and seeing **Me** up close and personal 13 years ago, **Myself** is here to tell you that **The Great I AM** is a God of miracles. Hang in there. One day, you will look back and see how far you have come when you believe and trust in God's mighty saving grace.

<u>Gift #14</u> – Appreciating the progress we are making.

Remembering a difficult day you have had, how heavy would you say the weight was?

Does it help to compare it to the weight Jesus carried when He bore our sins?

Record today's date and other notes you'd like to make:

The Great

I AM

The Spirit is God's guarantee that he will give us everything he promised and that he has purchased us to be his own people. This is just one more reason for us to praise our glorious God.
Ephesians 1:14 (NLT)

CHAPTER FIFTEEN

Our days on earth are like grass;
like wildflowers, we bloom and die.
The wind blows, and we are
gone - as though we had never been here.
Psalm 103:15-16 (NLT)

<u>Me</u>

The Game of Life

Monday, 28 Oct 2002

I saw him standing there in the shadows...one of the best home-run hitters of all times. It wasn't his best day. His team had just lost the seventh game of the World Series and he was not celebrating. This was not Heaven. This was torture—to have come so close and yet be so far from the light. How could it have escaped them? It would take time to run each play through his mind and figure all that out. But he would have that time now. The season was over. They would go home in 2nd place. Not bad, but his team had missed out on the best.

Is that our lives? Are we standing there in the shadows watching others celebrate theirs? Out on the field, out in the light, there was such joy. People were jumping up and down, yelling, laughing, running, and hugging! The fireworks went off, the crowd cheered, and the winners of this year's World Series "had arrived." The Angels did it! They were calling it Heaven, 7th heaven. After 42 years, they had finally made it. And they celebrated!

It probably came close to Heaven for those players, for those fans, in that moment. Their coach said they had taken it one day at a time. Now he could relax and enjoy what they had accomplished. Yes, the Angels were in "heaven."

Is that how it will be when we arrive in Heaven? Will those who have not made it stand in the shadows and watch us celebrate? Will they know that it is too late, that the game has been played, the last out has been made, and there is no turning back? What's interesting is that those on the field, those in the light celebrating, did not see those in the shadows. They were too busy being happy, rejoicing, to even notice. Is that why there are no tears in Heaven? Will there be too much joy to notice those left in the shadows? But those in the shadows watched, and they knew it was not their place to be out in the light celebrating. When I saw the tears in the children's eyes, carried away by their fathers who had played the game, it made me sad. I felt as I always do...everyone should have won. I don't like to see the pain on the faces of the team that lost. They tried so hard. They had come so far. They deserved it too...or did they?

There are rules. You win the most games out of seven, it's yours. No one argues that. That's the way it is. So why do we argue with God's rules? Why do we think they are not fair? You are either washed clean by His Son, Jesus Christ, and step into the light a winner, or you refuse what God has offered and you stay in the shadows. You lose everything when the last out is played, and you never know when that will be. Will the game of life go nine innings, or will it go into overtime giving you another chance to step up to the plate and accept God's offer?

My son Jimm and I went to a game a year or so ago and it lasted into the 15th inning, if I remember right. They had to start turning the lights on by the time this 1:00 o'clock game finished. I figured we got our money's worth that day in baseball. Those players went home tired, but they had had plenty of time to get the game right before it was finished.

Some lives will be like that. Some will have 95-100 years to get it right. Some will not. Some will get only nine innings, and they will be finished. If you're a pitcher in life, you won't even get that. You will be called out of the game early and someone else will come in to finish up for you. You may only have a short period of time to get the job done. Sometimes all you get is one batter to pitch to. That's all you're needed for. It's not that you're not important. It's not that you're not doing a good job many times. Hey, you've made it to the Big League, and you're part of the team. But you have a very specific job to do and when it is finished, you are called out of the game. The coach makes that decision. You really have nothing to say about it.

We have a Coach in life; His name is God. He calls the plays. He makes the changes that need to be made in the line-up as the game of life goes on. He has a perfect game plan, even though we may want to argue at times. He already knows who will win, and He knows who will lose. He knows how long we will be in the "game" and our reason for being there. He knows who will win this "World's Series" and who will be standing in the light rejoicing when the seasons are over. He knows who will be standing in the dark crying.

"And I tell you this, that many Gentiles will come from all over the world and sit down with Abraham, Isaac, and Jacob at the feast in the Kingdom of Heaven. But many Israelites - those for whom the Kingdom was prepared - will be cast into outer darkness, where there will be weeping and gnashing of teeth."
Matthew 8:11-12 (NLT)

I want to feast when the "World's Series" of life is over. I want to sit in the Kingdom of Heaven and celebrate the game that has been played. I want to be in the light of God, not standing in the shadows weeping. It took the Los Angeles Angels 42 years to "arrive." I'm already past that in my game, and I may have quite a few years left to play, but Phil made it Home after 16 years. Phil must have been a pitcher. He was not in the game long, but he was a very important part of it. He changed the whole game for me. He turned it around when it might have seemed I was falling behind. Perhaps I was distracted by the airplanes flying over—or the jeers of unhappy fans. Perhaps I was getting bored with the whole thing, and I needed a wake-up call? I don't really know God's reason for bringing Phil into the "game," but I am so grateful that He did. With just a few pitches from the mound by my son, I stood up and took notice of what the Coach was doing—who He had brought into the line-up in my life and where the game was going. I started to pay attention to the game more than ever before because it became much more important. Each play becomes significant because I know now that it has eternal reasons for being what it is. Each person becomes a unique part of the "series" of events because I know God has placed them on the field. The game is perfect, even though it seems there are errors. Those so-called "errors" may be exactly what helps lead us to that final game, that final out, and into the very light and presence of our Almighty God.

The Giants can come back next year, and the next, and they can try again. It's just a game. It's not life. It's just a part of life. But when we hear our final out called, it is our life, it is our death, and we cannot come back next year. Phil is not coming back. He has gone on to celebrate the victory, the feast! He will never be in darkness again.

And the city has no need of sun or moon, for the glory of God illuminates the city, and the Lamb is its light. The nations of the earth will walk in its light, and the rulers of the world will come and bring their glory to it. Its gates never close at the end of the day because there is no night.
Revelation 21:23-25 (NLT)

In Heaven the "game" is never over. The gates are never locked. The lights are never turned off. The celebration continues on and on and on for all of eternity. And the joy that we will know is greater than any joy seen after the 7th game of the World Series has been won. That is almost hard to imagine, a greater joy than we saw on the faces of the Angels last night when that last fly ball was caught in the outfield. I love knowing that our joy will be even greater than that.

What I don't love knowing is that there will be those lost in the shadows. I don't want there to be tears in the dugouts because everyone doesn't win the game. Everyone can win this game of life by simply choosing to. It's that simple. We don't have to know all the game strategies. We don't have to know everything contained in a large rule book. We don't have to start playing the game when we are five so we can be "good enough" when we grow up to be allowed to play. All we have to do is be willing to know the Coach, to tell our Father that we want to "play," and He will lead us, and guide us, and help us all along the way. The only practice we have to attend is the One He calls us to, which involves "walking" with Him each day of our life. But He makes it easy because on this walk He carries us. I know, it sounds like cheating, but it isn't. Jesus knows we are not capable of doing it on our own, and He loves us so much that He wants to help us. The only rulebook we have is the Bible, and the only rule that we must always follow is to love the Lord our God with all our heart, with all our soul, with all our mind, and with all our strength. And guess what? He gives us the strength, too!

God gives us everything we need to play the game of life. His only desire is for us to know Him and to finish this game in His Holy Light. He wants that none should perish in darkness.

The Lord isn't really being slow about his promise to return, as some people think. No, he is being patient for your sake. He does not want anyone to perish, so he is giving more time for everyone to repent.
2 Peter 3:9 (NLT)

Extra innings! How many will there be? Only God knows! Don't wait until that last out is made to come out of the dugout to play in the game. It will be too late then. Get out on the field and enjoy it all now. The Coach is calling you. He wants you in the game. He wants to show you all that He has for you. Sitting in the dugout is boring and tiresome, and you feel rejected and alone. You're wanted on the team! But the choice is yours. The neighborhood bully is not in control, although he thinks he is. The devil thinks he has control over you. But he doesn't. God does. If you've been bullied around all your life, it's time for it to stop. The "winning team" wants you!

The world would love you if you belonged to it, but you don't.
I chose you to come out of the world, and so it hates you.
John 15:19 (NLT)

God chooses us, and the devil hates us. When we run out onto the field to play ball with God, the devil is the bully still sitting in the opposing dugout. He is angry that we have decided to go with God's team. He knows he has already lost the game. Satan's not a dummy, but he wanted you to lose the game with him. Satan is not the Angels, he is the losing team, and he doesn't want to lose all by himself. He wants to take as many down with him as he can. His time is running short and he knows it. It may already be into extra innings...and God is just waiting for you.

Do you think those that submit to good Coaching are weak? Do you think they are dumb? Do you think they have no idea what they have gotten themselves into? Or do you think that they trust the Person they play for, their Coach, and that they know this Person has had many years of experience and probably knows the game even better than they do? And because of that, they are willing to go where they are told to go on the field, and to play as they are instructed to play, to get the best out of their performance. This is not weakness in their ability; this is strength in their knowledge of the game, because they trust the One who knows more than they do. The Coach's intention is not to make them look bad or to lose, His intention is to win the game, and eventually the "World's

Series." This requires a big person, a humble person, a confident person, to submit to someone else's instructions in the game. That's what makes them winners!

Is it easy to submit to God? No. I read that few things require more strength than submission. It is hard to completely and totally say, "I'm yours, God. I want Your will for my life, no matter what." Yet, what's one of the first things we think of if we're parents? Your will, Lord, except for my kids; God, I want to keep them. Oh, and my house, I'd really like to not be homeless. And my health, God, I really need to stay healthy. And we start taking things back after "totally submitting" all things to God. Why do we do this? FEAR! We think God is some great big meanie who wants what is ours, and the minute we tell Him He can have it, He will take it from us! Wrong! That's a lie from the evil one. God doesn't want what we have. He doesn't need what we have. He gave it to us in the first place. What He wants is our love.

When Phil died that night in his room, we prayed over him. I said something like this, "We give Phil back to You because You first gave him to us." If God had not given Phil to us for those 16 years, we would not be missing him now. We would never have known him. We would never have had the gift of his love in our lives. We would never have known what we had missed. But we do now, because God first gave him to us, and we are so grateful. God gives to us way more than is ever taken away. He gives to us because He loves us, and He wants the best for us. Then we get stingy and start telling God what He can and can't have. I did it, too. Like we have some control over that by just saying so. God is the Coach. God decides who plays when, and who plays where. And whether we fully submit or not is up to us, but it doesn't change the rules of the game. The only thing it changes is how much we enjoy the game while we are here—how much freedom we feel while we are here, how much joy we will have, and how much we will know the "Coach" on a personal level.

I feel that having experienced life here with Phil, and now experiencing life without Phil, it's like I have been pulled back in a large slingshot and shot into the air of life. That may sound strange, but let me explain. The pulling back is the hard part, the squeezing part, the part that feels so uncomfortable. It is the part of life that hurts and that we would rather not go through. But what happens after that is, we are flung into the air completely free of the gravity of life because we trust God completely to catch us. We are sailing towards an eternal future that holds nothing but light and joy. We see the world from a different angle and it is all fleeting. It doesn't make it any less real, but it doesn't tie us down anymore because we have felt the worst, and the worst did not kill us—it only set us free to enjoy the flight, the game, so to speak. We realize that every day we live now is only bringing us closer to our goal—and any we know, who are in Heaven, we will soon see again. Every step, every day, brings us closer to "winning" the game! So, we are free to fly!

How do you enjoy your life after saying good-bye to your son? By letting God heal your heart. And how do you do that? We completely submit to God's will for our life and trust Him for everything, even when the evil one tells us that if we do that, God will only take more away from us. It's not true. The more we submit, the more God blesses us with peace and joy, even if the game still has many bumps and bruises. The devil can and probably will strike again. But that's all he can do. And if he does, he will strike out! Jesus wins! Satan is the bully, and we can refuse to be on his team. We can listen to our Coach, and follow His game plan, until the final inning of Game Seven of the "World's Series." We will be on that field of light, jumping for joy, and it won't just feel like heaven, it will truly be Heaven!

Our days on earth are like grass;
like wildflowers, we bloom and die.
The wind blows, and we are gone -
as though we had never been here.
Psalm 103:15-16 (NLT)

The lights were shut down after the celebration ended. The grass they played on was mowed and the clippings hauled away. The field was readied for the next game to be played there the following season. The fans went home and slept, as did the players. The "heaven" the Angels had experienced blew away as quickly as it had come. It would be remembered. But the joy would fade, and those that had been left standing in the darkness would re-emerge another day to play another game and to try again. Their tears would dry, and their laughter would return, because...there's always tomorrow...or is there?

Living in His peace,
Diane

Myself

Is that our lives? Are we standing there in the shadows watching others celebrate theirs?

I sort of waited to write this chapter. I wanted to watch game seven of this year's World Series between the Giants and the Royals first. The game is over now, and the parade in the city is going on as I type this. It's a wet day out there, but I'm sure it is not dampening the celebration in San Francisco today. That's right, the Giants did come back to win, not only in 2014, but this is their third World Series Title in the last five years. That leaves a lot of teams in the shadows watching the Giants celebrate since I wrote the **Me** part of this book 12 years ago. The last time the Royals won the Series was in 1985. That was 29 years ago. And it sure makes me think about what was happening then in our lives—Phil was born that year. I just asked my phone when the World Series was played in 1985. My phone spoke back to me and gave me the site with the answer. It was played from October 19th to the 27th. Phil was born on the 16th. I don't think we were watching much of those games! We were celebrating our own "win"—Philip Andrew Shore, 8 lbs. 7 oz. of blessings!

Their coach said they had taken it one day at a time.

The Angels were a huge threat to the Oakland A's this year. Since I'm an A's fan, I watched those two teams battle it out for part of the season. Obviously, neither one of them made it to the finish line, but it was a good season for the most part. As in life, it has to be taken one day, one game at a time. When we bite off too big of a chunk, it chokes us. It scares us. We think it can't be done. If anyone would have told me that I'd be writing this journey for years, and that I would be sitting here today writing a second book about it all, I would have choked on the thought. I would have wanted to run off the field for the dugout and let someone else play the game. But one day at a time, God can bring us along. He can teach us. He can strengthen us. We can all be victorious with Jesus as our Coach in this life. Our Savior walked this earth. Jesus knows how it is done. He knows how difficult and painful it can be. Jesus doesn't diminish our struggles, or our sins, but He does help us through them, forgive us for them, as we trust in Him.

Is that why there are no tears in Heaven? Will there be too much joy to notice those left in the shadows?

This question comes up often in our minds, doesn't it? How can there be so much joy in Heaven if we're missing those who aren't there? I believe this whole concept is such a supernatural thing that our natural mind can't even wrap itself around it. The sad thing is, from what I know about Hell, those there will know what's missing. In Luke it says, "The rich man also died and was buried. And being in torment in Hades, he lifted up his eyes and saw Abraham afar off, and Lazarus in his bosom." Vs 16:22-23 (NKJV) There is NOTHING good about Hell, nothing comforting, nothing loving, nothing hopeful. And the exact opposite is true about Heaven. I heard today in a sermon that the enemy will tell us 99 things that are true before he tells us the one thing that is a lie. In this way there is a greater temptation to believe his lie. Satan is sly, he is a liar, and there is nothing good about him. We are all familiar with bad things, we have all experienced them. If we can just try to see the flip side of all that is dark, hard, and painful, maybe we can get just the tiniest glimpse of the wonder and the good of Heaven. Heaven is the exact opposite of Hell. Hell is torment and anguish. Heaven is Paradise.

There are rules. You win the most games out of seven, it's yours. No one argues that. That's the way it is. So why do we argue with God's rules?

God makes the rules. We may not like them. Many times we don't like God's decisions. We think God is taking too long, or He's having us go in the wrong direction. We think God's causing us too much pain, and on and on it goes... We can wrestle with these thoughts our whole lives, and we can still be headed Home as believers. But why would we want to live this way? If I wrestle every day with what has happened in my own life, allowing anger to rise up, and focus on how unfair I think it all is, those thoughts can overtake all that God is doing that is good. I would live in misery. I have that choice. And it is a tempting choice. But that would be choosing the one lie from Satan, and not focusing on the other 99 things true things that come from Jesus. We have to choose to trust in the ultimate goodness of God so we can live in His light of Hope that is eternal. It takes work, focus, time in the Word, and prayer, but it is possible when we follow God's guidance in these ways. Acts 7:51 (NLT) says, "You stubborn people! You are heathen at heart and deaf to the truth. Must you forever resist the Holy Spirit?" We were given the Holy Spirit to help us through each day. Hardening our heart to God's help is simply foolish. The Holy Spirit is the "Umpire" behind Home Plate. He can tell us when the pitch is a ball or a strike. And He is always right! No need to review the pitch. He sees it perfectly. We have to listen to His calls, and obey them to truly live in God's blessings of peace.

It's not that you're not doing a good job many times. Hey, you've made it to the Big League, and you're part of the team. But you have a very specific job to do and when it is finished, you are called out of the game. The coach makes that decision.

We can't know why things happen, most times. The picture is much too big for us to take it all in. Just like watching the World Series this year—Jim looked up at the screen one time, he's not much into sports, and he said he wondered why he didn't recognize any of the names of the players. It only took a split second for him to realize we were watching the Giants and not the A's. We don't know these guys. We haven't watched them play game after game. I don't know why it's better to put Perez in left field over whoever else was playing there before. I may have even gotten his name wrong, but you get the picture... I'm not part of this team. I haven't watched the whole season. I don't know the ins and outs of what is going on with the Giants. I'm an A's fan. That's why, in talking with my friend Ann about it, I told her I have to talk about how "they" are doing when referring to the Giants. I can't say "We won!" Because "they" are not my team. She said, "Yes, but the A's are out of it." I told her, "I know, but I'm a faithful fan. I can't suddenly act like this is 'my' team. I'm not going to jump on the bandwagon of a winning team." I will root for them because they are a Bay Area team, but they are not *my* team. She understood, and agreed. But we *are* on God's team when we say Yes to Jesus. We are part of the action. God has given us assignments, and He does have the power to put us in, or take us out, either one. He knows who to position where, and why. If we are willing to give ourselves over to His "game strategy," we can be a functioning part of the winning team.

He has a perfect game plan, even though we may want to argue at times.

There are many armchair quarterbacks and coaches. I saw a woman on the news last night celebrating the Giant's win. I heard her say how she would have put such and such a pitcher in earlier. I was surprised. Her team had won the game, and yet, still, she would have done things differently. Is that how we are with God? Even when we know the Victory is ours already? Our team has already won the game of life as Christians. We are on God's team, and He is the One making the calls. He knows who to put on first, who to put in left field, and who should pitch. We might have our own opinions about who should have gotten that job, been promoted, or been fired, but God knows what He is doing. He's already seen the end of the game. Our job, now, is to play our position as well as we can, and, "Trust in the LORD with all your heart and lean not on your own understanding; in all your ways submit to him, and he will make your paths straight." Proverbs 3:5-6 (NIV)

Phil must have been a pitcher. He was not in the game long, but he was a very important part of it. He changed the whole game for me. He turned it around when it might have seemed I was falling behind.

When the bases get loaded, and things are not looking good, the pitching coach will walk out to the mound and have a talk with the pitcher. The catcher usually joins them. I get a kick out of how they talk through their gloves. At least that stops them from spitting for a short time. Why do baseball players need to spit so much? Lest I digress... The whole game can change with a pitching change. A fresh arm comes in, and he can get three outs if needed, and leave all the runners on base. That's what they are hoping for in the change, anyway. Sometimes in our lives, things are not as they should be. Our walk with Jesus is distant, and that causes other problems in so many areas. Our addictions take hold, our relationships are rocky, our job performance is sub-par, etc... It's time for a change, and that change can come in many ways. God's main objective is to get our focus where it should be so that the life He blessed us with blesses Him back. When we get off the path that God makes straight, the results can hurt, not only us, but those around us. I was watching Tim Hudson in the game, pitching, and his wife in the stands. When he was doing well, she was all smiles. When he was pulled from the game, it hurt her, too. But when the Giants won the final game of seven, they all celebrated together. They could see that the coach had been right in pulling him when he did. At the moment, we are all focused on the one pitcher, in the one game, blaming him for getting behind in an inning, or even losing a game. But we can forget all that led up to it—a whole season of many baseball games. We can get shortsighted, worried, mad, frustrated...but God knows how to get the "win" in the best way possible for all concerned.

I don't really know God's reason for bringing Phil into the "game," but I am so grateful that He did.

I was more confused 13 years ago about Phil being in the "game," and being taken from the "game," than I am today. This is not to say that I have all the answers, I certainly don't. But I do have a lot less questions about it all. My heart is at peace. Not because I fully understand, but because I know Jesus better. I heard today that the antidote to sin is to fully understand the goodness of God. We want what we can't have because we are not satisfied with all that we have in Jesus. When Jesus is our all-in-all, we can live in peace even when we don't have everything else that we think we want or need. It almost seems too good to be true—that's because Jesus IS so very good! In Acts 6, when Stephen was addressing the Council, it says his "face became as bright as an angel's." God was certainly with him. Did it end well? Not in our eyes. Stephen was stoned to death shortly after that. But what Stephen understood, through it all, was the goodness of God.

The game is perfect, even though it seems there are errors. Those so-called "errors" may be exactly what helps to lead us to that final game, that final out, and into the very light and presence of our Almighty God.

Some errors are made on the field of baseball, but there are also some very excellent plays made. We have to be ready and willing to accept both. There is a rookie on the Giant's team, his name is Panik. But he didn't panic when a ball came to him just to the right of second base. He dove for the ball, snatched it up with his glove and flung it right from his glove to second base, resulting in a double play to first! They were saying it was probably the play of the game. If he had missed that catch, it might have been tallied up as an error. It would have depended on someone else's view of it. It may have been just out of his reach, and have been recorded as a single. They say it is a game of inches a lot of the time, and so is deep sorrow. Each day, we can go one way or the other with our choices. Will we reach for our Bible that sits on our nightstand, or will be go for the leftover beer from the night before? Will we pick up the phone and call a friend for prayer when we are hurting, or will we pick up our drugs to dull the pain? Will we roll to the right on Sunday morning and get up for church, or will we roll to the left and go back to sleep? Life can be a "game" of inches that changes the course of our lives.

And the joy that we will know is greater than any joy seen after the 7th game of the World Series has been won. That is almost hard to imagine, a greater joy than we saw on the faces of the Angels last night when that last fly ball was caught in the outfield. I love knowing that our joy will be even greater than that.

Sandoval (third baseman) played an amazing game for the Giants. I thought it was only fitting that he caught the final out. It was such a high pop-up that Posey (catcher) and Bumgarner (pitcher) had time to walk toward each other, glance at each other with smiles on their faces, and then turn and watch Sandoval catch the ball in foul territory. Sandoval fell to his back in joyfulness, and then hopped up and ran onto the field to celebrate with his teammates. Posey and Bumgarner were already hugging each other. These joys, these celebrations, are just small snippets of what we all have waiting for us when Jesus catches us up in the clouds with Him and takes us Home to Heaven. "For the Lord Himself will descend from heaven with a shout, with the voice of an archangel, and with the trumpet of God. And the dead in Christ will rise first. Then we who are alive *and* remain shall be caught up together with them in the clouds to meet the Lord in the air. And thus we shall always be with the Lord. Therefore comfort one another with these words." 1 Thessalonians 4:16-18 (NKJV) Are we talking about eternity with those we spend time with? Many think of it as a scary subject. It is not. It is comforting to know where we will spend eternity when we believe in Jesus!

Sitting in the dugout is boring and tiresome, and you feel rejected and alone. You're wanted on the team! But the choice is yours.

Too many are sitting this life out in the dugout, thinking they are not part of the game. Some aren't even on the field—they are hiding in the locker-room, not wanting to join the team. Can you tell I love sports? My poor husband, of all the women in the world he could have married, he picked me, and he doesn't like sports.

We are taking a spiritual gifts class at our church this month. The first day in class we took a test on our individual styles, having nothing to do with our gifts. We answered a few questions, added up the results, and charted them on a graph. It turns out...surprise, surprise, that Jim and I are exact opposites. He is task oriented and unstructured. I am relationship oriented, and structured. Years ago, this is probably the very reason we almost quit on our marriage. Thankfully, we made it through that, and have grown to not only realize our differences but to appreciate and blossom in them. We are two halves that God brought together to make us wholly able to serve Him. You would not be reading this book if not for my task oriented husband. Also, there would be no book without the relationships that I enjoy. We approach life from opposite directions, but we have learned, through God's grace, to meet in the middle and work together. We enjoy being teammates on God's team, but we realize that we play different positions, and that is okay. I don't "bat" well, and he can't "pitch" well, but that's how God designed us. And it's not boring or frustrating when we live in the fullness of it with Jesus. It's exciting as we watch God move us both forward in the different way He designed us.

The neighborhood bully is not in control, although he thinks he is. The devil thinks he has control over you.

Yesterday, I sat in a three hour session on spiritual warfare. It was amazing, and eye opening, even beyond what I already have learned about this verse, "For we do not wrestle against flesh and blood, but against principalities, against powers, against the rulers of the darkness of this age, against spiritual hosts of wickedness in the heavenly places." Ephesians 6:12 (NKJV) I won't go into yesterday's lessons in depth, but I will tell you one quote that I always want to remember. It is this: "Evil is small. If a butterfly in Heaven swallowed Hell in its entirety, it wouldn't even give it indigestion." I don't know if that is a direct quote from Mike Garner, the pastor teaching this class, or if it belongs to someone else, but I liked it. The bully, Satan, wants us to think he's in control of our lives, but he IS NOT! JESUS IS! Not even death could hold Jesus down. And if death and taxes are our worst fears, we have nothing to fear. Jesus conquered death, and He even got tax money right out of a fish's mouth. (Matthew 17:27)

Satan is not the Angels, he is the losing team, and he doesn't want to lose all by himself. He wants to take as many down with him as he can. His time is running short and he knows it.

Our enemy, Satan is working extra hard these days. World events are lining up with prophecy, and even if we don't believe Jesus is coming back any time soon, we do have to understand that He *is* coming back one day. I love the verse in 1 Thessalonians that says, "We loved you so much that we gave you not only God's Good News but our own lives, too." Vs 2:8 (NLT) I feel as I write these stories that I'm giving you the Good News about Jesus Christ, and my own life, too. It makes me vulnerable. I get lied to from the enemy. I hear his voice saying, "Who wants to read all this garbage anyway? Who do you think is interested in anything you have to say? Who do you think you are? You're not a scholar! There are so many who are so much wiser than you!" But I do this. I write these things, because I agree with God. I want that none should be lost...not only lost for all of eternity, but lost in this world. Too many are wounded, hurting, feeling hopeless, helpless, and confused. Too many don't know how loving God is because the lies of the enemy seem to crowd out God's goodness. Too many get buried in sin, not realizing there is a way of escape through Jesus. There are so many scars that have been inflicted on us by the enemy that sometimes we can't see around them to the love God is offering us. We wonder why He would let these bad things happen. Sadly, sometimes, it is because we open ourselves up to things that we shouldn't. This doesn't, in any way, account for things happening out of our will or by mean-spirited people around us. Something happened to them, and they allowed it to control their lives, and it spilled over into ours. But we can put a stop to that evil flowing from Satan. We can say "No" to the dark, and "Yes" to the light of Jesus. When once we say "Yes" to Jesus, accepting His gift of Salvation, all Jesus' power belongs to us. I guess I am getting into the lessons from yesterday, but why not? It is powerful to know that Jesus is in control of EVERYTHING, not Satan. The only power Satan has is the power we give to him. Our enemy thinks he still has a chance to win this "game." He doesn't. But he won't stop trying until the lights go out, and he's thrown into the bottomless pit. (Revelation 20:30)

It is hard to completely and totally say, "I'm yours, God. I want Your will for my life, no matter what."

The point of surrender in our lives does not come easy, and without cost, most times. That's a hard truth. If we can, we will skim along the surface of life and in our relationship with God, thinking all is well, and hoping it stays that way—it seems to be working. And then a gale force wind will hit us, and everything changes. (John 16:33) Up till that point, we were happy with God's will for our lives because it was pretty much our will for our own lives. But when God's will seems totally opposite of ours, we object! Just like in my marriage, I objected that Jim was completely opposite of me. We married young, had our children young, life was moving along at a good pace...but eventually life catches up with us. It's not all fun and games; it's a lot of hard work. And when it seems our partner isn't all *we* thought they should be, we object. We want to walk off the field and find a new pitcher, on a new team, thinking it might be better than this one. I had become very self-focused, and I wanted to throw in the towel. Jim reminded me recently that the song I used to sing back then was, "I'm Already Gone." (I had forgotten that.) In all this, I realized something recently in talking these things over with friends. When Phil got sick, instead of it tearing Jim and me apart even further, it brought us together as a team. We weren't as God-focused before Phil got sick as we should have been, but maybe just enough so that we didn't quit on God, or each other. I know I took the focus off myself at that point, and put it on Phil, helping him in any way I could. And Jim supported me. I had to leave Germany, where we were living, and fly to California with Phil for Phil's treatment. Jim remained in Germany with our other boys, holding down the fort there. Though separated in different countries, we became a team. God used what was sooo very dark, and sooo very hard, to work for our marriage instead of against it. It took years and years to realize that part of what Satan meant for harm, God was using for good to those who love Him, and are called according to His purpose. "You intended to harm me, but God intended it all for good. He brought me to this position so I could save the lives of many people." Genesis 50:20 (NLT) That is why I share all this, to give you my very life, to perhaps help you in some small way in yours.

God doesn't want what we have. He doesn't need what we have. He gave it to us in the first place. What He wants is our love.

God doesn't need our help, our marriage, our children, our job, our home...as my brother, Steve, always reminds me, his Father owns the cattle on a thousand hills. What God needs, and wants, is our love. Are we willing to give it to Him? Or are we choosing to be stingy with the very heart God created and filled with His love?

If God had not given Phil to us for those 16 years, we would not be missing him now.

We would have had nothing to give back to God if He didn't give us everything in the first place. That's hard to get through our heads most times. I have a husband who provides so well for me as I sit here and type these chapters for you. He is out there maintaining ATMs all over the Bay Area. Rain, sleet, or snow, as the U.S. Mail service would say, he is making sure that when you walk up to one of those, now very complicated, pieces of equipment, it will handle your money correctly. I know a few of the terms, and like to sound very smart when he heads out the door. "Is it a horizontal streak problem today?" I don't even know what that is. The other day I was cutting a gal's hair that works with Jim. She was talking about her work schedule, and it was so strange, because I understood it, totally. They work very strange hours, and all holidays, etc... All this to say, nothing I have in this home would be here if Jim didn't provide it for me. And nothing that we have together would be here if God didn't provide it for us. It is a food-chain of sorts...all reigning down from Heaven above where every good and perfect gift comes from. (James 1:17) We don't own what we have, it's all a gift. We don't own the air we breathe. God provides the breath we take from Him, and then we give it back to Him. He renews it for the next time, using the very world He created. It's not us; we didn't create any of it. We are dust, and He is KING! And He loves us!

God decides who plays when, and who plays where. And whether we fully submit or not is up to us, but it doesn't change the rules of the game. The only thing it changes is how much we enjoy the game while we are here.

God is not here to make us happy. We are here to bless God and bring Him glory. But in the meantime, we can find great joy in Him when we understand the rules of the game. They are written in the rule book, the Bible. But it's not like a baseball rule book, or a football rule book, where the rules can change from season to season depending on who is making the rules. Catchers now can't block home plate like they used to. Football players have to tackle only in certain ways, so as to save on injuries. But God's Book never changes, because God never changes. It has been the same Book from the beginning. It is a Book we can depend on because it was written by God. (James 1:17) That's why we can rest and enjoy the "game" while we are here, because we can have confidence in the Creator of the game. There will be no cheating, no changing, no unfairness from God's side. He is true, and right, and good. And we can depend on Him to see us through all things, because the end result is always, always, always the same—Jesus Christ, seated on the Throne, at the right hand of the Father. And until we see them face to face, they will give us the strength to face whatever challenges come our way every day of our lives.

The more we submit, the more God blesses us with peace and joy, even if the game still has many bumps and bruises.

The Royals catcher got hit in the thigh by a pitch. It hurt a lot! But this was the World Series. He wasn't about to leave the game. He practically hobbled down to first, once he got up off the ground and spent some time talking to trainers and physicians. He was not a huge threat to steal after that, since his movements were limited. When he got back behind home plate to catch once again, I'm sure it hurt each time he squatted down. But he kept on. I wondered if all the bruises on all the players were seen after a game, what a terrible site it might be. But this was **thee** Game of all games. This was what they had worked their whole lives for, and they kept focused, and they kept playing, through the pain. God asks the same of us. It seems like a lot to ask sometimes. We question God. "Really, God? Can't you just make it a little easier on us? It hurts so much!" God knows. And He cares. But He's not a quitter, and we shouldn't be either. Jesus didn't quit on us when we turned our backs on Him in the Garden. He could have. He could have just left this world behind, saying, "I'm done with all of you." Our Father practically did it once with the flood, sparing only Noah and his family. But God is sticking this out with us, now, until the last ball is pitched. His plan is to bring us Home, one day, where there will be no more of this mess. The least we can do is stick this out with Him, since we caused this chaos in the first place with the first sin in the Garden. I am loyal to the A's, and they lost. I am loyal to the Raiders, and they haven't won a game yet this season. The least I can do is be loyal to my God, since I know I already have the Victory in Him. To the end, Stephen looked heavenward—through the questioning and the stoning. His last words were, "Lord Jesus, receive my spirit." And then it says he fell to the ground, shouting, "Lord, don't charge them with this sin!" After that, he died. (Acts 7:59) The only thing that Stephen had was God's grace and power to sustain him. We, as believers, can have the same grace and power today. That should encourage us all!

The "heaven" the Angels had experienced blew away as quickly as it had come. It would be remembered. But the joy would fade...

My friend, Ann, is in the city today. She sent me a picture from her phone. It is cold, and wet, but she was there to welcome her S.F. Giants home. She said she didn't go the last time, but she wasn't missing it this time. I'm glad she didn't invite me. I'd much rather be here writing than be in the city with all those crowds of people. I would have had to refuse. I'm sure she found many loyal Giants fans to celebrate with. We need people like that in our lives. We need loyal God fans to be with us, to weather the storms, and to cheer on what God is doing in our lives. By this time next year, we will be cheering on another team in another World Series. This year will have faded, and the spotlight will be on another team, but the light of Jesus Christ never fades. It is the same yesterday, today, and forevermore. Next year at this time, many things will have changed, but God-willing, I will still be here, cheering on the same Jesus that I am this year. Go Jesus!

Their tears would dry, and their laughter would return, because...there's always tomorrow...or is there?

Our tomorrow lies in God's hands. He wants us on His team. He beckons to us each day to join up. God wants to write our name in the Book of Life. It is His Hall of Fame. We want to be found there because the "World's Series" is coming one day soon, and it's going to be AWESOME! It will be the best parade ever when Jesus returns to take us Home with Him. God will be creating a new Heaven and a new Earth to enjoy. Winners here on earth like to shout, "I'm going to Disneyland!" after they win a big game—and Disneyland does have a Tomorrowland. But the ultimate Tomorrowland is Heaven. Batter up!

Gift #15 – Knowing we are on God's Team, and the Victory is ours.

If you were ever picked last for a team, isn't it good to know God wants you on His team?

Who would you select to be on a team with you? Think of someone that compliments the position you play.

Record today's date and other notes you'd like to make:

The Great

I AM

*"The world would love you if you belonged to it,
but you don't. I chose you to come out of the
world, and so it hates you."*
John 15:19 (NLT)

CHAPTER SIXTEEN

*Therefore, from now on, we regard no one according to
the flesh. Even though we have known Christ according to the
flesh, yet now we know Him thus no longer. Therefore, if anyone
is in Christ, he is a new creation; old things have passed away;
behold, all things have become new.*
2 Corinthians 5:16-17 (NKJV)

<u>Me</u>

A New Life

Monday, 11 Nov 2002

*What this means is that those who become Christians become new
people. They are not the same anymore, for the old life is gone. A
new life has begun!*

*I am not the same anymore. A new life has begun. It feels like it
started today, but I know that is not true. What I believe is true is
that it starts every day of our lives. Each day we get up, we start a
new day with God—a day when the slate can be wiped clean. The
mistakes can be left in the past, the heartaches can be further*

healed, and the regrets can be left behind...that is, if we are willing. Most of us are not, and why not?
Is it because we think we don't deserve it? Well, that would be correct!
Is it because we can't let it go? Well, that is a hard one.
Is it because we think no one has sinned as badly as we have, and God would never forgive us for what we have done? Yes, we do feel alone in our sin most of the time.

What does God think? God KNOWS that we should give it all up to Him each and every day. That is His plan, and it is a perfect one. God wants to wipe our slate clean. He wants to take our regrets, our heartaches, our mistakes, and set us free from them all. He knows we don't deserve it, but He still wants to do it. He can, through His Son, Jesus. And He will, if we will let Him. WE are the only thing stopping our own freedom!

God has taken me so many places this year I can barely recount them all without forgetting at least one. I've traveled to San Diego, Nashville, Kansas City, Florida, the state of California, Tahoe, Canada, and lastly Cancun. We just returned last night from ten days on the white sandy beaches of Mexico.

I don't understand it really. In a year when I would have rather buried my head in the sand, God takes me to stroll along it instead. It was like He was saying, "Get back on the horse and ride." He wanted me to keep living; that I do know.

Phil and I traveled a lot together since he was out of school so much of the time. God knew how painful it would be for me to go again. Every airport would remind me of Phil. Every restaurant and every experience would cause a dagger to plunge into my heart, making it bleed and causing an agony like I had never experienced before. Every step would be difficult. Every trip would be a stretch beyond where I would choose to go. God knew that. And He knew that if I didn't start right away, I would probably choose to never start at all. These were things that God knew. I didn't.

Each trip held its own challenges. Each one, looking back now, was tailored by God as He carried me through them, and helped me to heal, although the healing was very painful at times. Sometimes it seemed to be more than I could bear, and it was. But God knew when those times came He would bear them. He would be my escape, my way out, and through that, I would learn where the "escape door" was. He is the Door, the Way, the Light, and my Salvation!

As we came up on this vacation, the last one we would take before the 14th of November arrived, the day of Phil's Homegoing, Jim and I were excited. We felt such a great sense of anticipation for the beauty and relaxation it would bring. And then, just before we left on this trip, oppression came upon both of us that was hard to explain. It weighed us down and brought tears to our eyes. It was a dark cloud that settled over us that we didn't understand. But we have come to realize, there is a lot that we don't understand. We have come to realize that when times like that come, there is only one place to go, and that is to God. We have to let Him fight the battle, to hide in the shadow of His wing, and to wait it out until the storm passes—until the dark cloud lifts and the sun shines again. We have learned a patience we never thought possible in this life. It has been such a hard lesson, but such a valuable one.

By the time we boarded the plane, this oppression was gone. Our spirits were lifted, and we were ready to begin a trip that we will never forget. It was all that we had imagined it would be! Back home this morning, as I sit here writing this, I am filled with a fullness of God that has no words. I am filled with a peace that goes beyond explanation. I type the words, but they cannot convey fully where God has brought us this past year. They can only scratch the surface in telling of hearts that have been shattered and are being put back together, piece by piece, in the most loving way possible. It is only possible with God. His compassion goes beyond anything this world could ever provide.

Yes, we made a trip to "paradise." When I look at my screen-saver now, the one of white sandy beaches and beautiful clear aqua-blue water, I say, "Yes. I've been there." I have drug my foot in that soft white sand and watched as the waves swirled around each step. I have felt the warmth of that sun and breathed in that tropical air. I was there, and I loved it. To me, that is what Heaven would be like if I could design it. But like I've said before, I would not want to limit God. I'm sure what He has planned goes way beyond what I think paradise should look like.

I will always remember Cancun. Yes, it is lined with hotels and restaurants, and there are times when it is probably hotter than you know where, and swarming with people—but not on our trip. The crowds were not large, and the weather was very comfortable. We stayed in a villa, and when we opened our sliding glass door, all we could hear were the waves crashing on the beach which was no more than 25 feet away from us. Imagine waking in the morning, throwing on some clothes, and then strolling along the beach, spending those first minutes of the day with God.
How can you not see Him there?
How can you not feel His healing touch upon your heart?
How can you not breathe in the air that He has provided and not be grateful for all that He has done in your life?
It is simply not possible!

Yes, God can be found anywhere. He lives in our hearts, and He is with me right now as I write this as much as He was on those beaches. But I believe He gives us those places on earth, those bits of "paradise," so that we can get a taste of Heaven right here—so that we can stop and soak in all that He wants for our lives—if we are willing to let Him into our hearts.

This year has been the TOUGHEST year of my life. It has held pain that is beyond description, and loss that seems so overwhelming I cannot begin to explain it. I have walked a path that I would not have chosen, and I have stumbled many times along the way. There have been times when it seemed so dark I didn't even care if the sun ever shone again. I have run and re-run the events of Phil's last days through my mind so many times that I have lost count. I have had regrets and heartaches that consume me, and seek to destroy every piece of me, until I would be nothing more than dust easily blown away by the slightest wind. It has been an absolutely devastating year, and yes there were times when I wondered if I could go on...if I wanted to—just take me now, God, because this life holds nothing that I desire anymore.

And then, day by day, step by step, God took my hand and led me through. He led me to places where I could see Him clearly. He helped me to heal in ways that I never thought possible. He continues to lead me, guide me, and amaze me each day I live.

I was thinking about footprints in the sand a little while ago and about that famous "Footprints" story of Christ. As I walked along the beach in Cancun, I stepped in another's footprints, remembering this story. As I thought about that again this morning, I realized something. Those footprints I stepped into in Cancun were made by man, they were not Christ's. I had no idea whose they were or where they were leading. They could have been heading the "wrong way." With Jesus I never need fear that He would lead me in the wrong direction. It's only His footprints that I should be following. They will lead me Home!

Early in our week in Cancun, I prayed for a shell. I had pictured in my mind a Conch shell, those beautiful ones that seem to only be found in gift shops. They twist around and become smooth as they turn inside themselves. We were on a beach with sand that was so soft, it was like flour. It was sand made from limestone. There were no shells in the area we were in. As I walked a distance down the beach I did find an area with a few shells, and I was excited to see them. I found a few interesting ones, and I picked them up to bring home. Still, my heart was not satisfied. I had prayed for a specific one. But I was grateful for what God had provided, and thanked Him for them. On the day before we were to leave, I was strolling down the beach on my morning walk, once again thinking about finding a Conch shell. (Although I didn't know the name at the time.) I laughed to myself because what would I do with one of those huge things anyway? We are down-sizing into an RV. I laughed because God knew that, too, and that was probably why I hadn't been given one. This was my thinking, because you know how thoughts go. Then shortly after that, I spotted it—a quarter-sized Conch shell in perfect condition. There, on the beach, for me, from God! I knew it was His gift to me. It is the best shell I have ever found in all my days on beaches. It was no coincidence. It was not an accident. It was a gift from a God who hears our prayers and answers them in His own timing, in His own way, and in His own "size." You can bet I brought it home and will keep it as a reminder of how very much God wants to bless us if we will only seek Him all our days.

We visited some Mayan Ruins called Chichen-Itza. Jim heard the easiest way to remember it is to think of Chicken Pizza. The people there are busy rebuilding these ruins to their original state, although it is very difficult because most of the stones have been taken away and used to build other buildings. It was amazing to me to be looking at things that were around at the time of Christ. But what also amazed me was to see the very things talked about in the Bible that should be avoided. (2 Kings 18:4, Deuteronomy 12:3) These were temples and idols built for other gods, places of sacrifices, and serpents which adorned almost every structure. These are the places that the Bible says should be torn down and destroyed. They were, for the most part, but now they are being rebuilt once again. Most seem unaware, I believe, of the harm they could cause in rebuilding them. It's being done to preserve a piece of Mayan archeological history. These are seemingly good people. They mean no harm. But that doesn't mean they can't get off track, and waste their time and energy on things that will bring them no gain. Maybe they have that time. Or perhaps, it's that they don't know God and His Son?

I'll never forget the day we took this bus ride to Chichen-Itza. We drove through many small villages of mostly Mayan people. There was such poverty there, small huts that they lived in, small dark stores that they shopped in. But they were not "dark" people. They were the most friendly, wonderful people, who seemed to have all the time in the world to just fellowship with one another. In fact, our bus got detoured because of road construction and we ended up where we shouldn't be. This was a huge bus, and the streets were very narrow. The driver had to make a sharp left turn that was almost impossible without taking down some walls. With lots of maneuvering, he finally accomplished it to an audience of village people watching. One man had even gone into the house to grab a bottle of coke and some glasses for his friends. We were the afternoon's "entertainment." They cheered us on, and directed us, and grimaced as we hit the stop sign on the corner. It seemed they had all the time in the world to sit and watch. Are they poor, or are they the richest people in the world who enjoy the simple things in life—having more time to spend with each other?

They mean no harm but...

How foolish are those who manufacture idols to be their gods. These highly valued objects are really worthless. They themselves are witnesses that this is so, for their idols neither see nor know. No wonder those who worship them are put to shame. Who but a fool would make his own god - an idol, that cannot help him one bit! All who worship idols will stand before the Lord in shame, along with all these craftsmen - mere humans - who claim they can make a god. Together they will stand in terror and shame.
Isaiah 44:9-11

Our guide told us about a game they played in this Chichen-Itza area where the winner, they believe, had his head cut off after his victory. This was his way to Heaven. Two times a year, in September and March, at the solstice, the sun shines in just a way where a serpent is seen on the side of the stairs of the pyramid. Thousands of people, more every year, gather to watch this event. Sure, it's interesting, just as it was interesting for us to be there touring all these places and hearing the "tales" of all that went on there, but does this make God happy? What does all this mean to God? Does this worship Him in any way, or does it do just the opposite, drawing people's attention from their Creator to the very one, the serpent, who is their enemy?

Some may say I've gone a little bit overboard. But being in God's Word, getting to know Him, and having a relationship that has

grown from an impersonal one, to one that is my very life's blood;
it all makes a difference. When God alone is the very One who has
brought you out of the darkness that the devil has tried to destroy
you with, it makes a difference. I don't care to worship serpents on
the sides of pyramids. That does nothing for me. It is my God who
has saved me this past year, not a serpent. The Serpent has only
sought to take my joy. God is restoring it!

"I will lead them and comfort those who mourn. Then words of
praise will be on their lips. May they have peace, both near and
far, for I will heal them all," says the Lord.
"But those who still reject me are like the restless sea. It is never
still but continually churns up mire and dirt. There is no peace for
the wicked," says my God.
Isaiah 57:18b-21 (NLT)

My brother, Steve, and his wife Marlene, were with us on this trip.
Steve had to rescue a man from the sea. We were sitting on the
beach one day and a man in his mid-fifties, in good shape, headed
out into the ocean. The waves were not large and there really was
nothing to fear, or so it seemed. He was not out there very long,
but as we sat resting in our chairs we noticed he was in trouble.
He was in very shallow water but the waves kept coming. "It is
never still but continually churns up mire and dirt." He was down
on his knees and it looked like he might be having a stroke. Steve
ran into the water to help him out as the waves continued to knock
him about. It seemed that both his legs had cramped up and he
could not get to his feet. He was going to drown unless someone
came to his rescue. It was not what he expected that day, I'm sure!
He was brought out of the water by Steve and a lifeguard, and they
settled him back into his lounge chair to recuperate. He didn't
know what had happened. A perfectly healthy man could have
drowned in waves no more than two feet high. The very next day
Steve saw him on the beach, jogging. I told you, he was in good
shape, but how quickly our lives can take a turn. How quickly the
waves of life can drown us when we get cramped up by the things
that seek to destroy us. But God is our Lifeguard.

We are hunted down, but God never abandons us. We get knocked down, but we get up again and keep going. Through suffering, these bodies of ours constantly share in the death of Jesus so that the life of Jesus may also be seen in our bodies.
2 Corinthians 4:9-12 (NLT)

That is why we never give up. Though our bodies are dying, our spirits are being renewed every day. For our present troubles are quite small and won't last very long. Yet they produce for us an immeasurably great glory that will last forever! So we don't look at the troubles we can see right now; rather, we look forward to what we have not yet seen. For the troubles we see will soon be over, but the joys to come will last forever.
2 Corinthians 4:16-18 (NLT)

Jim and I don't want to give up. We want to "look forward to what we have not yet seen."—the life that God has planned for us from this point on. We don't want to "look at the troubles," because they will soon be over. But the JOY will last forever—the joy that God gives to us.

But then God our Savior showed us his kindness and love. He saved us, not because of the good things we did, but because of his mercy. He washed away our sins and gave us a new life through the Holy Spirit. He generously poured out the Spirit upon us because of what Jesus Christ our Savior did.
Titus 3:4-6 (NLT)

This year has been unbelievable, amazing, heartbreaking, and difficult. It has taken us places we never thought we would go emotionally, spiritually, and physically. It has brought us to a place we never thought we would be. It has taught us to walk with God and to trust Him with everything, because life is just a breath that can be taken away by a wave when we are least aware. If God was not our Rescuer, we would not have a chance of survival. The Serpent seeks to destroy, and God seeks to rescue.

The hardest thing to do when you lose a loved one, I believe, is to let go. To give them back to God, completely. It seems disrespectful. It seems that if we let go, if we give them up, we have not loved completely. That is a lie. The lie that binds us is the one that will keep us from being completely free. It is the one that will hold us in sorrow, forever. Even if it is only partial, it will always tie us down. It is that last bit of string that needs to be cut that is the hardest.

I can't say I've done it yet, but I have the scissors in my hand. My mind is willing, but my heart clings to a piece of Phil that I don't want to let go of. I know he is with God, and I know he is not coming back, but it seems if I just open up my arms completely and release him I will lose him. It seems... The truth is that when I am able to do that, when I am able to take that pair of scissors and cut that string that ties me to him, only then will I be fully free to live again and fully heal. God is asking me to. I want to. And I will, when the time is right. If the struggles are not worked through and learned from, then nothing is gained. Through it all, I learn to trust God more and more.

That is what God wants for all of us. He wants us to cut that string that binds us to whatever it is we hold onto, and He wants us to live freely in Jesus. He wants us to walk down the white sandy beaches with the beautiful Caribbean waters and offer our hearts to our Savior, fully. He invites us to taste just a bit of paradise and look forward to all that He has in store for us in His real Paradise of Heaven—the one that will last for all of eternity.

They have a saying down in Mexico. If you have been there, you have probably heard it. They say, "Almost free," when trying to sell their wares to the tourists. We laughed so much about that on the way home. Of course it isn't free—they are trying to make a living. Sometimes because they "like you" (I was told that), they will drop the price a bit. But nothing is "free," except what God has to offer us through His Son, Jesus.

The Father's gift came at a very high price to Him. It was the price of His only Son dying on the Cross for our freedom. But it is offered to us free of charge. We must simply accept it. When accepted, it opens up a world that is Paradise gained. A New Life, filled with the Holy Spirit! Especially if the life you have known has ended. The life we knew ended on November 14, 2001 at 10:18 P.M. From that day forth, we started a new walk with God—one that is better and richer and more fulfilling than anything we have ever known, because we know this world is not all there is.

> *If it seems that we are crazy, it is to bring glory to God.*
> *And if we are in our right minds, it is for your benefit.*
> *Whatever we do, it is because Christ's love controls us.*
> *Since we believe that Christ died for everyone, we also*
> *believe that we have all died to the old life we used to live.*
> *2 Corinthians 5:13-14 (NLT)*

There will be no tears in the Paradise of Heaven. God reminded me of that as I sat on a swing by the ocean in Cancun. It was the only time during the trip that tears came to the surface and they were quickly "wiped away" by God. It was like He said, "No-no, there are no tears here. There is only peace, and joy, and love to surround you now."

I knew Cancun was not the true Paradise of Heaven, although at times it seemed to come close. I knew that God was with me every step of every day. And in one more way, He reminded me of what was to come...on earth and in Heaven.

A New Life we have been given, and it is to be enjoyed.

Living in His peace,

Diane

<u>Myself</u>

I am not the same anymore. A new life has begun!

I was reading quotations today out of a sweet book my sister-in-law, Sandy, gave me. The book is called, *Apples of Gold*. This one spoke to me: "No wise man ever wished to be younger." (There is no author noted for these quotations.) I like this. There is such value in not being the same anymore, in knowing just a tiny bit more than we did yesterday. Wisdom comes in mighty handy in life's circumstances, and there's no better wisdom than God's. In James 1:5 (NIV) it says, "If any of you lacks wisdom, you should ask God, who gives generously to all without finding fault, and it will be given to you." When would we not be lacking in wisdom? And when would we not need any wisdom that God is willing to give us? I ask daily, because with this new life that has begun, my gait is different. When Jesus says, "Walk this way," I want to. When He says, "Follow Me," it is the desire of my heart. When He says, "Jump," I want to jump before asking, "How high?" This new life involves being attached to the Vine, Jesus. Apart from Him we can do nothing. If we are cut off from what flows from Jesus, life makes no sense at all. Life is much too hard, much too vicious, and much too confusing. There was a woman in Oregon dying of a brain tumor. She decided she didn't want to go through the agony that was ahead of her in fighting that cancer. I'm not sure, but from what I heard and read, I didn't hear that Jesus was her Hope. Because of that, I understand why she decided to leave this world. Without Jesus, there is no Hope here. She had nothing to hold on to, so she let go... That is heartbreaking. But the even sadder part of what she did involves what came next for her if she didn't have Jesus as her Savior. She entered into Hell, real Hell, not just, "This life feels like Hell because of the pain and agony here." Things did not get better for her, they got worse if she went to Hell. The wisest decision she could have made was to say "Yes" to Jesus in the midst of the pain and agony. Then one day, the pain would have ended for her as she entered into Heaven. No wonder we are to go and make disciples in this world! Jesus knows what it is like for people who don't know Him. He doesn't want that for any of us. Jesus came to save us from such hopelessness.

God has taken me so many places this year I can barely recount them all without forgetting at least one.

What a year it was! That first year without Phil, God truly had me get back up on the horse and ride it out. That first year, there were lots of times when I was bucked off that horse. It did not want to be ridden, and I wanted to crawl into a hole and die. But day by day, and sometimes trip by trip, God healed my heart. He had me face the pain, and provided lots of help along the way.

Every step would be difficult. Every trip would be a stretch beyond where I would choose to go.

It's not that I didn't want to travel and have fun, it's that I had no energy or strength to do it. I could barely breathe in the church office where I worked, let alone fly to Cancun and make "happy." But it wasn't about making "happy," it was about walking it out with Jesus. He was showing me that life does go on, the world does keep spinning, and I was to be a part of it.

Sometimes it seemed to be more than I could bear, and it was. But God knew when those times came He would bear them. He would be my escape, my way out, and through that, I would learn where the "escape door" was.

"No temptation has overtaken you except what is common to mankind. And God is faithful; he will not let you be tempted beyond what you can bear. But when you are tempted, he will also provide a way out so that you can endure it." 1 Corinthians 10:13 (NIV) This is an awesome verse, but I think it is misunderstood so much of the time. How many times have we heard, "God won't give you more than you can handle"? Have you ever been given more than you can handle? I have! This verse is talking about temptation, and that God will show us a way to avoid temptation, so that we can endure it when it comes our way. But the burdens that we are given to bear is what I am talking about above. The burdens are more than we can bear in life when our child dies, when our spouse leaves, when we get the diagnosis of Stage IV cancer. The escape for these UNBEARABLE burdens is the same escape hatch, His name is Jesus. The difference is, avoiding temptation is our choice. Stage IV cancer, etc...is not our choice, but Jesus promises to help us through. He says, "Come to me, all you who are weary and burdened, and I will give you rest." Matthew 11:28 (NIV) If we come to Jesus, He will help us.

I type the words, but they cannot convey fully where God has brought us this past year.

I continue to type the words... I continue to try to explain, and share, and still...I wonder if it captures the true essence of this journey? As I handed "It Started in the Dark" to my friend, Jonnelle, today, she was excited to receive a copy of what she has been reading on my blog for years. I tried to explain to her what it is like to have it in book form, and I really couldn't. It's almost beyond what I am allowed to understand. As I read this morning about Saul's conversion in Acts 9, "The Lord said...'For Saul is my chosen instrument to take my message to the Gentiles...'" I love that. Saul was chosen to be Paul, and to do the Lord's work in this way. And he did it. I don't know who might be touched by these words I type. That thought is sort of hazy to me. It's like I just continue to write it, and I enjoy the work, but what results is totally and absolutely in God's hands. Like I'm a paintbrush. God dips me into the bucket and puts the color on the wall, and I just watch it from the angle of the brush. I'm not in control of the color, or the amount of paint, or how fast it dries. I'm just there for His use in the process of it all.

I believe He gives us those places on earth, those bits of "paradise," so that we can get a taste of Heaven right here—so that we can stop and soak in all that He wants for our lives—if we are willing to let Him into our hearts.

There are places where Jesus calls us so we can rest. The beach is one of those places for me, and Cancun beaches are amazing. Because they are limestone beaches, the sand is especially white and soft. Where we stayed, we were removed from the large crowds, and able to really relax. Each morning as I would go out walking—there was barely a soul around. I would spend those first moments of the day praying, probably trying to make some sense of it all when life didn't make much sense. Over the years, the conclusion I have come to is: "Life doesn't make sense without Jesus. And with Jesus, it doesn't matter if it makes sense, because He does." In reading the Word this morning, it is so crystal clear most days. Sure, there are times when I still need some interpretation, or further knowledge about what I am reading. But for the most part, it is clear. It is the story about man's fall, Christ's redemption, and where we are going when we leave here. But I do remember a time when I would pick up my Bible, and it didn't make sense. I'm not sure when that really changed. I just know that it has. It's probably like a baby taking its first steps. When did they start to walk with confidence? When could the toddler run? When was the child ready for sports, etc...? It will come all in time—all in time, if we will walk this life out with Jesus.

This year has been the TOUGHEST year of my life. It has held pain that is beyond description and loss that seems so overwhelming I cannot begin to explain it.

My friend, Jonnelle, shared some of her tough years with me today. We all have them. Sometimes it's just hard to find a person who will listen to our struggles. My brother, Rick, is on a temporary new job. He is driving a truck along with a couple other people. The other day they got into the truck and he said to the guy next to him, "I know your story." And then turning to the woman in the truck, he said, "But I don't know yours. What's your story?" She said, "Well, my husband left me and moved to Mexico, and I'm a single mom with five children." Rick didn't tell me any more, but I'm sure as they drove along they heard some "burdens" that she deals with in her life. We all have them. TOUGH times! TOUGH years! We need an even TOUGHER GOD to see us through them! And we have one! He was whipped, beaten, betrayed, spit upon, lied about, hung on a cross, shouldered all our sins, and cried out, "My God, my God, why have you forsaken me?" Matthew 15:34 (NIV) Jesus knows our pain! He understands what we are going through. He went through that, and worse, for us. Why would He do that? Because, Jesus *does* know our story, and He wants to give us a happy ending to it. He wants to provide a way into Heaven so we can live eternally with Him. And He has! And we can receive it! Not even death could conquer Jesus, because he is that TOUGH. He put our enemy in his place. And one day, our enemy will be in his final resting place, the bottomless pit, and we will be living with Jesus in Paradise!

It has been an absolutely devastating year, and yes there were times when I wondered if I could go on...if I wanted to—just take me now, God, because this life holds nothing that I desire anymore.

I just want to speak to this for a moment because it sounds so harsh. How could life not have held anything that I desired when I still had my husband, our other two sons, and so many close family members and friends? Sorrow blinds us for a time. It is not a reflection on anyone else, or how much we love them—it is just that our heart hurts so badly we want the hurting to stop. We want to find some relief, somewhere. As I said to Jonnelle today, we all hurt at different times in our lives, and we all need pain relief. Our selections of pain relievers are many, but most do us greater harm than good. That is why I didn't drink a drop of alcohol the first year Phil was gone. It would have been a temptation that could have overtaken me. I could have walked into a hornet's nest of problems since alcoholism is in my family. God made a way of escape for me to not get caught up in that mess, by the Holy Spirit urging me not to even get started. I listened. And I am grateful for His warning. Today, my heart is healed and I can embrace all that God has blessed me with. I always did; it's just that when I held those people close at that time, my heart was bleeding all over them. It was a messy, ugly time, and if not for the grace of God, I could have destroyed relationships, and myself. Today, I know that. Then, I was just trying to survive.

Early in our week in Cancun, I prayed for a shell. I had pictured in my mind a Conch shell, those beautiful ones that seem to only be found in gift shops. I laughed to myself because what would I do with one of those huge things anyway? We are down-sizing to an RV. I laughed because God knew that, too, and that was probably why I hadn't been given one. This was my thinking, because you know how thoughts go. Then shortly after that, I spotted it—a quarter-sized Conch shell in perfect condition.

Yes, I probably illegally removed the shell from Cancun. But it was such a gift! I couldn't leave it behind. It amazes me to this day that God answered that prayer so specifically—even tailoring it to fit in our RV. The beach I walked on each morning was a mile or two long. It was wide, and it was barren of any shells of any kind, except for one small section that had a few typical and also broken pieces of shells. And yet, in all that sand, I looked down at just the right time, in just the right spot, to spot a shell the size of a quarter. How did God place it there? I don't know. How did He get me to walk right to that spot so I wouldn't miss it? I don't know. But my broken heart felt such joy in His gift. I carried it back to breakfast where I met up with Jim, Steve, and Marlene. I sat down and showed them the shell saying, "Look what God gave me." I remember them looking at me a bit puzzled. I don't blame them. They had no idea I had been looking and waiting on God for it all week.

We visited some Mayan Ruins called Chichen-Itza... But what also amazed me was to see the very things talked about in the Bible that should be avoided...These were temples and idols built for other gods, places of sacrifices, and serpents which adorned almost every structure.

I've always been sensitive to evil movies. I never saw "The Exorcist" when it came out. Jim and I were in high school. I don't watch devil movies, and such... I always felt like it would open up my mind to things that I didn't want going into it. Today, I'm even more sensitive to these things. And now that I recently learned even more about spiritual warfare, I understand more how dark things are not to be messed with. I'm no expert, but I do know "...our struggle is not against flesh and blood, but against the rulers, against the authorities, against the powers of this dark world and against the spiritual forces of evil in the heavenly realms." Ephesians 6:10 (NIV) There is a dark vs. light battle going on in this world, and as children of the living God, we are the target Satan is after. Mike Garner describes strongholds like a climbing wall. He said when we open ourselves up to things of the enemy, we give him places to attach himself in our lives. The goal is to smooth out the wall so there's nothing there for Satan to grab on to. It's a simplistic way of looking at it, but it makes sense. There is so much more to this, but I'm just putting this in here so that we can all be more aware of how careful we should be when coming into contact with things that are not of God. They are not to be taken lightly.

They were the most friendly, wonderful people, who seemed to have all the time in the world to just fellowship with one another.

The people who pulled up a chair, grabbed a coke, and watched our bus fiasco that day have always been impressed upon my mind. In the U.S., there would have been horns blaring, and people angry at the delay as our bus tried over and over to make a turn in a space it was never designed to. But all I remember was how the people there enjoyed the "entertainment" that had come to them. No one got mad because we took out the sign. And once we made it through the turn, maybe they sat out there for a long while talking about what had happened in their neighborhood. God designed us for times of fellowship, and I would think Heaven is going to be full of it!

Some may say I've gone a little bit overboard. But being in God's Word, getting to know Him, and having a relationship that has grown from an impersonal one, to one that is my very life's blood; it all makes a difference.

We can't know what someone is going through unless we have walked in their shoes. No one could breathe for me when the sorrow sucked the air right out of my lungs. No one was there when I was on the floor next to my bed crying out in agony because of the tortuous thoughts that filled my mind. I battled back against the darkness that was trying to consume me in that moment saying, "I don't care. I love You, God! I don't care. I'll serve You, God!" The enemy was relentless in trying to kill, steal, and destroy me in the sorrow I felt. I was telling Satan I didn't care how badly it hurt, I was going to trust God, and stick this out with Him. Even to this day when I talk to my best friend, Deb, about how much I was hurting during that time, she says she wanted to help me in any way she could. She could only do so much, and that she did. But after that, and after the love of other good friends, and my family, I was on my own, and that "own" was filled with a lot of indescribable painful missing. When I began to discover that being in God's Word could start to fill up the empty places inside, and that meeting with God and getting to know Him was the perfect therapy and counseling that my heart and mind needed, I was all in. Call me a Jesus addict. That is fine. Call me, "overboard for Jesus," I don't care! When you have found the answer to what hurts most, and it doesn't hurt you back, it's a wise choice. Dangerous drugs start off seemingly good, from what I have heard, but then they take you down. Jesus starts off seemingly good, and lifts you up, up, up...to an even better place. No wonder Jesus is the reason for the Season! He is the answer to all of life's woes!

"I will lead them and comfort those who mourn. Then words of praise will be on their lips. May they have peace, both near and far, for I will heal them all," says the Lord.

Can you hear the words of praise on my "lips" in my typing fingers? I can't praise Jesus enough for the healing He has done. You may get sick of hearing Jesus' name in my writings, but I will not stop shouting it from the rooftops. Acts 5:38 talks about the preaching of Peter and the Apostles, being told to stop talking about Jesus. But they wouldn't. One Pharisee named Gamaliel suggested this: "If they are teaching and doing these things merely on their own, it will soon be overthrown. But if it is of God, you will not be able to stop them. You may even find yourselves fighting against God." (NLT) I write and I speak from what Jesus has brought me and my family through. We give Him all the praise and glory. That is who we are now. If Jesus had failed us, we would not be here today. He has not failed us, and never will!

How quickly the waves of life can drown us when we get cramped up by the things that seek to destroy us. But God is our Lifeguard.

You have your own "cramps" to deal with. I have mine. Life is crampy...but God is good. Life hurts, but Jesus heals. Life can be dark and dreary, but Jesus' light shines bright every day!

Jim and I don't want to give up. We want to "look forward to what we have not yet seen."—the life that God has planned for us from this point on.

Jim and I had no idea what our future held; we still don't. But we do know Who holds it, and we keep on keepin' on together each day, looking to the God who has seen us through everything so far. As I sat with Jonnelle and soaked up the wisdom that her 20 more years on this earth has given her, I valued the godly wisdom she shared. I'm just moving into "territories" that she has already well explored. God's Word says, "Likewise, teach the older women to be reverent in the way they live, not to be slanderers or addicted to much wine, but to teach what is good. Then they can urge the younger women to love their husbands and children, to be self-controlled and pure, to be busy at home, to be kind, and to be subject to their husbands, so that no one will malign the word of God." Titus 2:3-6 (NIV) I love to glean from women on the path ahead of me, and in turn, maybe help some coming up the path behind me. God's Instruction Manual has it all covered. It's all in the pages of His Good Book, if we will search it out. Our Lord helps us through this life, and we can be so thankful for the wisdom He gives to get us through each season.

If the struggles are not worked through and learned from, then nothing is gained.

If we get stuck in the dark, and don't end our journey in the light of God's wisdom, then what we have to give to those coming up behind us is missing so much of the richness of God's love. If we only offer them our complaints, and woes, that's not encouraging. If we can offer them God's Hope and help, it's a blessing. In Heaven, we will be in direct face-to-face contact with our Father. And from what the Bible has to say about Heaven, no one there will be old. But for now, there is much to learn from those who have gone ahead of us. Let's be those that learn from Jesus along the way, so we can be of value in the Kingdom of God. Let's be a "chosen instrument" He can use!

There will be no tears in the Paradise of Heaven. God reminded me of that as I sat on a swing by the ocean in Cancun.

One last story about Cancun, and then I will let you go. I was walking on the beach, and there was an old swing up to the left of me, on the back side of the beach away from the water. I went over and sat down on it. I wasn't there long when the tears started to well up in my eyes, and then just as quickly as they came, it seemed God "wiped" them away. It seemed the Holy Spirit impressed upon my heart, "There are no tears in paradise." I knew this wasn't Heaven, and I knew there would be many more tears to come on this journey, but in that moment, I believe God was giving me a glimpse of what His true Paradise would be like. He knows us so intimately, that He chose that moment, in a setting which was close to Heaven for me, to bring that Hope to my heart. Cancun was not an easy vacation, as we neared the first year of Phil being gone for us, but it was a memorable one in so many ways. I wouldn't have wanted to miss it and all the healing moments that it contained.

Gift #16 – Continuing to find healing moments as we journey on.

Where has God met you and healed a broken piece of your heart?

Have you been able to share this healing moment with someone close to you?

Record today's date and other notes you'd like to make:

The Great

I AM

We are hunted down, but God never abandons us. We get knocked down, but we get up again and keep going. Through suffering, these bodies of ours constantly share in the death of Jesus so that the life of Jesus may also be seen in our bodies.
2 Corinthians 4:9-12 (NLT)

CHAPTER SEVENTEEN

The Lord's loved ones are precious to him;
it grieves him when they die.
Psalm 116:15 (NLT)

<u>Me</u>

Simply Amazing

Saturday, 16 Nov 2002

Hope Will Endure!

I don't understand it, I only know what is
I have no answers, with any of this
My heart overflows, with gratefulness
My mind's at peace, and in stubbornness
I say you can't have it, no not this day
My God's in control, that's all I have to say
He will make it all that it should be
You are the enemy, get away from me!

There's no rule book, that I can find
That says just how, and just what kind
Of human emotions I should feel
No, not today. But what is most real
Is my God who carries the weight of this
When life is hell, it can still be bliss
It's way beyond what I can comprehend
It goes way past the furthest end
Of anything I've ever done
And without God's One and only Son
I have no idea, where it would lead
except to the pit where broken hearts bleed

But not today! No, not with God
He is the Truth. He is no fraud
He wants what's best, and nothing less
He wants our lives, so He can bless
Each day we live, in trials and strife
Each day we live, as we deal with life
He never leaves us, of that I'm sure
After all I've seen, I can concur
With every Word the Good Book says
Jesus saves us from any mess
We aren't removed, that's not the plan
But by our side, He'll always stand

And we can rest in Him each day
I've lived. I've breathed; and I've found the way
To deal with what can hurt the most
And even still, of God I boast
In Him alone I rest assured
When day is done, Hope will endure

That's not how I planned this e-mail. It's not that I plan out any of
them. But when I started to write what was way down deep in my
heart—sometimes it seems to be best expressed with poetry. And so
it flowed this morning. It's probably because no simple sentence

will do. Not when a heart is so full of gratitude like mine is this morning.

How do I begin to tell you what Thursday held for me—the one-year anniversary of Phil's Homegoing. I have to be honest with you, I really don't understand it. I can't comprehend how God can take something so tragic, so heart breaking, and then experience what He does with it. It seems to confuse every "human" emotion I have inside. He transposes it into something beyond my ability to explain. I try, but God's Word says it best.

> *Don't worry about anything; instead, pray about everything. Tell God what you need, and thank him for all he has done. If you do this, you will experience God's peace, which is far more wonderful than the human mind can understand. His peace will guard your hearts and minds as you live in Christ Jesus.*
> *Philippians 4:6-7 (NLT)*

How can a mother go into her child's room, lay down on his bed, exactly one year from the night he left her, and find peace?
How can a mother look at his things, the pictures on the walls, the toys on the shelves, and find peace?
How can a mother open the last book he was reading to the page saved by a bookmark and know that those were some of the last words he read, and find peace?
How can she lie in the very spot her son was in when he breathed his last breath on this earth and feel no pain in her heart?—to have it strangely missing, because she knows it well—that pain. But tonight instead, to feel only the softness of the bed underneath her, and to thank God for the comfort that He has brought to her.

I am that mother, and yet I have no explanation except for the verse above in Philippians. God knew we would not be able to understand such peace, and yet He still gives it to us when we ask Him for what we need, and thank Him for all He has done.

Oh, how I want you to get this! And yet I feel frustrated that I can't help you understand because I don't understand it myself. I pray that God will take these simple words and convey the feeling behind them for all of you!

One year has passed. I have lived without Phil for 367 days as of today. Each day has been an experience in itself. No day was lived lightly, without thought. No day was spent ignoring God, because I don't have that "luxury" now. I can't put God off until I have time, as I have done in previous years, because I NEED Him every day now. My choice is to either sink in a pit of despair, or rest in God's Hope. Which would you choose? It seems an easier answer for me now. I am learning that the pit of despair is horrendous; Jesus' Hope is everything I will ever need—this day and for eternity.

A good friend asked me a question the other day. I can't remember the exact words she used, but it was something about being in those deepest, darkest moments of grieving, and what was found there. Did I even think it was possible to go on? I told her that no matter how bad it got, there was always Hope. That never died, even though I, myself, wanted to die.

The pain is so excruciating, the thoughts are so unbearable, and the missing is so unbelievable, that the human mind and body says, no way. It's only the Spirit of God that lives within that says hold onto the Hope you have been given. This Hope is only in our Savior, Jesus Christ, and His work on the Cross. He is the One who came to conquer death. He even calls death an enemy.

Talking about Christ coming back in 1 Corinthians 15:24-26 (NLT), it says:

After that the end will come, when he will turn the Kingdom over to God the Father, having put down all enemies of every kind. For Christ must reign until he humbles all his enemies beneath his feet. And the last enemy to be destroyed is death.

Death is an enemy to be destroyed! I 2nd and 3rd that!! I think of a young boy who is perhaps dying of cancer as I write this, if he has not already gone "Home." Do you think that pleases our God? Do you think Jesus doesn't weep over the heartache in that home?

> *The Lord's loved ones are precious to him;*
> *it grieves him when they die.*
> *Psalm 116:15 (NLT)*

That may seem strange. Why should it? The Lord's loved ones go on to be with Him. He is not missing them. But think about what is left behind? Think about the heartache that the Lord has to watch from Heaven, and even those who will not call out to Him for help in their time of trouble. Too many will suffer alone, in silence, covering up their pain with the things of this world that will never heal their broken heart. I don't think it is the dying that grieves Him, as much as it is those still living that are left here to grieve. (Just my opinion)

As I sat at my desk on Thursday (Yes, I went to work.), there was no one more amazed than me that I was able to be there. I knew last month, for Phil's first birthday in Heaven, it was time to get away and enjoy God's beautiful earth and retreat. On this first anniversary of his Homegoing though, I felt God telling me to go to work. It made no sense to me. The enemy tried to tell me it was disrespectful. And there was no book that I could go to with "instructions" for this day. But as God has so clearly taught me, trust in Him, and He will make my paths straight before me. Even when I have no idea what is in store, just trust in Him.

On Tuesday at Bible study, I learned something new from Pastor Jodie. I learned that the Hebrew word for Work and Worship is the same word. I learned that God designed work in the Garden of Eden before the fall, not after. So when I thought of work on Thursday, I thought of it as a way to Worship God and all He has done for me.

Thursday was a great day! I was surrounded by so many wonderful people who gave me hugs and support. I received flowers from my parents, and telephone calls from friends. I was visited by people who came by to simply encourage me on a day that could be most difficult. I came home to cards and flowers that had been delivered to the house, and I knew that God was blessing us in more ways that we could even imagine. He was not only with us, He sent a multitude of others to be with us, or to pray from afar, and it was a good day.

At lunch, I left the office to go to the park and sit with God for an hour. It was a beautiful day...and I realized in that moment that I had no idea what the weather was like one year ago on this day...no idea. I could not say, "Oh, this day is like that one." Or how, "This day reminds me of Phil's last day." So this was a new day, unto itself, and it was beautiful. It was a short sleeves and sunshine day—with fall colors and blue skies. Yes, it's mid-November in California. We've had some bad weather recently, but we were in Mexico and not sorry to have missed it.

When I arrived home from work, Jim was getting ready to leave for practice. He is playing at church this Sunday with the worship team, which he does every so often. He has been fighting a terrible cold that is going around, so when I asked him about watching the video of Phil's Memorial Service, he declined. That was fine, because I understood, he was already too tired. It is good to know where the boundaries are in grief, and allow them to be there. I told him I would go ahead and watch it while he was gone then. But as I went to get the video tape, there, next to it, was the video of Phil's baptism and his hot air-balloon ride. For a minute I thought maybe I would watch those, and then I thought, no. That was outside the boundaries for me on this day. Those would push me into a place I did not belong if I was going to allow God to carry me. It was a choice that God would leave up to me, but the results would be mine, not His. I said, "No."

Watching Phil's service was such a blessing. What I noticed most was that with all the songs that were sung, with all the words that I heard on that day a year ago, I was now living the reality of that. On that day, a year ago, I hoped for what I had not yet seen. I hoped that God would "turn our mourning into dancing." I hoped that He would "lift my sorrows." I knew that was what He promised, but I had not experienced that yet. One year later, I see God's faithfulness. I see that when Jesus asks to stay focused on Him, we can "walk on water" like Peter did—not literally, perhaps for us, but emotionally. If you don't think that being able to work joyfully on the first anniversary of your son's death is "walking on water," then we need to get together for lunch and talk. It's a miracle!

I took my shell to work—the one I talked about in my last e-mail— my gift from God. I thought, if I start to waver, if my mind wants to "go there," I will look at that shell and remember how very good God is to us. It also gave me the joy of sharing it with others at work, which was fun!

Thursday evening, after eating my bowl of popcorn and watching Phil's service video, it was then that I went into his room for a bit. I stayed there for about a half hour. Then I was tired, and I thought about going to bed—but it felt sort of wrong—to go to sleep before the "appointed hour." Where was that book with the instructions I needed? I laughed a bit to myself because Phil would understand. He knew I didn't stay up late. He, like his dad, was an early riser and a late night person. They don't need 8-10 hours of sleep a night. I do.

I crawled into bed and read for a bit, and then decided to go to sleep. I drifted in and out, hearing Jim come in from practice. And then, at one point, I wondered what time it was, so I lifted my head to look...it was 10:19 P.M. Of course it was. God would not want me to miss the moment. It needed to be recognized. I needed not to miss it. And then, my head hit the pillow and I was gone. Sound asleep. Jim said he coughed a lot during the night and was worried he was disturbing me. I never heard a thing. I slept through without interruption. How is that possible? Peace from God alone. The day was done. I had been obedient to what God had asked me to do when it made no sense, and He had blessed me the entire day. He had taken care of everything that needed doing. I simply had to show up and "worship" Him as He asked of me.

Now, the devil had lost that round. So on Friday, he started in with how I was in denial about everything. That was the only way I could feel as I do, could work as I had...and so it goes. The enemy lies, and I pray for God's protection against his attacks. Satan is only out to destroy any good there could ever be. And there can be good, even out of the rubble of destruction that lies in his wake. The good is God. Always! With Him we are victorious!

In Phil's video, the song was sung, "God is good, all the time." We sang those words with broken hearts one year ago. I heard them now knowing all the more how very true they are if we will only walk in God's ways, and let Him lead us out of the rubble.

Last night we were watching the movie, "Singing in the Rain." There is a scene where Gene Kelly is dancing down the street in the rain with his umbrella. He is a man in love, and not caring one iota about the pouring rain. In fact, he stomps and splashes in the gutters as a small child would without a care in the world. Along comes "Mr. Policeman." He never says a word, standing there in his black hat and coat. But just the look on his face says it all, "Move along. You're having way too much fun here. This is not the way it's supposed to be. It's raining!" Gene Kelly slowly smiles at him, and sings, as he dances away, "I'm dancing...and singing...in the rain..."

I love that! It's raining in my life. It's pouring, I'm soaking wet, and I don't care! Grief cannot consume me any longer because God has put His joy in my heart! And I don't care if the enemy in black says it's disrespectful to work on Phil's Homegoing day, or if the enemy in black says I'm in denial because I'm way too joyful for the "rain that is pouring down." I don't care if he says, "Move along. You're having way too much fun here. This is not the way it's supposed to be." It doesn't matter. The only thing that matters is what God says. And God's Word says:

> *No, despite all these things, overwhelming victory is ours through Christ, who loved us.*
> *Romans 8:37 (NLT)*

Their life will be like a watered garden, and all their sorrows will be gone. The young women will dance for joy, and the men - old and young - will join in the celebration. I will turn their mourning into joy. I will comfort them and exchange their sorrow for rejoicing.
Jeremiah 31:12b-13 (NLT)

It's time to dance, even in the rain! It's time to sing praises to God for all that He has done! The man in black has no control over this situation. Satan can't tell me to move on. He can't spoil this. He can't steal my joy. God is in control! And when the rains come in the future, I will continue to stand firm in them, to splash in them, knowing the Son always shines behind the darkest clouds!

*One year—367 days now... It's hard to believe. The whole thing is hard to believe. It is a long journey with no way around it—straight through is the only way. Some never come out on the other side. Some stay in the dark, in the rain, and I believe it grieves the Lord. I won't be one of those. I won't! No one has ever loved their child more than I love Phil at this very moment. My love for Phil still grows as he lives on in my heart. I was asked if I would visit his grave on Thursday? I said no. Phil lives in my heart, not in the ground. This is my way. Your way may be different. God has called us all to walk different paths. But as long as we are following Jesus, we will never be led astray. Some grieve much longer, some less, some cry lots, some cry little, some talk, some stay silent, some are busy, some are still... There is no real book that tells us **how** to do it. There is only Thee Book, the Bible, that shows us the way **THROUGH IT.***

Romans 8:1 says, "So now there is no condemnation for those who belong to Christ Jesus."

Let no one tell you how things should be. Let them be what God designs them to be. Don't let the world tell you what to do on any day. Don't even let me tell you. It's between you and God. Listen to God, and God alone.

He showed me this verse for last Thursday:

"Today you must listen to his voice."
Hebrews 3:7b (NLT)

That is what I held onto all day long. Whenever the enemy moved in, I ignored him and I only listened to God's voice, over, and over again. Let Jesus be your Teacher. He will show you things you can't possibly imagine. I could not imagine this one year ago, but now I have lived it. God is bigger than anything! And all things are possible when God is the One in control.

God is good, all the time!

Living in His peace,
Diane

Added note: In my last e-mail I said the time of Phil's death was 10:18 P.M. As I wrote that, I asked Jim in the other room if that was correct and both of us thought it was. As I watched the video of Phil's service tonight, Pastor Dave talked about it being 10:19 P.M. which was the correct time. I was mistaken. But God knew just when to lift my head off the pillow to glance at the clock, even if we had forgotten. God is always faithful!

Myself

I don't understand it. I only know what is... I have no answers, with any of this.

As I finished up the first year of missing Phil, I still had so many questions. My heart was still very broken, but also very determined. I was finding out what worked and what didn't work on the grief journey. As I told my new friend, June, the other day, the first part of the journey is muddy. It's like being on the narrow path, headed in the right direction with Jesus, but it's so slippery that we keep falling off into the pits on each side of the trail. The "Trial Trail" might be a good way of describing it. But now, 13 years later, I've traveled on down that trail for long enough that it's turned into solid rock; the Rock is Jesus Christ and the Hope we have in Him. It's not that the muddy part of the trail isn't on Rock, also, it's just that it's buried so deep in our pain we can lose sight of what's holding us up. Of course this line of thinking comes out of a verse like, "He lifted me out of the slimy pit, out of the mud and mire; he set my feet on a rock and gave me a firm place to stand." Psalm 40:2 (NIV) We all have our slimy pits in life, but Jesus can rescue us. He promises to, if we choose to walk this life out with Him.

It's way beyond what I can comprehend.
It goes way past the furthest end
Of anything I've ever done.
And without God's One and only Son
I have no idea, where it would lead,
Except to the pit where broken hearts bleed.

There's that pit again. Like I said, we keep falling into it in the beginning—at least I did. Maybe you can relate. It reminds me of one of those game shows where the people have to traverse all the slippery, water-shooting, bumper-guarding challenging courses. And if they can make it through without falling into the water, they win! I rarely watch those, but when I do, I am intrigued. Any of us, no matter what we are going through in life, are on a course that sort of resembles that. Things come along each and every day that can knock us off our feet. Can we duck it fast enough? Do we see it coming? Can we make our way around it, or through it? It takes focus, concentration, and a great deal of effort. And yet, sometimes, we expect our walk through this life with Jesus to be easy. It's not. He never promised us that it would be. Too many times we want to soften the Gospel, but the Gospel is very straightforward. It pulls no punches. In Hebrews 3:13 (NLT), it says, "You must warn each other every day, as long as it is called 'today,' so that none of you will be deceived by sin and hardened against God." Keeping our hearts soft toward our Savior and all He offers us is not just for His benefit, it is for ours. Jesus won't take away all our pain, but He will take away our sin when we ask Him, as we turn from it. He also helps life make some sense when the mud of our pain is so thick we are slipping all over the place. Jesus doesn't want us in those pits of despair. He wants us to be in His arms of care.

How do I begin to tell you what Thursday held for me—the one-year anniversary of Phil's Homegoing?

How do I begin to tell you any of this, and yet here we are in book two still talking about just one year of grief. Today it is November 10, 2014. Thirteen years ago, this week, life changed forever in the Shore household. How many of us have had moments like that? Many, if not all, of us have. What do we do in those moments, and the moments that follow? How we answer those questions will play a big part in how we will live out the rest of our lives. If we don't know what we will do, because we don't know what to do, find someone who knows Jesus and ask for help. If they can't help you, maybe they can direct you to someone who can. Keep searching for your answers from God and not from any other source. All others paths lead to further destruction. How can I say that? Because there is only one holy path, and that is the One where Jesus is. Anything else is temporary at best. But understand, even with Jesus, we have to keep bringing Him our hearts, our hurts, our failures, our questions, our everything. If we turn away from Him, if we decide to go it on our own, we are in for a much bigger struggle. I'm not here 13 years later writing this story because it was an easy journey. I'm here because it was extremely difficult. I understand how easy it is to get stuck in the mud along the way. It is very tempting to just sit down in it, and give up. The other night, just driving down the freeway, the feeling of despair started to creep in...it seemed like a warm cozy blanket. I was so tempted to curl up with it. But I recognized the pit, and that the "cozy warm blanket" was a lie. I refused it in the mighty name of Jesus. I told despair it had no right or power in my life. The despair stuck its tail between its legs and left almost instantly. This type of talk against the enemy works when we learn to speak in the power of Jesus' name. It takes practice, like in the "Karate Kid," when he was practicing in the "Wax on. Wax off" scene. Then he had to paint the fence, up and down—then the house, side to side. When he was finished, and the physical attack came, he responded instantly and correctly in fending off the blows because he had been trained in that way. We can train spiritually that way, too. We can be in the Word, daily, reading of others who have been there, and using their example of faith to lead the way through our troubles. There is so much more to life than the pain you feel today. It will get better with the Holy Spirit as your Guide. Trust the Father, and Jesus will see you through this mess.

How can she lie in the very spot her son was in when he breathed his last breath on this earth and feel no pain in her heart?—to have it strangely missing, because she knows it well—that pain.

That pain came back. I'm not saying this to discourage you, but just to be real with you. It will go away, and God's peace will reign, for a time. And then it will come back again, and again. That is why grief is a process. We have to practice "Wax on. Wax off." But these moments of peace, especially early on, are such a relief. To know that the pain can go away, even for a short time, is helpful and Hope-filled. It gives the sorrow a break, and the joy a chance to start taking hold. Little by little that joy will grow into a full blossom of beauty. It can't be rushed, but it can be strived for as we get to know Jesus better and better. Spending time with God is the only way. Even in that, it is hard. So many things get in the way. But let's not let anything get in the way of our healing. It is our life—the one that God gave to us. And the enemy needs to get his hands OFF!

One year has passed. I have lived without Phil for 367 days as of today.

How many days are there in 13 years? The answer is 4,745, plus a few leap years in there. That's how many days have passed, and that's how many days **closer** I am to seeing Phil again! That's a lot of sun ups and sun downs! That's a lot of tears and smiles. That's a lot of pain and healing. That's a lot of everything, with so much more to go. But like a baby, we eventually do stop counting the days, the weeks, and even the months. We probably count the years for a lifetime. Time moves on, and that is not disrespectful, it just is.

No day was spent ignoring God, because I don't have that "luxury" now. I can't put God off until I have time, as I have done in previous years, because I NEED Him every day now. My choice is to either sink in a pit of despair, or rest in God's Hope.

That "luxury" of being lukewarm toward God is a bit nearer now, but I fend it off. I don't want it. I fight to keep close to God, to stay in His Word, to learn from Him. I listen to sermons even when it's not Sunday. I read the Bible almost every day. I talk with others about God, and His goodness, and His commands. I go to Bible studies, and I'm even going to start a Bible study here in my home in a week or so. Some have asked, "What are you going to study?" And my answer is, "The Bible." I have been to many good Bible studies that use videos and workbooks, and I have learned much from them. But right now, I want to open our home, and open the Word, and draw nourishment from it—so many need that, as do I. I'm not an expert. But I don't have to be, because God is. He will draw close to us when we draw close to Him. He assures us of that.

Did I even think it was possible to go on? I told her that no matter how bad it got, there was always Hope. That never died, even though I, myself, wanted to die.

Yes, I wanted to die. The pain was so unbearable. If you're in those shoes today, you know what I'm talking about. Sorrow burrows in deep, and stays a long time. But God can burrow in deeper, and stay even longer. "Guard your heart above all else, for it determines the course of your life." Proverbs 4:23 (NLT) You might be needing someone to encourage you along the way—that's the reason why I write. Thank you for reading. And may God bless your journey with His abiding peace and joy. We always have Hope because Hope is eternal. It comes from Jesus, and it will always be with Jesus, as will we when we leave here as believers in Him.

I felt God telling me to go to work. It made no sense to me. The enemy tried to tell me it was disrespectful.

So many things that God asks us to do seem opposite of what the world leads us into. Just yesterday, our son, Jimm, had to make a difficult decision, and move forward with it. He prayed a long time about it, and even though it seemed like things would get worse when he obeyed what He thought the Holy Spirit was telling him to do, it actually brought him great peace when it was done. I was surprised. He was surprised. But we rejoiced together in God's goodness. We experienced something similar years ago when Jimm was in a situation that called for some tough love on our part as his parents. He was in high school at the time. We sat him down at the table, which in our family is not the place you want to be. When you get "called to the table," things are brewing! Jimm sat down, and we began our discussion with him. We had people praying for this time with Jimm. He came to the table bound up in darkness, resistant to our talk, and very angry. When the truth was presented to him, he didn't want to hear it. But we kept on, and there came a moment when I saw something that I have never forgotten. It was like chains fell off of our son. His body relaxed, and the tears came. The fight was over, and the freedom that Jesus brings settled on him. Supernatural things happen when people pray and parents obey. "My child, pay attention to what I say. Listen carefully to my words. Don't lose sight of them. Let them penetrate deep into your heart, for they bring life to those who find them, and healing to their whole body."
Proverbs 40:20-22 (NLT)

I realized in that moment that I had no idea what the weather was like one year ago on this day...no idea. I could not say, "Oh, this day is like that one." Or how, "This day reminds me of Phil's last day."

I went to a work meeting recently. Our owner, Don, conducted this meeting instead of the normal manager handling the meeting. Don was just returning from time spent away from the business. He, his brothers, and his mom, had been caring for his dad. His dad's kidney failure eventually took his life, but not before they all had the blessing of spending these last few weeks with him. I was reminded of Don's focus on his dad, instead of the business, as I read this part of my journey. The weather outside could have been "frightful," as we sing in a familiar song, but I wouldn't have known it. All my energy, all my attention, all my prayers were focused on Phil, lying in his bed, in his room, getting ready to leave us. I share that with you here to say, "It's okay to do what needs to be done." Those are the important times in life. It's okay to take your focus off this world, off your work, when God is calling your loved one Home. Cherish those moments, release the regrets, and know that you did all you could do with the ability and strength you were given. Remember the good things, toss the bad, and hold onto the things you can be thankful for. Sometimes, there are strange things to be thankful for in those moments. But that's okay, too. I was grateful when they wheeled Phil out of our house, down the front porch, and into the waiting van. The reason I was grateful was because it was 2:30 in the morning, and none of the neighborhood kids were out playing—strange thoughts from a grieving mom—but I remember. I do remember there was fog that night, as I stood on the porch. I may not have known what the day had been like, but I do know the night was cold, and that's where this journey of sorrow began...in the cold dark of night. But it didn't end there!

It is good to know where the boundaries are in grief, and allow them to be there.

Jim and I somehow knew to give each other grace on this journey. I hope you are finding others giving you the same grace. I hope I am in these writings. I don't mean to rush you, or diminish your pain, in any way. Whatever it is you are going through, whatever your sorrow or struggle is on this day, I hope you will be comforted to know that God knows every intimate detail, and is concerned with them all. Take the time you need, take the space you need, and follow God through it, prayerfully. Jesus will work to heal your heart as you rest in Him.

Those would push me into a place I did not belong if I was going to allow God to carry me. It was a choice that God would leave up to me, but the results would be mine, not His. I said, "No."

Some choices don't seem harmful, but they aren't always what is best for us. It reminds me of the verse in 1 Corinthians 10:23 (NLT) which is, "You say, 'I am allowed to do anything'—but not everything is good for you. You say, 'I am allowed to do anything'—but not everything is beneficial." Would I have lived through watching the other video of Phil? Of course. Would it have harmed me for life? Probably not. But when the Holy Spirit gently guides us away from something, it is best to listen. God knew I needed encouragement and strength more, in that moment, than I needed to cry through something else. Our Savior is trying to help us, not hinder us...if we will listen and obey.

On that day, a year ago, I hoped for what I had not yet seen. I hoped that God would "turn our mourning into dancing." I hoped that He would "trade my sorrows." I knew that was what He promised, but I had not experienced that yet.

Another deep breath just now, and a strong realization that God has done a mighty work. For that, I am grateful. Is there a difference in the gratitude I felt on that foggy night as they took Phil away from our home, compared to the gratitude I feel in my heart as I write this? I wonder...that dark night was a wispy fog-like gratitude. Being grateful during such a horrendous time is almost a ludicrous thought. It caused barely a ripple in my mind, and yet I remember it like it was yesterday. Parents don't quickly, if ever, forget those moments in time, or the thoughts that come with them. But what I am grateful for on this day is HUGE! These past 13 years built upon that first moment of foggy gratitude on the porch. This long journey of healing started the minute I went back into the house and closed the door. It was in infancy when I had to go to bed and wonder how I was going to get up the next morning with no one to take care of. That baby grief cried out with gratitude when the phone rang and Tony needed a ride to school, giving me a purpose for getting out of bed. With fresh sorrow, there were so many dark days...but there can be many sunny ones, too, when we cling to the Hope we have in what Jesus died to give us. That Hope has never failed us all these years later. That Hope in Jesus has remained the same. The Solid Rock has taken over where the mud used to make me falter. I see the clear path ahead of me now...not without its trials, temptations, sadness, and challenges, but knowing with Jesus all things are possible. I have experienced the Lord's goodness through the sorrow. His light is bright. No wonder Moses had to wear a veil when he came down from the mountain after being with God. He saw the Lord's goodness up close and personal. It lit up his face with an overwhelming joy. Oh, how the Lord loves us!

I took my shell to work—the one I talked about in my last e-mail—my gift from God. I thought, if I start to waver, if my mind wants to "go there," I will look at that shell and remember how very good God is to us.

Tools like this are so important. Whatever God gifts us, we can use to add to the life God has given us. I don't remember how many times I needed to focus on my shell that day, but I have looked at it many times since.

We sometimes put a lot of focus and energy into just getting through our day, acting like everything is right with our world, when it isn't. What if we put that energy and focus into a relationship with our Savior, instead? What if we made choices that worked toward adding to our life instead of subtracting from it? What if over time, we **added** to the holy side of our life, and **subtracted** from the unholy side of our life? Whatever we feed, grows. And whatever it is we do, we are drawn to do more. So let's do the healthy, God-filled things on our journey. Let's feed life and starve death! Let's live as fully in Jesus, as He lives in us!

Then I was tired, and I thought about going to bed—but it felt sort of wrong—to go to sleep before the "appointed hour."

We have strange ways of looking at things. I had never heard that it was wrong to not be awake at the exact time of Phil's departure for Heaven a year later, but it seemed so. But I also knew, like I said, that Phil would understand. I also knew that getting overly tired caused so many tears, and I probably didn't want to push it.

I wondered what time it was, so I lifted my head to look...it was 10:19 P.M. Of course it was. God would not want me to miss the moment.

I don't know that this moment was important to God, but He must have known it was what I needed. It reminds me of when I glanced at the clock when my friend, Barbara, went Home to Heaven. The time was 8:40 exactly. Later when I asked God why it was that time, being surprised that I had even looked at the clock, He said, "Because you met in 8th grade, and you were friends for 40 years." Seriously, that is what He whispered to me on my drive home from the hospital. Time may not be important in Heaven, since we will have FOREVER, but God knows we live by the clock here— especially those of us who don't like to be late! I believe God includes these moments to simply remind us how involved He is in our lives. It is good to know, isn't it.

Grief cannot consume me any longer because God has put His joy in my heart!

Sorrow can be all-consuming. I know. I have felt it. It zaps our strength. It steals the air from our lungs. It makes us not care about things we have always cared about, etc... But it does so much more than that. It can help us know the value of Jesus' death and resurrection. It can take the words of worship songs and turn them into 3-D images on the screen as we sing about our life. It can build an inner strength in us through Jesus that we never thought was possible. It can fill our lungs to such a capacity that we can't help but speak out and share the Good News of Jesus Christ with those we meet, especially those who are hurting and looking for Hope. When God turns our mourning into dancing, it doesn't literally mean that we become John Travolta, or Fred Astaire. It's an inside job—one done in the heart of those who trust in the only true God. There is no other way around sorrow. The world does not provide what is needed. It's simply not here. Our healing is found in another dimension—just as Heaven is. "No eye has seen, no ear has heard, and no mind has imagined what God has prepared for those who love him." 1 Corinthians 2:9 (NLT) That's why words fail to capture it, why cameras can't take a picture of it, and why our minds can't conceive it. To find God's healing power and live in it, is truly supernatural. It's something that has to be experienced.

God is in control! And when the rains come in the future, I will continue to stand firm in them, to splash in them, knowing the Son always shines behind the darkest clouds!

The sun is shining, today, and the Son is shining, today! The first year didn't fully end in the light, but it *was* a beginning, so that 13 years later the ending **would** be in the light. The sun comes out little by little along the way, until it is a full blown blue sky! Thirteen years later fall colors are beautiful again, and my heart doesn't break when the leaves cover the ground—they are enjoyed instead of dreaded, except for the raking! Thanksgiving, which is just around the corner, will be a day of gratitude. And Christmas, which holds the promise of Jesus, means more each and every year. Resurrection Sunday is IT!! He is Risen! He is risen indeed! What better event in all of His-story to celebrate!

One year—367 days now... It's hard to believe. The whole thing is hard to believe. It is a long journey with no way around it— straight through is the only way.

Thank you for travelling with me through this book. And if you also read "It Started in the Dark," thank you for your time spent there, too. I hope you have found it to be of some help and comfort. I love this verse: "All praise to God, the Father of our Lord Jesus Christ. God is our merciful Father and the source of all comfort. He comforts us in all our troubles so that we can comfort others. When they are troubled, we will be able to give them the same comfort God has given us." 2 Corinthians 1:3-4 (NLT) AMEN!

Some never come out on the other side. Some stay in the dark, in the rain, and I believe it grieves the Lord. I won't be one of those. I won't!

I believe the Lord selected me for this "mission" because He knew I would "choose to accept it." He knew I wouldn't get stuck in the dark because He knew how stubborn and determined He made me. He knew no matter how much it hurt, I wouldn't quit. I'm not saying, as you have read, that my mind didn't go there. But God knew it wouldn't be the end of me...that it would be much more the beginning of me. I met a beautiful woman this last week. Her name is Dodie, and she is in her 80's. I love to ask questions about people's lives, and especially when they have lived enough years to really share about the goodness of God they have seen in their own trials. Dodie had plenty to share, and I was blessed during our time together. Dodie could have gotten stuck along the way in her own life, but she didn't. I could have gotten stuck along the way, but I didn't. *Now it's your turn!* I pray that one day you will be able to give to others the same comfort that God has given you. I'm going to pray for you right now, even though I don't know your name—God does. "Lord Jesus, teach me how to pray for those that will read these words about Your healing power. Help them to see You in what is written here. Open their eyes to Your goodness, and Your strength on their very difficult path, whatever it might be. There might be brokenness, there might be sin, there might be anger, or depression... Help them to reach up with their hands, maybe in this very moment, and grab hold of the Hope You are offering them. Help them to accept the forgiveness You are offering. Help them to open their heart to the healing You are offering. Let them know how much You love them, how much You care about them, and how You long to have them with You when their time on earth is through. You have brought them to this book for a reason. The greatest reason would be to know You and Your gift of eternal life. I pray that becomes true for each person that reads this prayer today. Thank You for Your love, Father. For

Your forgiveness, Jesus. And for Your strength, Holy Spirit.
Amen, Come, Lord Jesus."

*Some grieve much longer, some less, some cry lots, some cry little,
some talk, some stay silent, some are busy, some are still... There is
no real book that tells us **how** to do it. There is only Thee Book, the
Bible, that shows us the way **THROUGH IT.***

The quickest way through our sorrows is taking them to the One
who understands them. Jesus is "a man of sorrows, acquainted with
deepest grief." Isaiah 53:3 (NLT) Why would our Father in
Heaven not have given us a Savior who understands one of our
deepest hurts on this earth—the separation from our loved ones? If
God had provided for everything else, but not that, it would seem
like He had missed the mark. But He didn't. He gave us Jesus.
Even Jesus wept. Jesus is the answer to our questions. He is the
cure for what ails us, and He is just waiting to return to this earth,
when the time is right, to take us all Home with Him. Our sins
have been forgiven through His blood shed on the Cross. We can
bypass the exit sign to Hell because of Jesus. There is no other way
to enter into the gates of Heaven. We must be washed clean from
all the grime of this world, and that is only possible with the
sacrifice of Jesus. If it doesn't make sense, and you want it to,
there are many who are willing to share this Good News with you.
Those are the people we should spend time with. We can't expect
the world to act like Christians, because they aren't. They don't
have the Holy Spirit living in them so they don't have the same
Hope we have. Find those that know Jesus and gather with them,
and be encouraged by them. Find a great church that preaches the
Gospel Truth about Jesus Christ, and start going. Open the Bible
daily, even if it's to start by reading one sentence a day. There's
enough bad news subtracting from your life in this world; why not
spend time immersing yourself in the Good News and add to your
life today!

*Let Jesus be your Teacher. He will show you things you can't
possibly imagine.*

If your heart is broken today, you're not alone. Look around you if you're in a bookstore, or in a coffee shop, or at a park...see those people, they all have wounded hearts. Some wounding started in childhood, some as a teenager, some early adulthood, and some not until later in life. But the wounds are there. One of our pastors, Tyler, spoke this last Sunday. He did an amazing job. He is always so transparent. He told of a time when he was about middle school age and was wounded by what others had said to him. Just hearing the story hurt my heart for what a young boy had to endure from his classmates. Wounds come in all shapes and sizes, but they come to us all. They appear in different forms. Some of us wear them boldly by being angry. Some of us wear our wounds silently by suffering with different types of depression. Some of us wear our wounds in an outlandish way by being an obnoxious life of the party. Some of our wounds cause us to stand in the shadows, unwilling to join in at the party. How do you wear your wounds? Have you found the one who came to bind up the brokenhearted? Jesus "heals the brokenhearted and bandages their wounds." Psalm 147:3 (NLT) You're on a personal journey, and your personal God is with you. He has all the supplies you need to make it through. Depend on God all of your days, and one day your heart will desire nothing more than to give Jesus all the glory for all that He has done! The Lord our God will show you things you can't possibly imagine!

God knew just when to lift my head off the pillow to glance at the clock, even if we had forgotten! God is always faithful.

This might seem like a strange ending after all that has been written here. But I think it is very fitting. God is in the details of our lives, more so than we can comprehend. That's important to know. We all want to be loved, and known. God provides that for us even if no one else in the world will love us or take time to know us. I hadn't even gotten the time of Phil's Homegoing exactly right, but that didn't stop God from getting it right. Talk about a personal Savior! "See, I have written your name on the palms of my hands." Isaiah 49:16 (NLT) He knows our name. Our Father in Heaven also knows the day and hour we are born, and the day, hour, and minute we will leave this earth. I don't know why

Phil's hour and minute was 10:19. I know why Barbara's was, for me personally. For someone else, it may have spoken to them in another way. But for whatever reason, 2:21 P.M. was when Phil entered into this world, and 10:19 P.M. was when he left. In four days from today, Phil will have lived in Heaven for 13 years. I couldn't count all the people that I have shared his story with in person. I don't know how many read my blogs through the years. It is yet to be seen how many will read the books I write. It's not something I really need to know, because I know that God knows. But if I am to hear the words, "Well done, good and faithful servant," when my hour comes to leave this earth, it will make it all worth it—all the pain, all the missing, all the unanswered questions, all the fears, all the tough stuff of this world will have all been worth it if my Savior is pleased. "After all, what gives us hope and joy, and what will be our proud reward and crown as we stand before our Lord Jesus when he returns? It is you! Yes, you are our pride and joy." 1 Thessalonians 2:19-20 (NLT) If what I have written here has drawn you to Jesus for the first time, or brought you closer to Him on your journey, then this mission is a success. That is not disrespecting Phil's memory, he would agree with me. But the enemy just lied to me about that as I wrote it. Yet I know the truth is, no one would be happier than Phil to have people meet Jesus, or grow closer to Jesus, because of what he endured while he was here. So if you get to Heaven before me, please give Phil a big hug from his mom. And tell him how much I love him, and miss him, and can't wait to see him again! Maybe that will bring him a moment like at his baptism, when those in attendance raised their hand, letting him know there was a reason for his suffering—because his journey had encouraged them in their own walk with Jesus. I pray my journey has encouraged you.

Thank you for joining me in the pages of this book. It's always a high point in my day when I get to sit and write to you. I started this chapter with a poem, so I'll end with this one written just one year ago, this week, on what would have been Phil's 28th birthday. Sometimes, it is the best way I can express to you what is in my heart.

It started in the dark, so many years ago

It started in the dark, and I really didn't know

Where I was heading, what I should do

All that I would learn...I just knew I needed You

You came to me, You helped me, Your healing was there

If only I would cling to You, but I was just so scared

How my heart bled, would I even live?

But Your powerful amazing love, had so much more to give

More than I could ever imagine, in the darkness of my soul

The process seemed so grueling...You worked to make me whole

As each minute of each day, turned into months and years

You healed my bleeding heart, and wiped away my tears

You turned the ashes into beauty, and the pain turned into peace

Now all these years later I can say, You set the captives free

What started in the dark, ended in the Light of You

Thank You Lord Jesus, the Conqueror, the One who sees us through

<u>Gift #17</u> – Taking the comfort we have been given, and giving it to another hurting heart.

What has been the greatest thing you have learned so far in your sorrow?

Has there been a moment that changed your perspective of God's involvement in your life?

Record today's date and other notes you'd like to make:

The Great

I AM

Their life will be like a watered garden,
and all their sorrows will be gone.
The young women will dance for joy,
and the men - old and young - will join
in the celebration.
I will turn their mourning into joy.
I will comfort them and exchange their
sorrow for rejoicing.
Jeremiah 31:12b-13 (NLT)

EPILOGUE

It's hard to believe "It Ended in the Light" is finished. I didn't know if there would be enough of this journey to fill another book, but you are holding it in your hands. Whether it is helpful information or not, remains to be seen. I just feel called by God to keep moving forward, keep sharing, and enjoy the process. So I do. In all that, it seems to me that all these thousands and thousands of words could be summed up in just a couple of sentences. And yet, I continue to type. But I would like to summarize what it seems those sentences could be, if I may.

Sorrow, trials, temptations, etc...of any kind are hard to go through, and they come to us all.
The only way through them is with Jesus as our Savior, the Holy Spirit as our Guide, and our Father God watching over us all.
Our main source of information comes from the Holy Bible.
If we are willing to allow Jesus to bring us through the "fires," cooperating with Him, listening to Him, and turning away from the enemy and his traps, then Jesus will bring us through the tough stuff, in His own way, and in His own time.
The end result of a faith in Jesus Christ is the forgiveness of our sins, and living eternally with Him in Heaven, where all the pain, sorrow, and tears are gone forever. Amen

Story-telling seems to be what I do now, and it is fun work! If you like reading real-life stories, then we're a good match. It doesn't mean I'm an expert on the things of God. I'm just a traveler here on earth, just like you. The only difference is that I write about it. You share your walk with Jesus in other ways. As Jim and I are presently in a spiritual gifts class, it becomes clear that God made each one of us uniquely different. Our Father in Heaven sure knew what He was doing. His system works! We went around the class of about 25 people, and everyone shared what their gifts are. And then we talked about how they might look in being used for God's Kingdom work. Even though we might have a couple of the same gifts, it became obvious how they all play out differently. It's what makes the world go 'round,' and when it is done in cooperation with our Father's will, it doesn't have to squeak. It can be a smooth operation.

Yes, I can summarize what "It Started in the Dark" and "It Ended in the Light" contain in just a few sentences. But what fun would that be? I never do a quick "coffee chat"—two to three hours is about normal for me...hence the 300 or so pages you are holding in your hands, talking about how well Jesus does in bringing us through our trials. I get excited to tell you all about our Savior, how the Holy Spirit works in and through us, and how we can go boldly into the Throne Room and speak to our Father—we have every right to be there as His children. These are exciting things! We **must** share!

As I finish up this book, I will be starting a Bible study in my home with a group on Wednesday mornings. I have never done that before. I was hesitant, and I learned why. I have the gift of Faith, Encouragement, and Mercy. I score high in the Shepherding area, too. But, I score low in Apostleship and Hospitality which means inviting people into my home and starting a small group is a very shaky area for me. Our teacher, in the class, had us write our name on the first day, with the hand opposite our writing hand. So as I placed the pen in my left hand and tried to write my name, it was a very shaky signature. Then she had us write our name with our writing hand. Of course, using my right hand, I was as sure and confident as could be. We all were. What that impressed upon me is how confident we can be operating in the gifts we have been given. I can't stop myself from encouraging people. But operating in the gifts I'm shaky in, is more challenging. But if we are called to do something by God, even if we're not super strong in that area, we still need to be obedient to His request. What better way to strengthen what is weak in us spiritually than to allow Jesus to make us strong in Him in those areas!

How do I relate that to this book, and all that is written here? When sorrows and trials come into our lives, it's a shaky time. Our faith may flounder, our doubts may be on the rise, and our willingness to reach out for help from God and others may be the last thing we choose to do...we might just want to curl up in a blanket and pull the covers over our head. But if we will step into the light of Jesus, on shaky legs, with a quaking body, and barely enough air to breathe, Jesus will fill us up and make us strong in the weakness we feel. He can do that for all those who **call** upon His name. But, we need to call, and accept His help with a willing spirit.

If you haven't met Jesus as yet, even after reading this entire book, and you are still wondering how you can get your heart in the right place to find the healing you have been reading about, let me take you through a simple prayer that will usher you right into the Throne Room of Heaven and into a relationship with the Savior. It's not difficult. It's a choice you make. Jesus can open the door to an eternity in Heaven for you with a key called prayer. Pray this with me if you will:

Lord Jesus, I don't know You as yet, but I want to. I have heard so many things about You, and You seem like the One I need to help me in my struggles and my sin. I want to open my heart up to Your healing, and Your forgiveness. Please forgive me for the things I've done that are not of You, but are of this world—I turn from them. Wash me clean, and bring me into a relationship with You that is beyond what I can imagine at this moment in time. I want to be in the family of God. I want to live eternally with You, and be filled with Your Holy Spirit as I walk out the rest of my days on this earth. I want to follow You each day, learning more about You as I go along, until You are my very Best Friend. Please come into my heart, live in me, and help me want Your will above my own. I will look forward to learning to trust You in all things. It's in Your name, Jesus, that I put my Hope, and offer this prayer up to You. Amen.

We have come to the end of our stories for today, but there may be more in the future. I can't say that as Thanksgiving approached at the end of that first year, it was any easier. The second Christmas was equally as hard. But with time and God, healing came, and the writings continued for many years. Perhaps a book called "Living in the Light" will be written, and it will take us further on this journey of **Me**, **Myself**, and **The Great I AM**.

My message and my preaching were not with wise and persuasive words, but with a demonstration of the Spirit's power, so that your faith might not rest on human wisdom, but on God's power.
1 Corinthians 2:4-5 (NIV)

All praise to Jesus Christ my Lord!

Diane

The Gifts We Receive Along The Way.

1. A blessed Hope comes with Jesus.

2. Finding that surrender is the only way to win the battle.

3. Heaven. Pure Heaven. Forever, and ever, and ever. Amen!

4. Beginning to know that God is God, no matter what comes our way.

5. Learning to Believe.

6. Discovering the call(s) of God on our lives.

7. Seeing new gifts from God showing up on the grief journey.

8. Learning to rest in what is, instead of fighting for what isn't.

9. There's a reason, there's a way, and Jesus will show us!

10. Finding that we have absolutely everything we need in Jesus.

11. Recognizing the 'gators and winning the battle against them.

12. Learning, living, and sharing with others.

13. God can turn miserable into memorable.

14. Appreciating the progress we are making.

15. Knowing we are on God's Team, and the Victory is ours.

16. Continuing to find healing moments as we journey on.

17. Taking the comfort we have been given and giving it to another hurting heart.

Giving Thanks

"So the last will be first, and the first will be last."
Matthew 20:16 (NIV)

This may be the hardest page of the book for me to write. Not
because I don't have anyone to thank, but because there are so
many I would like to acknowledge. Eighteen years ago this
journey began at the bedside of our son in Munich, Germany
when he was diagnosed with Leukemia. It would take a book just
to mention all those who have helped us/me along the way. So, I
will limit those I mention on this page to those who have been
personally involved in getting this in print. I hope the rest of you
will find yourselves somewhere in the stories shared, as you
were so much a part of the healing process. It took **all** of you
with your prayers, cards, letters, flowers, food, hugs, time spent,
listening ears, phone calls, words of encouragement, thoughtful
acts of service, etc... No one thing brings a person through
something so difficult. But each small kindness helps in its own
significant way. So THANK YOU!!

Those who helped to put these pages into book form:

I would not be here today writing this if not for Jesus, my Lord
and Savior, the only begotten Son of our Father in Heaven, and
the power of the Holy Spirit who lives in me and keeps me
going. Lord, You fill me up, and help me pour out Your Hope
and Love through my typing fingers.

I would have no way to accomplish all the technical things
required without my husband, Jim. No one else would have the
patience for the "millimeter" changes I make along the way
when we work together on these projects. Jim, you always
support me, love me, and encourage me in so many ways!! God
has shown me after 39 years of marriage that we are two halves
He brought together to make us wholly able to serve Him.
I love you more every day! Thank you for all you do!

I would have laid my "pen" down if not for Connie Dixon, who encouraged me over and over to keep writing. It seemed that enough had been written, but she strongly disagreed. And then, she agreed to edit the things I did write! Not only did you edit what I wrote, Connie, you encouraged me by liking it and wanting more! I pray God blesses you even more than you have blessed me! Thank you!

Jenn Ackerman, I'm thankful God brought us together through "Closer Coins." The idea for this book came by using these 12-year-old writings to help you when you needed encouragement after your daughter Zeyah Grace entered Heaven. God has used your precious Zeyah to hopefully touch many lives through these pages.

Thank you Debbie Clemmons, for blazing the self-publishing trail for me. In seeing you share Randy's story, "In His Grace, Grappling with Mesothelioma," I was encouraged to do the same.

Thank you to Mockingbird Primitive on etsy.com for handcrafting our window frame that is pictured on the cover. This frame hangs in our home with a poster-sized picture of all our grandchildren displayed in it. I wanted to be able to sit in our living room and always be able to "see" our grandchildren playing "outside." It continually reminds me of Job's blessings, and how God restored his life and ours.

In finishing up the final details of this book, I appreciate all those who helped smooth out any left over rough edges. You are usually the same team that helps me with my own rough edges!

Thank you to my best friend, Debbie LeBlanc, for taking pictures of a Florida sunrise. Only God knew you were providing the morning "light" for this book's front cover. Well done!

Soli Deo Gloria

(To God Alone The Glory)

ABOUT THE AUTHOR

diane.dcshorepublishing.com

Diane C. Shore lives in Danville, California with her
husband Jim of 39 years. They have been blessed with three sons.
They greatly enjoy being the grandparents of
Denell, Kylie, Jackson, Maren, Laila, and Cooper.
Diane has been using writing as a ministry for many years.
As God pours His love into her heart, she pours it out to others in
many written forms. She enjoys telling the story of God's Hope
and Love through the darkest times. She shares her testimony at
churches, and speaks to women at gatherings both large and small.
Her favorite thing to do is converse about the things of God,
one-on-one, over a cup of coffee.

...he set my feet on a rock
and gave me a firm place to stand.
Psalm 40:2b (NIV)

Photo taken by Aimee D. Harris at Lake Tahoe, CA

Other Books by Diane C. Shore

For more information go to:
http://diane.dcshorepublishing.com

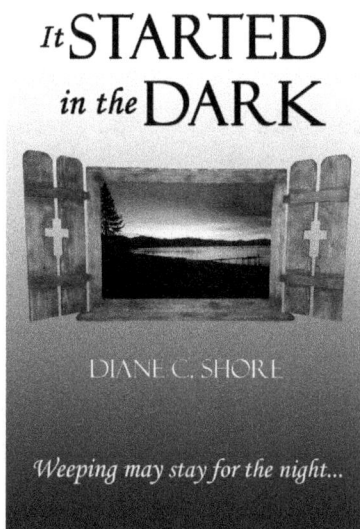

It STARTED *in the* DARK

DIANE C. SHORE

Weeping may stay for the night...

The SAND Room

Searching And Noticing the Divine

Volume 1

Thus Joseph stored up grain in great abundance like the sand of the sea, until he stopped measuring it, for it was beyond measure. Genesis 41:49 NASB

Diane C. Shore

How does a person go from questioning to knowing, from doubting to believing, from hurting to healing?

We all experience grief of some sort in our lives. Where do we find the healing and answers we are looking for? Will our joy return one day? Will the pain ever stop? How do we not give up? With Jesus, we not only have an eternal Hope in Heaven, we also have hope for each day we live. We can find that Jesus is enough! What starts in the dark can truly end in the light.
(This is the first six months of the first year of grief.)

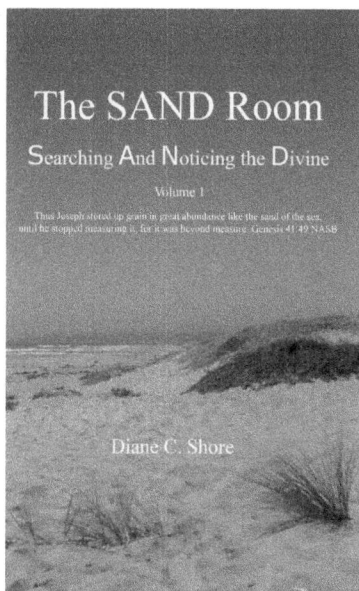

52 Short Stories that help us see God in our every day.

Our Lord is always with us, and when we notice Him, it connects our world with His Heavenly one.

Miracles happen around us all the time...but sometimes we explain away Divine moments by calling them coincidences or good luck.

These simple, yet very true, stories will help you see God in your own life. Your faith will be strengthened as you experience God's love for His children in the pages of this book.

www.ingramcontent.com/pod-product-compliance
Lightning Source LLC
LaVergne TN
LVHW051108080426

835510LV00018B/1964